Problem-Solving
Therapy

Thomas J. D'Zurilla, PhD, University of Illinois at Urbana-Champaign, is a Professor in the Department of Psychology at Stony Brook University. He has published a number of pioneering theoretical and research articles on social problem solving and problem-solving therapy. His 1971 article with Marvin R. Goldfried, "Problem Solving and Behavior Modification," published in the *Journal of Abnormal Psychology,* was recognized as a Citation Classic in *Current Contents,* No. 50, December, 1984. Together with Arthur Nezu and Albert Maydeu-Olivares, he has also published a new self-report measure of social problem-solving ability, the *Social Problem-Solving Inventory—Revised.* His writings and measuring instrument have been translated into Spanish, Japanese, Chinese, German, and French. Dr. D'Zurilla is a member of the American Psychological Association, the Society for a Science of Clinical Psychology, the Eastern Psychological Association, and the Association for Behavioral and Cognitive Therapies. He has also been a practicing clinical psychologist for more than three decades.

Arthur M. Nezu, PhD, ABPP, State University of New York at Stony Brook, is Professor of Psychology, Medicine, and Public Health at Drexel University. He is a Fellow of the American Psychological Association, the Association for Psychological Science, the Society of Behavior Medicine, the American Academy of Cognitive and Behavioral Psychology, and the Academy of Cognitive Therapy. Currently a Trustee of the American Board of Professional Psychology, Dr. Nezu previously served as President of the Association for Advancement of Behavior Therapy (now known as the Association of Behavioral and Cognitive Therapies), the Behavioral Psychology Specialty Council, the World Congress of Behavioural and Cognitive Therapies, and the American Board of Cognitive and Behavioral Psychology. He has contributed to over 170 scientific and professional publications, many of which have been translated into various foreign languages. He serves on numerous journal editorial boards, was previously Editor of *the Behavior Therapist,* and currently is a standing member of the Interventions Research Review Committee of the National Institute of Mental Health. Dr. Nezu has received awards for his professional and scientific contributions to the field by both the Association for Advancement of Behavior Therapy and the World Congress of Behavioural and Cognitive Therapies. He has been a practicing psychologist for over 25 years and is board certified by the American Board of Professional Psychology.

Problem-Solving Therapy

A Positive Approach to Clinical Intervention

3rd Edition

Thomas J. D'Zurilla, PhD
Arthur M. Nezu, PhD, ABPP

SPRINGER PUBLISHING COMPANY

NEW YORK

Springer Publishing Company, LLC
11 West 42nd Street
New York, NY 10036

Acquisitions Editor: Sheri W. Sussman
Production Editor: Emily Johnston
Cover design: Joanne E. Honigman
Composition: Apex Publishing, LLC

07 08 09 10/ 5 4 3 2 1

Library of Congress Cataloging-in-Publication Data

D'Zurilla, Thomas J.
   Problem-solving therapy : a positive approach to clinical intervention / Thomas J. D'Zurilla, Arthur M. Nezu. -- 3rd ed.
       p. ; cm.
   Includes bibliographical references and index.
   ISBN 0-8261-1488-1
   1.   Problem-solving therapy. I. Nezu, Arthur M. II. Title.
   [DNLM: 1. Psychotherapy--methods.   2. Problem Solving.   3. Social Adjustment.   WM 420 D999 2006]

RC489.P68D98 2006
616.89'14--dc22

                                                            2006018590

Printed in the United States of America by Bang Printing.

To my parents, Thomas and Mary D'Zurilla, for letting me solve my own problems.

To my wife, Lola, for her continuing love, support, and understanding. —— T.J.D

To my wife and best friend, Christine, who makes every dream a reality. —— A.M.N

Contents

II. CLINICAL APPLICATIONS

List of Tables and Figures

Preface

The term "problem-solving therapy" (PST) refers to the clinical application of training in constructive problem-solving attitudes and skills. PST was developed during the early 1970s as part of the growing trend toward clinical interventions that focused on the facilitation of social competence (Gladwin, 1967; Ullman & Krasner, 1969). The aim of this positive approach was to not only reduce psychopathology, but also to enhance functioning in a positive direction so as to maximize positive therapy outcomes and prevent relapses and the development of new clinical problems. Since the early 1970s, a rapidly growing number of PST programs have been reported in the clinical, counseling, and health psychology literature. Focusing on children, adolescents, and adults, PST has been employed as a treatment method (alone or as part of a treatment package), a maintenance strategy, and a prevention program (see previous reviews by D'Zurilla & Nezu, 1982 & 1999; Durlak, 1983; A. M. Nezu & D'Zurilla, 1989; A. M. Nezu, Nezu, Deaner, & D'Zurilla, 1997; Pellegrini & Urbain, 1985; Spivack, Platt, & Shure, 1976; Spivack & Shure, 1974; Urbain & Kendall, 1980). Like the second edition of this volume, this new third edition focuses on PST for adolescent and adult populations.

Since the publication of the second edition in 1999, there have been a number of important advances in theory and research on social problem solving (i.e., problem solving in the real world) and PST. In this new edition, we present a revised social problem-solving model based on an integration of the original theory and subsequent new research data. We also present a completely revised therapist's manual that is based on our revised social problem-solving model and is designed to be more "user friendly" than the original manual. The new manual is organized into a set of modules that each focus on a different set of principles and procedures that can easily be adapted by a therapist or researcher to any individual patient or group of patients with a particular disorder. Since 1999, there has also been an explosion in research on the relations between social problem solving and a wide range of adjustment variables, as well as studies on the efficacy of PST with a variety of different patient populations, including people with different psychological and behavioral disorders as well as individuals with different medical conditions, such as cancer and diabetes. The present edition provides updated reviews of these two important areas of research. It also describes several new measures of social problem-solving ability that have been developed for use in research and clinical practice since the publication of the second edition of this volume.

This new third edition has a similar structure as the second edition. Section I focuses on the theoretical and research foundations of PST, including our updated review of studies on the relationship between social problem solving and adjustment. Section II deals with clinical applications, beginning with a description of the revised problem-solving training manual for therapists. Several case studies are then presented that illustrate the application of PST for different clinical problems, including a patient with cancer. We then present our updated review of outcome studies on the efficacy of PST for a variety of populations. The book concludes with a discussion of our recommendations for future research on social problem solving and PST.

This book is intended for therapists and counselors in the mental health professions and education who are interested in improved methods for enhancing the adaptive functioning and stress-management ability of their clients. The book will also be of interest to community psychologists and social workers who are concerned with prevention programs and methods for increasing the effectiveness of individuals and groups in the community with the responsibility of solving community problems and making policy decisions. In addition, the book will be of interest to theorists and researchers in the areas of positive psychology, social problem solving, self-control, stress and coping, social cognition, decision making, and social information processing. Finally, college instructors will find the book useful in their courses in psychotherapy and counseling, behavior modification, cognitive-behavioral therapy, abnormal psychology, personal adjustment, personality, self-management, stress management, community psychology, and prevention.

The individuals who have influenced our work on social problem solving and problem-solving therapy are too numerous to list here. However, there are three people whom we would like to specifically acknowledge because they have had a major impact on the creation and early development of the problem-solving approach to clinical intervention. First, there is Marvin Goldfried, who collaborated with TJD in the early development of the social problem-solving model on which the present approach is based (see D'Zurilla & Goldfried, 1971). The second influential individual is Richard Lazarus, whose work on stress and coping has helped us to recognize the parallels between social problem solving and the stress and coping process as viewed from a transactional or relational perspective. Third, we would like to acknowledge the important influence of Sidney Parnes's work on creative problem solving, which has contributed much to the present conceptualization of the social problem-solving process and to the PST methods described in this book.

We would also like to acknowledge and thank a number of our students and collaborators who have contributed much to the theory and research on social problem solving and problem-solving therapy presented in this book: Chris Maguth Nezu, Albert Maydeu-Olivares, Mike Perri, Edward Chang, Larry Burns, George Ronan, Collette Sheedy, Peter Houts, and Stephanie Felgoise.

REFERENCES

D'Zurilla, T. J., & Goldfried, M. R. (1971). Problem solving and behavior modification. *Journal of Abnormal Psychology, 78*, 107–126.

D'Zurilla, T. J., & Nezu, A. (1982). Social problem solving in adults. In P. C. Kendall (Ed.), *Advances in cognitive-behavioral research and therapy* (Vol. 1, pp. 202–274). New York: Academic Press.

D'Zurilla, T. J., & Nezu, A. M. (1999). *Problem-solving therapy: A social competence approach to clinical intervention* (2nd ed.). New York: Springer Publishing.

Durlak, J. A. (1983). Social problem solving as a primary prevention strategy. In R. D. Felner, L. A. Jason, J. N. Moritsugu, & S. S. Farber (Eds.), *Preventive psychology: Theory, research, and practice.* New York: Pergamon.

Gladwin, T. (1967). Social competence and clinical practice. *Psychiatry: Journal for the Study of Interpersonal Processes, 3*, 30–43.

Nezu, A. M., & D'Zurilla, T. J. (1989). Social problem solving and negative affective conditions. In P.C. Kendall & D. Watson (Eds.), *Anxiety and depression: Distinctive and overlapping features* (pp. 285–315). New York: Academic Press.

Nezu, A. M., Nezu, C. M., Deaner, S. L., & D'Zurilla, T. J. (1997). Problem-solving approaches: State-of-the-art [El estado de la cuestión en los enfoques de resolución de problemas] (pp. 171–179). In I. Caro (Ed.), *Handbook of cognitive psychotherapies: State-of-the-art and psychotherapeutic processes.* Barcelona, Spain: Paidós.

Pellegrini, D. S. & Urbain, E. S. (1985). An evaluation of interpersonal cognitive problem solving training with children. *Journal of Child Psychology and Psychiatry, 26*, 17–41.

Spivack, G., & Shure, M. B. (1974). *Social adjustment of young children.* San Francisco: Jossey-Bass.

Spivack, G., Platt, J. J., & Shure, M. B. (1976). *The problem-solving approach to adjustment.* San Francisco: Jossey-Bass.

Ullmann, L., & Krasner, L. (1969). *A psychological approach to abnormal behavior.* Englewood Cliffs, NJ: Prentice-Hall.

Urbain, E. S., & Kendall, P. C. (1980). Review of social-cognitive problem-solving interventions with children. *Psychological Bulletin, 88*, 109–143.

SECTION I

Theoretical and Empirical Foundations

CHAPTER ONE

Introduction and Historical Development

Down through the ages, philosophers, educators, and psychologists have long recognized that humans are problem solvers and that there are individual differences in their problem-solving ability. These observers of human nature have generally assumed that successful problem solving reduces maladjustment and enhances positive adjustment as everyday life is replete with problems that must be solved in order to function effectively. Despite these early views, as well as the fact that the study of human problem solving has a long history in experimental psychology (see Kleinmuntz, 1966; Newell & Simon, 1972), the question of whether social and behavioral adjustment can be improved through training in problem-solving skills did not receive serious scientific study until the second half of the twentieth century. Likewise, the issue of whether such training might be useful as an intervention to treat psychopathology, or as a strategy to prevent relapses or the development of new clinical problems following treatment, received very little research attention before the 1970s.

There have been at least two major reasons for the past failure to recognize the potential value of problem-solving training (PST) in clinical and counseling psychology. One has been the dominance of the medical or disease model of psychopathology throughout most of the history of clinical psychology. The second reason has been the lack of relevance of most of the research on human problem solving in experimental psychology for understanding and improving problem solving as it occurs in the real world.

The medical model defines psychopathology primarily in terms of the presence of deviant or maladaptive responses (cognitive, emotional, and behavioral), which are presumed to be signs or symptoms of underlying intrapsychic conflicts. Within this conceptual model, normality is viewed primarily as the *absence* of abnormality. Positive or adaptive functioning is believed to be disrupted or inhibited by psychopathology and is expected to improve when psychopathology is reduced. Clinical interventions based on this model have focused on the removal or reduction of psychopathology through the use of psychodynamic insight therapy. Direct re-educational or coping skills training approaches have been viewed as merely supportive and only temporarily effective. It has been assumed that the old symptoms or new symptoms will eventually appear if the underlying conflicts are not identified and resolved through psychodynamic intervention.

With regard to past research on human problem solving in experimental psychology, most studies have focused on impersonal intellectual problems such as water jar problems, jigsaw puzzles, mechanical problems, mathematical problems, and concept formation tasks. The cognitive abilities required to solve these problems do not include many of the abilities that appear to be important for social problem solving (Guilford, 1967; Spivack et al., 1976). Moreover, theories of human problem solving have focused on *descriptive* models, which are concerned with the question of how individuals *typically* solve problems. The problem-solving approach to clinical intervention requires a *prescriptive* model, which specifies how individuals *should* solve problems in order to maximize their effectiveness.

PST was originally developed in the late 1960s and early 1970s and has continued to be refined and improved up to the present day. Four different streams of historical development have had a significant influence in shaping this approach: (a) the growing research interest on the nature and nurturance of creativity, including creative problem solving; (b) the rise of the positive approach to clinical intervention, (c) recognition of the importance of cognitive processes and self-control in behavior therapy, and (d) the development of Richard Lazarus's relational model of stress, which identifies negative cognitive appraisals and coping deficits as major causes of stress and stress-related disorders.

CREATIVITY RESEARCH

The arousal of interest in the nature and nurturance of creativity that occurred in the 1950s led eventually to the first training and research programs in applied problem solving, which were developed in the fields of education and industry. In his American Psychological Association (APA) presidential address in 1950, J. P. Guilford called for a major research effort to study creativity, which he believed could have great practical significance for the future of our society, particularly in the area of problem solving. Guilford (1977) saw much overlap between creativity and problem solving:

> In problem solving and creative thinking we find intellectual abilities working together, if the problem and its solution are at all complex. The two kinds of exercise are intimately related, for the solving of a problem calls for novel steps in behavior, and this means creative performance. (p. 198)

The traditional concept of general intelligence (IQ) was criticized by Guilford for failing to include many of the abilities that are important for creative performance and "social intelligence." Through his own research on creativity and intelligence, Guilford developed a new model of intellect, called the "Structure of Intellect," which includes important creative abilities, as well as the traditional intellectual abilities. These creative abilities include associational and ideational fluency, spontaneous and adaptive flexibility, originality, and a sensitivity to problems.

Coming from a different field and perspective (industry), Alex F. Osborn (1952, 1963) was a strong voice calling for the development of training methods and techniques to nurture and enhance creative performance. He was instrumental in the development of one of the earliest and most influential PST programs, which was named the Creative Problem-Solving Program. Beginning over 30 years ago at the University of Buffalo, this training program focused initially on the stimulation of productive thinking and creative performance using Osborn's "brainstorming" techniques, which tap several of the creative abilities identified by Guilford. Later, under the directorship of Sidney J. Parnes, who was influenced by both Osborn and Guilford, the goals and methods of the program were broadened considerably to focus on the facilitation of general social competence (Parnes, 1962; Parnes, Noller, & Biondi, 1977). An extensive, controlled two-year evaluation of this program was conducted by Parnes and Noller (1973). The program was administered to 150 college freshmen as a four-semester curriculum of creative problem-solving courses. Another 150 college freshmen were assigned to a control group that did not take any of these courses. The results of the study indicated that the creative problem-solving program significantly enhanced the participants' problem-solving abilities as well as their confidence in their ability to cope effectively with life's problems. Most importantly, these gains in ability and confidence tended to translate into actual improvements in problem-solving competence in the natural environment. Since the 1970s, creative problem-solving programs based on the original Osborn-Parnes program have multiplied at a rapid rate in courses, seminars, workshops, conferences, and institutes in educational and industrial settings throughout the United States and abroad.

THE POSITIVE APPROACH TO CLINICAL
INTERVENTION

As PST programs were multiplying in education and industry, a challenge was mounting in clinical psychology against the medical model of psychopathology and psychotherapy. Clinicians were becoming increasingly doubtful about the general applicability and validity of this approach. Investigators were questioning whether understanding or "insight" concerning the underlying causes of maladaptive behavior could produce positive therapy outcomes without also teaching more adaptive alternative behaviors. Instead of viewing normality simply as the absence of abnormality, theorists were beginning to argue for a separate dimension of normality or positive functioning, using such terms as *positive mental health* and *social competence* (see e.g., Jahoda, 1953, 1958; White, 1959). This view led to the hypothesis that an inverse relationship might exist between social competence and psychopathology such that higher levels of social competence might be associated with less severe symptomatology. In the early 1960s, a series of investigations with psychiatric patients by Zigler and Phillips provided empirical support for this hypothesis (Phillips & Zigler, 1961; Zigler & Phillips, 1961, 1962).

The finding of an inverse relationship between social competence and psychopathology has been interpreted in two ways. One interpretation is that social competence acts as a buffer or preventive factor against the negative life experiences that cause psychopathology. The second viewpoint is that psychopathology may actually result from deficiencies in the skills and abilities that constitute social competence, such as social skills, problem-solving skills, and other coping skills (D'Zurilla & Goldfried, 1971; Lazarus, 1966; Phillips, 1978; Spivack et al., 1976). According to this view, deficits in social competence lead to ineffective or inappropriate attempts to cope with life's problems and demands, which in turn, result in negative psychological consequences (e.g., anxiety, anger, depression, and low self-esteem).

Stimulated by the work on the relationship between social competence and psychopathology, a group of highly respected mental health professionals met with staff members from the National Institute of Mental Health (NIMH) at a conference in 1965 "to explore ways in which clinical interventions might be facilitated through placing a greater emphasis upon improving the social competence of persons who seek or need professional help in dealing with emotional or adjustment problems" (Gladwin, 1967, p. 30). Particularly significant for PST is the fact that the conference participants defined social competence in terms of three components that are also major components of social problem solving as it is defined in this volume (see chapter 2). The three components of social competence are:

1. The ability to use a variety of alternative pathways or behavioral responses in order to reach a given goal, which implies also the ability to choose among a range of goals, both instrumental and ultimate.
2. The ability to use a variety of social systems and resources within the society in order to achieve one's goals.
3. Effective reality testing, which involves not merely the lack of perceptual impairment, but also a positive and sophisticated understanding of the world.

During the three decades following, the most successful positive interventions were developed and implemented within the young fields of behavior modification and behavior therapy, using such learning methods as prompting, modeling, behavior rehearsal, performance feedback, positive reinforcement, and shaping (Spiegler & Guevremont, 2003; Ullman & Krasner, 1969). In the early 1970s, problem-solving training was added to this group of interventions (D'Zurilla & Goldfried, 1971). At the turn of the century, APA President Martin Seligman (1999; Seligman & Csikszenthihalyi, 2000) called for a greater emphasis on *positive psychology* in the field of psychology in general. According to Seligman, the aim of this approach is to change the focus of psychology from a preoccupation with reducing and eliminating things that are "wrong" (i.e., maladaptive, self-defeating) to a greater emphasis on identifying and facilitating things that are "right" (e.g., adaptive, self-enhancing). In recent years, positive psychology has become a major force in the field of psychology and problem-solving training is a major part of this trend.

COGNITIVE PROCESSES AND SELF-CONTROL IN BEHAVIOR THERAPY

Initially, positive clinical interventions focused on the direct facilitation of behavioral competence in specific problematic situations using behavioral skills training methods, such as modeling and behavior rehearsal, as well as contingency management methods (e.g., prompting, positive reinforcement, and shaping). This situation-specific approach was found to be very effective in improving performance, but behavior changes were often limited to the specific training situations—generalized improvements in competence did not always occur. Thus, whereas this approach was very useful for specific behavioral deficits, it was much more difficult to deal with clinical problems that involved more generalized deficiencies in social competence, which may have resulted in many cases from deficits in problem solving and other general coping skills.

The problem of limited behavior changes helped to instigate a trend in behavior modification in the late 1960s toward a greater emphasis on cognitive mediation in an attempt to facilitate self-control and produce greater generalization and maintenance of behavior changes (Kendall & Hollon, 1979). Hence, behavior therapy was broadened to become *cognitive-behavioral therapy.* The cognitive activities focused on in this expanded approach to behavior modification have ranged from specific thoughts and cognitive appraisals, to a broader level of underlying beliefs and assumptions, to more complex processes such as information processing and problem solving (Murphy, 1985; A. M. Nezu, Nezu, & Lombardo, 2006; Turk & Salovey, 1985).

At a symposium on the role of cognitive factors in behavior modification at the 1968 APA convention, T. J. D'Zurilla and M. R. Goldfried argued that behavioral skills training programs should include training in problem-solving skills to facilitate broader and more durable behavior changes. This presentation was later expanded and published in 1971 under the title "Problem Solving and Behavior Modification." In this article, D'Zurilla and Goldfried argued that problem-solving training can be conceived as a form of self-control training, where individuals learn how to change their own behavior for the better and, thus, function as their own therapist. With these new problem-solving skills, individuals can increase their coping effectiveness across a wide range of problematic situations and, consequently, reduce stress in daily living which, in turn, helps to reduce and prevent stress-related symptoms and disorders.

A few years later, Spivack et al. (1976) published their influential book, *Problem-Solving Approach to Adjustment,* which presented evidence on the relationship between problem-solving ability and psychopathology and described several early studies on PST with both children and adults. At about this point in time, Mahoney (1974) described the promise of PST as follows:

> The potential relevance of problem solving to both clients and therapists needs little elaboration. In terms of adaptive versatility and the ability to cope with an ever-changing array of life problems, these cognitive skills may offer an invaluable personal paradigm for survival. Their potential contribution to therapeutic efficacy and independent self-improvement will hopefully become an issue of priority in future empirical scrutiny. (p. 212)

RICHARD LAZARUS'S RELATIONAL MODEL OF STRESS

While the preceding developments were occurring, Richard Lazarus and others in the field of stress research were developing a transactional or relational theory of stress (Lazarus, 1966, 1981, 1999; Lazarus & Folkman, 1984; McGrath, 1970, 1976). Within this framework, stress is viewed as a particular type of person-environment transaction or relationship in which demands are appraised as taxing or exceeding coping resources and endangering well-being (Lazarus & Folkman, 1984). Cognitive appraisal and coping are viewed as important mediators of the relationship between stressful situational demands and emotional stress responses. In this view, negative cognitive appraisals and coping deficits are assumed to be important causes of stress and stress-related disorders. In the 1970s and early 1980s, it soon became apparent that there was much conceptual overlap between this model of stress and social problem-solving theory. This led to the development of an integrated relational/problem-solving model of stress in which problem solving plays a central role as a general coping strategy that can significantly affect a person's ability to reduce, manage, and control stress and its negative effects across a wide range of situations (see chapter 6). This model provides a strong theoretical rationale for the use of PST as a treatment and prevention method.

Since the early 1970s, PST programs have been applied within a variety of clinical and counseling settings, including individual, group, marital, and family therapy and counseling. In addition, there have been preventive applications in nonclinical settings such as workshops, academic courses, and seminars. Target populations have included a wide range of people, including patients with depressive and anxiety disorders, substance abusers, people with mental retardation, patients with schizophrenia, various medical patient populations, family caregivers, individuals with lesser maladjustments (e.g., academic underachievement, weight-control problems), as well as normal individuals who are interested in maximizing their social and behavioral competence and managing stress more effectively. The types of problems focused on in training have ranged from personal problems (e.g., emotional, behavioral, and health), to relationship problems (e.g., marital and family conflicts), to broader community and social problems (e.g., crime and poverty). These PST programs will be described in chapter 10.

SUMMARY

Before the 1970s, the fields of clinical and counseling psychology had failed to recognize the potential value of problem-solving training for clinical intervention. Two major reasons for this neglect were (a) the dominance of the "medical" or "disease" model of psychopathology throughout most of the history of clinical psychology, and (b) the lack of relevance of most of the past experimental research on human problem solving for *social problem solving*, or problem solving as it occurs in the real world. The present problem-solving approach to clinical intervention had its beginnings in the late 1960s and early 1970s and has continued to develop and improve since that time. Four streams of historical development have shaped this approach: (a) the growing interest in the nature and nurturance of creativity, including creative problem solving; (b) the rise of the positive approach to clinical intervention; (c) recognition of the importance of cognitive processes and self-control in behavior therapy; and (d) the development of Richard Lazarus's relational model of stress, which identifies negative cognitive appraisals and coping deficits as major causes of stress and stress-related disorders. The next chapter describes the attitudes, skills, and abilities that are involved in the social problem-solving process.

CHAPTER TWO

Social Problem-Solving Processes

DEFINITIONS OF MAJOR CONCEPTS

Any adequate theory of social problem solving must clearly define three major concepts: (a) *problem solving,* (b) *problem,* and (c) *solution.* It is also important for theory, research, and practice to distinguish between the concepts of problem solving and *solution implementation.* The definitions presented below are based on concepts previously discussed by Davis (1966, 1973), D'Zurilla and Goldfried (1971), D'Zurilla and Nezu (1982, 1999), and Skinner (1953).

Problem Solving

As it occurs in the natural environment, *problem solving* may be defined as the self-directed cognitive-behavioral process by which a person attempts to identify or discover effective or adaptive solutions for specific problems encountered in everyday living. More specifically, this cognitive-behavioral process (a) makes available a variety of potentially effective solutions for a particular problem, and (b) increases the probability of selecting the most effective solution from among the various alternatives (D'Zurilla & Goldried, 1971). As this definition implies, problem solving is conceived here as a conscious, rational, effortful, and purposeful activity. Depending on the problem-solving goals, this process may be aimed at changing the problematic situation for the better, reducing the emotional distress that it produces, or both.

In the fields of clinical, counseling, and health psychology, *social problem solving* has become the most popular term for this phenomenon

(D'Zurilla & Nezu, 1982, 1999), although other terms have been used by some investigators, including *interpersonal problem solving* (Shure, 1981), *interpersonal cognitive problem solving* (Spivack et al., 1976), *personal problem solving* (Heppner & Petersen, 1982), and *applied problem solving* (Heppner, Neal, & Larson, 1984). It is important to note that the adjective *social* in the term social problem solving is not meant to limit the study of problem solving to any particular type of problem; rather, it is used only to highlight the fact that the focus of study is on problem solving that occurs within the natural social environment. Thus, theory and research on social problem solving has dealt with all types of problems in living, including impersonal problems (e.g., finances and personal property), personal/intrapersonal problems (i.e., cognitive, emotional, behavioral, and health), interpersonal problems (e.g., marital and family conflicts), and even broader community and societal problems (e.g., crime and public services).

Research on real-life problem solving has also been conducted in other areas of psychology, including cognitive, developmental/gero-psychology, and organizational/industrial psychology. Terms used by investigators in these areas have included *practical problem solving* (Denney & Pearce, 1989), *everyday problem solving* (Cornelius & Caspi, 1987), *everyday cognition* (Poon, Rubin, & Wilson, 1989), and *practical intelligence* (Sternberg & Wagner, 1986). The work in these areas has focused on such topics as problem solving in the elderly, age differences in problem-solving ability, and the role of problem solving in job performance.

Social problem solving is at the same time a learning process, a general coping strategy, and a self-control method. Because the solving of a problem results in a change in performance capability, social problem solving also qualifies as a learning process (Gagné, 1966). Because effective problem solving increases the probability of adaptive coping outcomes across a wide range of problematic situations, it is also a versatile coping strategy. Finally, because social problem solving is a *self-directed* learning process and coping strategy, it can also be viewed as a self-control method that has important implications for the maintenance and generalization of treatment effects (D'Zurilla & Goldfried, 1971; Mahoney, 1974; A. M. Nezu, 1987; Rehm & Rokke, 1988).

Problem

A *problem* (or problematic situation) is defined as any life situation or task (present or anticipated) that demands a response for adaptive functioning, but where no effective response is immediately apparent or available to the person due to the presence of one or more obstacles. The demands in a problematic situation may originate in the environment (e.g., objective task demands) or within the person (e.g., a personal goal, need, or commitment). The obstacles might include novelty, ambiguity, unpredictability, conflicting stimulus demands, performance skills deficits, or lack of resources. A person might recognize that a problem exists immediately, or only after repeated attempts to respond effectively have failed. A specific problem might be a single time-limited event (e.g., missing a train to work, an acute illness), a series of similar or related events (e.g., repeated unreasonable demands from one's boss, repeated violations of curfew by one's teenaged daughter), or a chronic, ongoing situation (e.g., continuous pain, feelings of loneliness, or medical illness).

An *interpersonal problem* is a special kind of real-life problem in which the obstacle is a conflict in the behavioral expectations or demands of two or more people in a relationship (Jacobson & Margolin, 1979). Within this context, *interpersonal problem solving* may be described as a cognitive-interpersonal process aimed at identifying or discovering a resolution to the conflict that is acceptable or satisfactory to all parties involved. Hence, according to this view, interpersonal problem solving is a "win-win" approach to resolving conflicts or disputes, rather than a "win-lose" approach that is likely to be ineffective in the long run.

As it is conceived here, a problem is not a characteristic of either the environment or the person alone. Instead, it is best described as a person-environment relationship characterized by a perceived imbalance or discrepancy between demands and coping response availability. As such, a problem can be expected to change in difficulty or significance over time, depending on changes in the environment, the person, or both. This relational view of a problem has major implications for problem-solving assessment as it suggests that problems are very individualist—that is, what is a problem for one person may not be a problem for another person. This issue will be discussed further in chapter 4.

Solution

A *solution* is a situation-specific coping response or response pattern (cognitive and/or behavioral) that is the product or outcome of the problem-solving process when it is applied to a specific problematic situation. An *effective* solution is one that achieves the problem-solving goal (i.e., changes the situation for the better and/or reduces the distress that it produces), while at the same time maximizing other positive consequences and minimizing negative consequences. The relevant consequences include effects on others as well as one's self, and long-term outcomes as well as short-term effects. Given this definition, it should be noted that the quality or effectiveness of any particular solution may vary for different individuals or different environments, depending on the norms, values, and goals of the problem solver or significant others who are responsible for judging the problem solver's solutions or coping responses.

With specific reference to an *interpersonal problem,* an effective solution is one that resolves the conflict or dispute by providing an outcome that is acceptable or satisfactory to all parties. In other words, the solution minimizes negative consequences and maximizes positive consequences for the two or more people involved in the dispute. This outcome may involve a consensus, compromise, or negotiated agreement that accommodates the interests and well-being of all concerned parties.

Problem Solving Versus Solution Implementation

Our theory of social problem solving distinguishes between the concepts of problem solving and *solution implementation.* These two processes are conceptually different and require different sets of skills. Problem solving refers to the process of *finding* solutions to specific problems, whereas solution implementation refers to the process of *carrying out* those solutions in the actual problematic situations. Problem-solving skills are assumed to be general, whereas solution-implementation skills are expected to vary across situations depending on the type of problem and solution. The range of possible solution-implementation skills includes all the cognitive and behavioral performance skills that might be required for effective functioning within a particular person's environment. Because they are different, problem-solving skills and solution-implementation skills are not always correlated. Hence, some individuals might possess poor problem-solving skills but good solution-implementation skills, or vice versa. Because both sets of skills are required for effective functioning or social competence, it is often necessary to combine PST with training in other social and behavioral skills in order to maximize positive outcomes (Goldfried & D'Zurilla, 1969; McFall, 1982; Sarason, 1981; Wrubel, Benner, & Lazarus, 1981).

Based on the definitions in the previous paragraph, it should now be clear that social problem solving represents one set of social skills that are important for social competence. Hence, PST is one form of social skills training. In the past, social skills training programs have focused almost exclusively on situation-specific behavioral skills (Bellack, 1979). However, the concept of social skills has since been broadened to include cognitive skills, and in recent years an increasing number of investigators have been including general problem-solving skills in these training programs (Kagan, 1984; Liberman, McCann, & Wallace, 1976; McFall, 1982; Sarason, 1981; Trower, Bryant, & Argle, 1978; Sprafkin, Gershaw, & Goldstein, 1980).

LEVELS OF PROCESS VARIABLES

Social problem solving has been defined here as a cognitive-behavioral process that results in the discovery of a solution to a problem. The variables involved in this process can be described at three different levels, each having differential effects on problem-solving performance. At the metacognitive level is a set of *orienting responses* which serve a motivational function. At the performance level is a series of *problem-solving skills* that are necessary for effective problem-solving performance. Underlying the performance level are the *basic cognitive abilities* that affect the ability to learn and implement the required problem-solving skills.

Orienting Responses

Orienting responses are the immediate cognitive-emotional responses of a person when first confronted with a problematic situation. They include an attentional set to either recognize or ignore problems and a set of relatively stable cognitive-emotional schemas (e.g., beliefs, appraisals) which describe how a person generally thinks and feels about life's problems and his or her ability to solve them, independent of any specific problem. This generalized response set is based primarily on the person's problem-solving history. Depending on the nature of these orienting variables, they may produce either positive affect and approach tendencies that are likely to facilitate problem-solving performance, or negative affect and avoidance tendencies, that tend to inhibit or disrupt performance. However, these variables do not include the skills that are necessary for effective problem-solving performance.

Problem-Solving Skills

Problem-solving skills may be conceptualized as a set of specific goal-directed tasks that must be performed in order to solve a particular problem successfully. Each task has its own unique purpose or function in the problem-solving process. They include the tasks of defining and formulating the problem, generating a list of alternative solutions, making a decision, implementing the solution, and evaluating the solution outcome (D'Zurilla & Goldfried, 1971). In behavioral terms, this series of problem-solving tasks can be conceived of as a behavioral chain, where the successful completion of each task reinforces task performance, and the general reinforcing outcome for the entire series of tasks is the discovery of a solution to the problem. In the next chapter, these specific problem-solving skills will be discussed in more detail.

Basic Cognitive Abilities

These involve the specific abilities that underlie and affect the learning and performance of the problem-solving skills identified previously. Although it has not yet been established which basic abilities are most important for effective problem solving, they are likely to include some of the specific cognitive abilities described by Spivack and colleagues (1976), such as *causal thinking* (ability to understand that thoughts, actions, and feelings are in response to prior events in the social environment), *consequential thinking* (ability to anticipate the effects of behavior on oneself and others), *means-ends thinking* (ability to conceptualize relevant means to a goal), *alternative thinking* (ability to produce alternative solutions to problems), and *perspective taking* (ability to perceive a situation from another person's perspective). The alternative thinking ability may be linked to the capacity for creative thinking and imagination (Guilford, 1977; Osborn, 1963; Parnes, 1962).

These cognitive abilities and other potentially important basic abilities are likely to be found in Guilford's *Structure-of-Intellect* model (1967, 1968). This model has three dimensions: (a) *contents* (major kinds of information), (b) *products* (how information is structured or organized), and (c) *operations* (intellectual processes). In Guilford's model, there are five kinds of informational content (visual, auditory, symbolic, semantic, and behavioral), six kinds of products (units, classes, relations, systems, transformations, and implications), and five kinds of operations (memory, cognition, convergent production, divergent production, and evaluation). Each cell in the model represents a specific ability. The abilities that are measured by traditional IQ tests are included in the intellectual operations of *memory* (storage and retrieval of information), *cognition* (knowing and understanding), *convergent production* (focused search for one correct answer or conclusion), and *evaluation* (comparing and judging information). The operation of *divergent production* (broad search for alternative ideas or solutions) is not included in traditional IQ tests and is not correlated with traditional IQ measures. However, divergent-production abilities are major determinants of creativity. They include abilities such as *fluency* (ability to produce a large number of ideas), *flexibility* (ability to produce a variety of kinds of ideas), and *originality* (ability to produce unusual or novel ideas).

Guilford (1977) has emphasized the overlap that exists between creativity and social problem solving. In his Structure-of-Intellect Problem Solving (SIPS) model, all five intellectual operations are represented, but divergent production is particularly emphasized. Within the informational content dimension, the abilities associated with the categories labeled semantic (verbal, meaningful information) and behavioral (personal-social information) are most relevant for social problem solving. According to Guilford, the behavioral category, in particular, entails a large number of abilities that are important for social problem solving (e.g., information processing abilities, alternative thinking). The operation of memory is important because it involves the storage and retrieval of information as needed during the problem-solving process. The operation of cognition focuses on two important problem-solving events—awareness that a problem exists (i.e., cognition of implications) and comprehension of the nature of the problem (i.e., cognition of relations and systems). Convergent production and divergent production both contribute to the generation of solutions, divergent production being more important because of the emphasis on fluency, flexibility, and originality. In addition, the abilities associated with the product category of *transformations* (ability to modify and improve information or ideas) are considered important for the generation of good-quality solution alternatives. Finally, the operation of evaluation is necessary for comparing and judging solutions and assessing solution outcome.

More research is needed to determine exactly which basic abilities account the most for individual differences in social problem-solving performance in both normal and clinical populations. Tests that have been developed to measure the abilities described in Guilford's model could contribute much to this research (Guilford, 1967, 1977; Parnes & Noller, 1973). In addition, the rigorous methodology developed in recent years in cognitive psychology and social cognition for studying the parameters of social information processing should also help to identify and assess these basic abilities (e.g., Bodenhausen, Macrae, & Hugenberg, 2003; Leighton & Sternberg, 2003; Morris, Bellack, & Tenhula, 2004).

One clinical population that is likely to have significant deficits in the basic cognitive abilities required for effective social problem solving involves individuals with schizophrenia. A model of cognitive dysfunction in schizophrenia proposed by Cohen and his colleagues (Braver, Barch, & Cohen, 1999, as described in Morris et al., 2004) might help to stimulate research that could shed more light on these basic cognitive deficits. According to this model, the core neurocognitive deficit in schizophrenia is the failure to exert adequate control over thoughts and actions, which results in significant impairments in task performance, including problem solving. These authors propose that in order to selectively attend to relevant stimuli, ignore extraneous sensory input, manipulate information, access relevant memories, and select appropriate actions, a person must maintain an adequate mental context. Mental context is defined as task-relevant information that facilitates selective activation of neural pathways that are necessary for effective task performance. According to Braver et al., the dopamine (DA) neurotransmitter system in the prefrontal cortex modulates the availability of context information to active memory. They further propose that the pathology of schizophrenia lies in a disturbance of the DA system, resulting in significant deficits in the effective maintenance of timely context information. Hence, in order to improve social problem-solving performance in schizophrenic patients, this model suggests that it would be necessary to address this core neurocognitive deficit, which might require pharmacological interventions, as well as behavioral interventions (for a further of discussion of this issue, see Morris et al., 2004).

RELATIONSHIP BETWEEN SOCIAL PROBLEM SOLVING AND INTELLIGENCE

A number of studies have investigated the relationship between real-life problem-solving performance and general intelligence as measured by traditional IQ tests and tests of academic aptitude. These studies have consistently found nonsignificant or low correlations (see Cantor & Kihlstrom, 1987; Epstein & Meier, 1989; Heppner & Petersen, 1982; Spivack et al., 1976; Sternberg & Wagner, 1986; Sternberg, Wagner, Williams, & Horvath, 1995). Tests of Guilford's divergent-production ability also show low correlations with IQ tests (Guilford, 1977). However, according to Guilford, there is an interesting relationship between divergent production ability and IQ. Individuals with low IQs have only low scores on divergent production tests. However, when IQs are high, divergent production scores vary. Thus, it appears that IQ puts an upper limit on divergent-production performance, but high IQ does not ensure high divergent production ability. According to Guilford, this relationship must be qualified in that it has been established only with divergent-production tests that focus on semantic content. If divergent production is important for social problem solving, as Guilford suggests, then there may be a similar relationship between IQ and social problem-solving ability. Such a relationship would be consistent with the observation that mentally retarded individuals are generally deficient in both general intelligence and adaptive social functioning, whereas individuals with higher IQs show greater variability in social competence.

TRAINING IN SOCIAL PROBLEM SOLVING

Training programs may focus on any one or all of the three levels of process variables described in this chapter, depending on where the significant deficits are found. To date, most programs for adolescent and adult populations have focused primarily on the first two levels—orienting responses and problem-solving skills. There are two reasons for this emphasis. One is the assumption that most adolescents and adults already possess the basic cognitive abilities that are required for the learning of positive orienting responses and effective problem-solving skills. The second reason is the lack of knowledge about the basic abilities that are most important for social problem solving. As more knowledge is acquired about these basic abilities and appropriate methods are developed for assessing and enhancing them, training programs can be extended to include these methods with populations that are likely to have significant deficits in these abilities, such as patients with schizophrenia.

SUMMARY

Social problem solving is defined as the self-directed cognitive-affective-behavioral process by which an individual attempts to identify or discover solutions to specific problems encountered in everyday living. A *problem* is defined as a life situation that demands a response for effective functioning, but for which no effective response is immediately available to the person confronted with the situation. A *solution* is a situation-specific coping response or response pattern that is the product or outcome of the problem-solving process. An *effective* solution achieves the goal of changing a problematic situation or one's own personal reactions to it so that it is no longer perceived as a problem, while at the same time maximizing other positive consequences (benefits) and minimizing negative consequences (costs). It is important to distinguish between the concepts of problem solving and *solution implementation*. The former refers to the process of finding an effective solution, whereas the latter is the process of carrying out the solution in the actual problematic situation. These two processes consist of different sets of skills that are not always correlated.

The variables involved in the social problem-solving process may be described at three different levels. At the metacognitive level are *orienting responses* which serve a motivational function. At the performance level are *problem-solving skills* which are necessary for effective problem-solving performance (i.e., the discovery of effective solutions). Underlying the performance level are *basic cognitive abilities* which affect the learning and performance of the problem-solving skills. The most important basic abilities for social problem solving might be Guilford's divergent production abilities (1967, 1968), which are important determinants of creativity. Studies on the relationship between social problem-solving ability and general intelligence as measured by traditional IQ tests have consistently found nonsignificant or low correlations. However, it is possible that IQ might put an upper limit on social problem-solving ability. To date, training programs have focused primarily on orienting responses and problem-solving skills. As more is learned about the basic cognitive abilities that are most important for social problem solving, training programs can be extended to include methods for assessing and enhancing them with populations that might have significant deficits in these abilities, such as individuals with schizophrenia.

CHAPTER THREE

A Five-Dimensional Model of Social Problem Solving

The majority of PST programs reported in the literature have been based on a model of social problem solving originally developed by D'Zurilla and Goldfried (1971) and later expanded and refined by D'Zurilla and Nezu (1982, 1990, 1999; A. M. Nezu & D'Zurilla, 1989). Based on the collective research of D'Zurilla, Nezu, and Maydeu-Olivares (2002; Maydeu-Olivares & D'Zurilla, 1995, 1996), this model has been further revised in recent years, resulting in a new five-dimensional model of social problem solving.

ORIGINAL SOCIAL PROBLEM-SOLVING MODEL

The original model assumed that problem-solving outcomes in the real world are largely determined by two major, partially independent processes: (a) *problem orientation,* and (b) *problem-solving skills* (later referred to as "problem-solving proper" by D'Zurilla & Nezu [1999] and more recently as "problem-solving style" by D'Zurilla et al. [2002]; D'Zurilla, Nezu, & Maydeu-Olivares [2004]). *Problem orientation* is a metacognitive process that reflects a person's general awareness and perceptions of problems in living, as well as his or her own problem-solving ability. This process primarily serves a motivational function in problem solving; it does not include the skills that are required to solve problems effectively. *Problem-solving skills,* on the other hand, refer to the cognitive and behavioral activities by which a person attempts to understand problems in everyday living and find effective *solutions,* or ways of coping with them.

Problem Orientation

According to this model, a positive or constructive problem orientation produces positive emotions and approach tendencies, sets the occasion for problem-solving behavior, keeps attention focused on constructive problem-solving activities, and maximizes effort, persistence, and tolerance for frustration and uncertainty. In contrast, a negative or dysfunctional problem orientation generates negative emotions and avoidance tendencies, increases destructive worrying, and reduces effort, persistence, and tolerance for frustration and uncertainty.

The model identifies five major problem orientation variables: (1) problem recognition, (2) problem attribution, (3) problem appraisal, (4) perceived control, and (5) time/effort commitment. *Problem recognition* refers to the general tendency or readiness to recognize problems when they occur during the course of daily living rather than ignoring or denying them. Problem recognition is important because it activates the other problem orientation schemas and sets the occasion for the application of problem-solving skills. *Problem attribution* refers to a person's causal beliefs concerning problems in living. A positive problem attribution is the belief that problems are normal and inevitable events in life for everyone, whereas a negative problem attribution is the belief that problems are caused by stupidity, incompetence, or psychological disturbance. *Problem appraisal* is based on Richard Lazarus's concept of "primary appraisal" (Lazarus & Folkman, 1984). It refers to a person's evaluation of the significance of a problem for well-being (psychological, social, or physical). A positive problem appraisal involves viewing a problem as a challenge or an opportunity for benefit or gain (e.g., mastery, achievement), whereas a negative problem appraisal involves the perception that a problem is a threat to well-being (e.g., harm, loss).

Based on Albert Bandura's (1997) concepts of "self-efficacy" and "outcome expectancy," *perceived control* has two components: (a) problem-solving self-efficacy, and (b) problem-solving outcome expectancy. The former refers to the general belief that one is capable of solving problems and implementing solutions effectively, whereas the latter refers to the general belief that problems in living are solvable. *Time/effort commitment* also has two components: (a) the likelihood that an individual will estimate accurately the time it will take to solve a particular problem successfully, and (b) the likelihood that the individual will be willing to devote the necessary time and effort to problem solving. This variable is important for problem solving because many problems in life are complex and difficult, requiring effort, persistence, and a tolerance for frustration and uncertainty.

Problem-Solving Skills

The model identifies four major problem-solving skills: (1) problem definition and formulation, (2) generation of alternative solutions, (3) decision making, and (4) solution implementation and verification. These four skills may be viewed as a set of specific goal-directed tasks that enable a person to solve a particular problem successfully. Each task has its own unique purpose or function in the problem-solving process. The function of *problem definition and formulation* is to gather relevant, factual information about the problem, clarify the nature of the problem (i.e., identify demands, obstacles, and/or conflicts), and set a realistic problem-solving goal. The purpose of *generation of alternative solutions* is to produce a list of potential solutions in such a way as to maximize the likelihood that the best solution will be among them. This is accomplished by applying three principles: quantity, deferment of judgment, and variety. To apply the quantity principle, the person generates as many solutions as possible. When using the deferment of judgment principle, the person suspends judgment or critical evaluation of solutions until later in the problem-solving process (i.e., during the decision-making task). To apply the variety principle, the person generates as many different types of solutions as possible.

The purpose of *decision making* is to evaluate (judge and compare) the available solutions and choose the best one(s) for implementation in the problematic situation. In the present model, the best solution is the one that is most likely to achieve the problem-solving goal while maximizing positive consequences and minimizing negative consequences. Finally, the function of *solution implementation and verification* is to assess the solution outcome and verify the effectiveness or utility of the chosen solution in the actual problematic situation.

Based on this theoretical model, D'Zurilla and Nezu (1990) developed the Social Problem-Solving Inventory (SPSI), which consists of two major scales: the Problem Orientation Scale (POS) and the Problem-Solving Skills Scale (PSSS). The items in each scale were designed to reflect both constructive and dysfunctional problem-solving characteristics (cognitive, emotional, and behavioral). The assumption that problem orientation and problem-solving skills are different, albeit related, components of social problem-solving ability was supported by data showing that the POS items correlated relatively high with the total POS score and relatively low with the total PSSS score, whereas the reverse was true for the PSSS items (D'Zurilla & Nezu, 1990).

REVISED SOCIAL PROBLEM-SOLVING MODEL

Several years later, Maydeu-Olivares and D'Zurilla (1995, 1996) conducted exploratory and confirmatory factor analyses on the SPSI in a large sample of young adults and found only moderate support for the original two-factor model (i.e., problem orientation and problem-solving skills). A five-factor model consisting of two different, albeit related, problem orientation dimensions and three different problem-solving styles was found to be more appropriate. The two problem orientation dimensions are *positive problem orientation* and *negative problem orientation*, whereas the three problem-solving styles include *rational problem solving* (i.e., effective problem-solving skills), *impulsivity/carelessness style*, and *avoidance style*. Positive problem orientation and rational problem solving are constructive or facilitative dimensions, whereas negative problem orientation, impulsivity/carelessness style, and avoidance style are dysfunctional or inhibitive dimensions. As would be expected, the constructive dimensions are positively correlated with each other and negatively correlated with the dysfunctional dimensions, and vice versa (D'Zurilla et al., 2002). Each problem-solving dimension is described more specifically in the following paragraphs.

Problem Orientation Dimensions

Positive problem orientation is a constructive problem-solving cognitive set that involves the general disposition to (a) appraise a problem as a challenge (i.e., opportunity for benefit or gain), (b) believe that problems are solvable (i.e., optimism), (c) believe in one's personal ability to solve problems successfully (i.e., problem-solving self-efficacy), (d) believe that successful problem solving takes time and effort, and (e) commit oneself to solving problems with dispatch rather than avoiding them. In contrast, *negative problem orientation* is a dysfunctional or inhibitive cognitive-emotional set that involves the general tendency to (a) view a problem as a significant threat to well-being (i.e., psychological, social, or economic), (b) doubt one's own personal ability to solve problems successfully (i.e., low problem-solving self-efficacy), and (c) easily become frustrated and upset when confronted with problems (i.e., low frustration tolerance).

Problem-Solving Styles

Rational problem solving is a constructive problem-solving style that is defined as the rational, deliberate, and systematic application of effective problem-solving skills. As described in the original model, there are four major problem-solving skills: (1) problem definition and formulation, (2) generation of alternative solutions, (3) decision making, and (4) solution implementation and verification. In *problem definition and formulation,* the problem solver tries to clarify and understand the problem by gathering as many specific and concrete facts about the problem as possible, identifying demands and obstacles, and setting realistic problem-solving goals (e.g., changing the situation for the better, accepting the situation, and minimizing emotional distress). In the *generation of alternative solutions,* the person focuses on the problem-solving goals and tries to identify as many potential solutions as possible, including a variety of different conventional and original solutions. In *decision making,* the problem solver anticipates the consequences of the different solutions, judges and compares them, and then chooses the best or potentially most effective solution. In the final step, *solution implementation and verification,* the person carefully monitors and evaluates the outcome of the chosen solution after attempting to implement it in the real-life problematic situation (see chapter 8 for a more detailed description of these four problem-solving skills).

Impulsivity/carelessness style is a dysfunctional problem-solving pattern characterized by active attempts to apply problem-solving strategies and techniques, but these attempts are narrow, impulsive, careless, hurried, and incomplete. A person with this problem-solving style typically considers only a few solution alternatives, and often acts impulsively by choosing the first idea that comes to mind. In addition, he or she scans alternative solutions and consequences quickly and unsystematically, and monitors solution outcomes carelessly and inadequately.

Avoidance style is another dysfunctional problem-solving pattern characterized by procrastination, passivity or inaction, and dependency. The avoidant problem solver prefers to avoid problems rather than confront them head on, puts off problem solving for as long as possible, waits for problems to resolve themselves, and attempts to shift the responsibility for solving his or her problems to other people.

These five dimensions of social problem-solving ability are measured by the Social Problem-Solving Inventory-Revised (SPSI-R; D'Zurilla et al., 2002), which is described more specifically in chapter 4 of this volume. The five-dimensional model has been cross-validated in samples of young adults (D'Zurilla et al., 2002), as well as with adolescents (Sadowski, Moore, & Kelley, 1994). Using translated versions of the SPSI-R, the model has also been cross-validated in samples of Spanish adults (Maydeu-Olivares, Rodríquez-Fornells, Gómez-Benito, & D'Zurilla, 2000), German adults (Graf, 2003), and Chinese adults (Siu & Shek, 2005).

Based on the revised social problem-solving model, the hypothesized social problem-solving process is depicted in Figure 3.1. As the figure

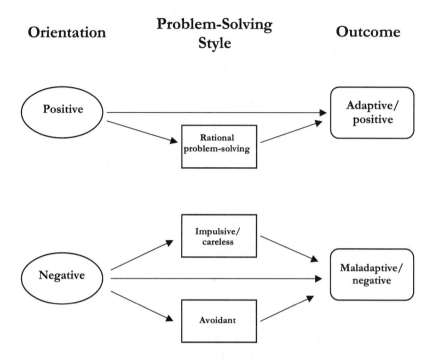

FIGURE 3.1 Schematic representation of the social problem-solving process based on the revised, five-dimension model of social problem solving.

shows, problem-solving outcomes are assumed to be determined by two general processes: (a) problem orientation, and (b) problem-solving style. The figure also shows the two differing problem orientation dimensions and three different problem-solving styles that comprise the revised social problem-solving model. Positive and negative problem orientation are shown as having direct effects on outcomes as well as indirect effects via the problem-solving styles. Constructive or effective problem solving is depicted as a process in which a positive problem orientation facilitates rational problem solving (i.e., the systematic application of effective problem-solving skills) which, in turn, is likely to produce positive problem-solving outcomes.

Dysfunctional or ineffective problem solving is depicted in Figure 3.1 as a process in which a negative problem orientation contributes to either impulsive/careless problem solving or problem-solving avoidance which, in turn, is likely to produce negative outcomes. Hence, our revised social problem-solving model predicts that negative or maladaptive outcomes are most likely to be produced by individuals who score relatively high on measures of negative problem orientation, impulsivity/carelessness style, and avoidance style, and relatively low on measures of positive problem orientation and rational problem solving. In contrast, positive or adaptive outcomes are most likely to be produced by individuals who score relatively high on positive problem orientation and rational problem solving, while scoring relatively low on negative problem orientation, impulsivity/carelessness style, and avoidance style. This model of effective problem solving serves as our prescriptive model for PST (see chapter 8).

All of the hypothesized relationships in Figure 3.1 have been supported by results from experimental and/or correlational research. A selective review of relevant experimental studies is presented in the following paragraphs. The relevant correlational research is reviewed in chapter 7.

Empirical Evaluation of Model Components

Several components of the social problem-solving model have been evaluated in experimental studies that provided training in the particular component(s) and then observed the effects on some measure of problem-solving performance. The model components that have been studied include positive problem orientation and three of the four rational problem solving skills, namely, problem definition and formulation, generation of alternative solutions, and decision making. The subjects in most studies were normal college students. However, one study included both depressed and nondepressed college students, another study focused on after-care psychiatric patients, and a third study focused on alcoholic in-patients.

Positive problem orientation was evaluated in a study by Cormier, Otani, and Cormier (1986). Subjects who received instruction in positive problem orientation performed significantly better than control-group subjects on a problem-solving task in which they were asked to select the best alternative from a list of solution alternatives to several socially oriented problems. In addition, there is much experimental support for the effects of one particular problem orientation variable on coping performance, namely, perceived self-efficacy (Bandura, 1997). According to this research, people avoid tasks they believe exceed their coping capabilities, but they willingly undertake activities they judge themselves capable of managing successfully. In addition, Heppner and his associates (Heppner, 1988; Heppner & Petersen, 1982) have reported studies that suggest that problem-orientation variables, such as problem-solving confidence and perceived control, have a positive influence on problem-solving performance.

Several studies have provided evidence supporting the efficacy of training in *problem definition and formulation* (PDF). In one study, subjects who were given specific training in PDF did significantly better on a decision-making task than subjects who received no training (A. M. Nezu & D'Zurilla, 1981a). In another study, subjects who were trained in PDF produced more effective solution alternatives on a problem-solving task than did a control group that did not receive such training (A. M. Nezu & D'Zurilla, 1981b). Results supporting the important role of PDF in problem solving were also found by Cormier et al. (1986). In this study, subjects trained in problem-solving skills that included PDF selected significantly better solution alternatives after a one-month follow-up than did subjects whose training did not include PDF. These results are consistent with those reported by A. M. Nezu and D'Zurilla (1981b) while providing additional evidence for the durability of training effects.

Several studies have investigated the efficacy of principles involved in the *generation of alternative solutions* component of the model. Brilhart and Jochem (1964) found that "brainstorming" instructions (i.e., quantity principle, deferment of judgment principle, and variety principle) resulted in more good-quality solution ideas than instructions requesting subjects to produce only good ideas. D'Zurilla and Nezu (1980) found that subjects who received training in the use of the quantity principle produced significantly more effective solutions than control subjects who received no training. These results were later replicated by A. M. Nezu and D'Zurilla (1981b) and by A. M. Nezu and Ronan (1987). The latter study found significant training effects with depressed as well as nondepressed college students. Several studies have focused on creative problems, such as finding new uses for an ordinary broom or wire coat hanger and inventing brand names for new products. Results supporting brainstorming instructions have been found by Meadow, Parnes, and Reese (1959), Parnes and Meadow (1959), and Weisskopf-Joelson and Eliseo (1961). Evidence for the deferment of judgment principle has been provided by Bayless (1967) and Parloff and Handlon (1964).

Four studies have been reported that provide support for the model's *decision making* component. A. M. Nezu and D'Zurilla (1979) investigated the effects of training in decision making on the ability of subjects to make effective decisions when asked to choose the best solution from among a list of alternative solutions to socially oriented test problems. The results showed that subjects who received specific training in the decision-making component made more effective choices than control subjects who received no training or who were provided only with a general definition of the expected utility model of decision making. These results were later replicated in studies by A. M. Nezu and D'Zurilla (1981a) and A. M. Nezu and Ronan (1987). The latter study found significant results for both depressed and nondepressed college students. Results supporting the role of the decision-making component were also reported by Cormier et al. (1986). Focusing on a task in which subjects were required to describe in detail the behaviors they used to solve problems, Cormier et al. found that subjects trained with the decision-making component described significantly more problem-solving behaviors at a 1-month follow-up assessment than did subjects trained without the decision-making component.

In addition to providing evidence supporting the individual contributions of positive problem orientation, problem definition and formulation, and decision making to problem-solving effectiveness, the study by Cormier et al. (1986) also assessed the effects of training in all three of these components together *plus* the generation of alternative solutions component. Compared to an untrained control group, they found that the trained subjects selected significantly better solution alternatives and described significantly more problem-solving behaviors at posttesting and at the 1-month follow-up.

In a study that focused on seven chronic psychiatric patients enrolled in an aftercare program, Hansen, St. Lawrence, and Christoff (1985) used a multiple-baseline design to evaluate the effectiveness of training in the following problem-solving skills: (a) problem identification (specific statement of a problem); (b) goal definition (specific statement of a desired end); (c) solution evaluation (specific benefit or cost statement regarding a solution); (d) evaluation of alternatives (specific benefit and/or cost statement regarding at least two solutions); and (e) selection of a best solution (explicit choice of one of the proposed solutions as the best course of action).

A group training format was used, with sessions conducted twice weekly. Training focused on the first skill component until the subjects demonstrated skill acquisition, and then the next component was trained, and so on. Following each training session, skill acquisition and the effectiveness of solutions were assessed with four of the problematic situations used in training and four unfamiliar generalization situations. A social validation assessment was also conducted by comparing the patients' problem-solving effectiveness with that of 20 average, nonpsychiatric persons living in the community. All of the problematic situations used for training and assessment approximated actual situations that the patients were likely to encounter in the community and that were reported as problematic by the patients and the program staff.

Results showed that each component skill rapidly improved with the introduction of training for that particular skill, with the improvement generalizing to the untrained problematic situations. Moreover, problem-solving effectiveness (i.e., the effectiveness of solutions as rated by independent judges) improved significantly over time, with the largest increase occurring during the solution evaluation phase of training. With regard to the social validation assessment, prior to training the patient sample showed a significant deficit in problem-solving effectiveness compared to the criterion nonpsychiatric sample. By the evaluation of alternatives phase of training, however, the patient's problem-solving effectiveness had improved to the point where it was equivalent to that of the criterion sample.

In a similar multiple-baseline study focusing on five alcoholic inpatients, Kelly, Scott, Prue, and Rychtarik (1985) provided training in problem definition and formulation, generation of alternative solutions, and decision making. Training resulted in significant improvement in all three component skills; however, no concurrent improvement was found on a problem-solving performance test using personally relevant problematic situations related to alcohol.

The negative results for the problem-solving performance test in the aforementioned study conflict with the positive results found with college student subjects in the A. M. Nezu and D'Zurilla studies (1981a, 1981b) and the A. M. Nezu and Ronan study (1987), as well as with the chronic aftercare psychiatric patients in the Hansen et al. study (1985). An informal observation reported by Kelly et al. (1985) suggests a possible explanation for their negative findings. On the problem-solving test, subjects were asked to generate alternative solutions and then choose the best one. According to the investigators, their alcoholic subjects often generated more effective solutions but rejected them, either because of negative beliefs about the solution or because of a desire to avoid a stressful encounter, such as an assertive confrontation. This observation supports the view that negative cognitive and emotional factors can have a detrimental effect on problem-solving performance, especially in a clinical population, and that PST programs must include procedures to assess and control these disruptive factors. As the positive problem orientation component of the present problem-solving model is designed for this purpose, it would appear to be a very important component for PST programs with clinical populations (Heppner & Anderson, 1985; A. M. Nezu & Perri, 1989).

No experimental studies have specifically examined the solution-implementation and verification component of the model. However, it is an undisputed fact that an objective assessment of outcome is necessary to establish clearly the success of any behavior change procedure. Thus, the evidence supporting the use of self-monitoring and self-evaluation in behavioral assessment in general can be used to support the efficacy of solution implementation and verification (see Barlow, Haynes, & Nelson, 1984; Cone & Hawkins, 1977).

In conclusion, there is empirical support for the efficacy of positive problem orientation and three of the four problem-solving skills that comprise the rational problem-solving dimension of the social problem-solving model. All components contribute significantly to problem-solving effectiveness. The strongest evidence appears to favor the problem definition and formulation component. These results argue for a careful definition and formulation of the problem before proceeding to the tasks of generating alternative solutions and decision making.

SUMMARY

A model of social problem solving is described that consists of two major, partially independent components: (a) problem orientation, and (b) problem-solving skills. *Problem orientation* is a metacognitive process that reflects a person's general awareness and evaluation of problems in living and his or her own problem-solving ability. This process primarily serves a motivational function in problem solving. *Problem-solving skills,* on the other hand, refers to the cognitive and behavioral activities by which a person attempts to understand problems and find effective solutions or ways of coping with them. A self-report instrument called the Social Problem-Solving Inventory (SPSI) was developed to measure these two components of social problem solving.

Factor analytic research using the SPSI has produced a revised, five-dimensional model of social problem solving consisting of two different problem-orientation dimensions and three different problem-solving styles. The two problem-orientation dimensions are positive problem orientation and negative problem orientation, whereas the three problem-solving styles are rational problem solving (i.e., effective problem-solving skills), impulsivity/carelessness style, and avoidance style. This model has been cross-validated in samples of young adults, adolescents, Spanish adults, German adults, and Chinese adults. The model predicts that positive or adaptive problem-solving outcomes are likely to be produced by individuals who score relatively high on measures of positive problem orientation and rational problem solving and relatively low on measures of negative problem orientation, impulsivity/carelessness style, and avoidance style. In contrast, negative or maladaptive outcomes are most likely to be produced by individuals who score relatively high on negative problem orientation, impulsivity/carelessness style, and avoidance style, while scoring relatively low on positive problem orientation and rational problem solving. Experimental research was reviewed that provides support for several components of this model.

CHAPTER FOUR

Measures of Social Problem-Solving Ability

This chapter discusses assessment methods and instruments that have been used to measure social problem-solving ability in research on social problem solving and PST, as well as in clinical settings. Before describing the most popular and promising measures, we will discuss the important distinction between process measures and outcome measures, as well as the differences between verbal and observational measures.

PROCESS VERSUS OUTCOME MEASURES

It is useful to distinguish between two major types of problem-solving measures: (a) process measures, and (b) outcome measures. Process measures directly assess the general cognitive and behavioral activities (e.g., appraisals, beliefs, skills) that facilitate or inhibit the discovery of effective or adaptive solutions for specific problems, whereas outcome measures assess the quality of those specific solutions. Hence, process measures are used to assess specific strengths and deficits in social problem-solving ability, whereas outcome measures are used to evaluate problem-solving performance, or the ability of a person to apply his skills effectively to specific problems. An outcome measure can be viewed as a global indicator of social problem-solving ability, but unlike a process measure, it does not provide any information about the specific components of social problem-solving ability.

Process measures can be subdivided into inventories and process performance tests. As the term is used here, a problem-solving inventory is a broad survey of a person's problem-solving attitudes, strategies, and techniques, both positive (facilitative) and negative (inhibitive). Some inventories also estimate the extent to which the person actually uses the problem-solving skills that he or she possesses, as well as the manner in which these techniques are typically applied (e.g., efficiently, systematically, impulsively, carelessly, etc.). Most problem-solving inventories are pencil-and-paper questionnaires that employ Likert-type items, but other formats can be used for this purpose as well, such as structured interviews, audiotape procedures, and computer-assisted methods.

The major disadvantage of a problem-solving inventory is that it does not actually *test* the person's problem-solving skills, that is, it does not assess the ability of individuals to apply their skills effectively to a specific problem-solving task. A process performance test, on the other hand, is specifically designed to make this assessment. The performance test format presents the person with a task that requires him to use a specific skill or ability (e.g., problem recognition, problem definition and formulation, generation of alternative solutions, decision making). The individual's performance is then judged or evaluated, and this measure is viewed as an indicator of his level of ability in that particular area (see D'Zurilla & Nezu, 1980; A. M. Nezu & D'Zurilla, 1979, 1981a, 1981b; Spivack et al., 1976). Because performance tests more closely approximate real-life problem-solving behavior than inventories, these measures might be expected to have greater external validity, although this is an issue that has not yet been adequately researched.

All outcome measures are performance tests. However, instead of testing one particular component of the problem-solving process, outcome measures tend to assess overall problem-solving performance by presenting a person with a problem and asking him or her to solve it, after which the quality of the solution is evaluated. Most outcome measures employ hypothetical test problems, but subjects' solutions for their real current problems have also been assessed (see Camp, Doherty, Moody-Thomas, & Denney, 1989; Marx, Williams, & Claridge, 1992; Schotte & Clum, 1987). When real problems are used, the subjects may be asked to report their solutions verbally, either before or after they implement their solutions, or solution implementation may be directly observed, either in the natural environment or in some simulated or role-played problem-solving situation.

Rather than assessing process and outcome separately, some outcome measures have been designed to assess one or more process variables as well, thus providing more information about the person's problem-solving ability (Donahoe et al., 1990; Getter & Nowinski,

1981; Goddard & McFall, 1992; C. M. Nezu, Nezu, & Arean, 1991; Plienis et al., 1987; Sayers & Bellack, 1995; Schotte & Clum, 1987). For example, before instructing the person to report a solution to a test problem, the person might be instructed to list as many alternative solutions as possible, which provides a measure of one problem-solving skill, namely, the ability to generate alternative solutions. As most process variables are cognitive processes (e.g., decision-making), a useful method for assessing these processes during a problem-solving task is the "think aloud" method described by Meichenbaum, Henshaw, and Himel (1982), or the *Articulated Thoughts During Simulated Situations* procedure developed by Davison, Robins, and Johnson (1983).

Two general types of scoring procedures have been used in problem-solving outcome assessment: *quantitative* scoring and *qualitative* scoring. In quantitative scoring, some relevant solution variable is identified and a frequency count is taken. For example, in the scoring system for the Means-Ends Problem-Solving procedure (MEPS; Platt & Spivack, 1975; Spivack, Shure, & Platt, 1985), quantitative scores are computed for *relevant means* (discrete steps that enable the problem solver to move closer to the goal), *obstacles* (interferences with goal attainment), and *time* (references to the fact that problem solving takes time or that appropriate timing is an important ingredient of an effective solution). Qualitative scoring, on the other hand, usually involves a rating or classification of the subject's overall solution on some dimension of solution quality, such as effectiveness, appropriateness, active, passive, or avoidance (Fischler & Kendall, 1988; Freedman, Rosenthal, Donahoe, Schlundt, & McFall, 1978; Getter & Nowinski, 1981; Linehan, Camper, Chiles, Strosahl, & Shearin, 1987; Marx et al., 1992).

Several investigators have suggested that quantitative scores may not provide sufficient relevant information about a person's solutions to distinguish between different levels of problem-solving competence and adjustment. In one study, Fischler and Kendall (1988) found that qualitative scores (i.e., social appropriateness ratings), but not quantitative scores, were related to adjustment in school children. In another study, Marx et al. (1992) found that only qualitative scores (i.e., effectiveness ratings) distinguished between depressed psychiatric patients and nondepressed patients. However, until more studies are done on this issue, the best recommendation to researchers at the present time is to analyze their data using both types of scoring procedures.

When solution effectiveness ratings are used, they are typically assessed for interrater reliability, but are generally assumed to have external validity. However, adequate reliability does not guarantee validity. A major threat to the validity of these ratings occurs when they are performed by unqualified raters who are not sufficiently familiar with the criteria that are generally used to judge coping performance in the particular target environment. Qualified raters would include authority figures or experts who routinely evaluate coping behavior in a particular setting (e.g., supervisors, instructors, counselors), as well as members of the target population who have previously been judged as competent on the basis of such criteria as grades, peer ratings and nominations, letters of recommendation, and/or scores on a valid measure of social problem-solving ability.

Unfortunately, a study by Marsiske and Willis (1995) has raised serious questions about the construct validity of some problem-solving outcome tests. These investigators conducted a confirmatory factor analysis on three outcome tests in an attempt to show that they are all measuring a single problem-solving construct. The tests were the Everyday Problem Solving Inventory (EPSI; Cornelius & Caspi, 1987), the Everyday Problems Test (EPT; Willis & Marsiske, 1993), and a modified version of the Practical Problems (PP) test (Denney & Pearce, 1989). Unexpectedly, the results showed that the three tests were virtually unrelated to each other, sharing less than 5% of their variance. The conclusion was that these tests are measuring quite different coping constructs.

These results are not surprising considering the fact that none of these tests are based on any specific theory of social problem solving. At the very least, the construction and selection of test items (real or hypothetical problems) must be based on clear and interrelated definitions of the terms *problem, problem solving,* and *solution.* Earlier in this chapter, a problem was defined as a life situation that calls for an effective or adaptive coping response, but no such response is immediately available to the person. As such, a problem is likely to set the occasion for problem solving, which is defined as a rational cognitive-behavioral process aimed at finding a solution, or effective coping response. Because this coping response is the product of a rational problem-solving process, it can be viewed as an indicator of social problem-solving ability. On the other hand, if some percentage of the test items are familiar stress situations for which the person has a ready coping response based on past experience, then the test results may be confounding social problem solving with automatic processing, or the direct, single-step retrieval of coping responses from memory (see Burns & D'Zurilla, 1999; Logan, 1988). For a discussion of test construction guidelines that may help to maximize the construct validity of social problem-solving measures, see D'Zurilla and Maydeu-Olivares (1995).

VERBAL VERSUS OBSERVATIONAL MEASURES

In this context, a verbal problem-solving measure is a self-report measure that focuses on the subject's oral or written responses using a pencil-and-paper questionnaire or an interview format. An observational measure focuses on the subject's actual problem-solving behavior in the natural environment or in some simulated or role-play problem-solving situation. Both approaches can be used to assess problem-solving processes as well as outcomes. However, each approach has its own advantages and limitations.

Verbal problem-solving assessment has two major advantages: (a) it is the most practical, efficient, and cost-effective way to obtain a measure of problem-solving ability from a large number of subjects across a wide range of problematic situations; and (b) it is the only way to obtain a direct, comprehensive assessment of *covert* problem-solving processes, which constitute the major part of the overall problem-solving process.

The limitations of verbal problem-solving assessment include the threats to validity that are associated with any other self-report measure, including faking or deliberate distortion, expectancy effects, response sets, forgetting, recall biases, and comprehension problems. The external validity of verbal problem-solving measures may also be limited because such variables as emotionality, motivation, and self-efficacy expectancies are less likely to influence the person's problem-solving performance in a test situation than in a real-life problem-solving situation. It should be noted that some of these threats to validity apply only to inventories and not to performance tests. Because the latter tests focus on a person's *present* ability to solve problems (or make decisions, generate alternative solutions, etc.) rather than on past problem-solving performance, forgetting or recall biases are not an issue with these tests.

Due to the limitations of verbal assessment, some investigators have argued that social problem-solving assessment should focus more on observational methods (Butler & Meichenbaum, 1981; Krasnor & Rubin, 1981; Tisdelle & St. Lawrence, 1986). However, although an observational approach would avoid most of the limitations of verbal assessment, it has its own unique disadvantages. In addition to being costly, inefficient, and time-consuming, this approach also has some serious threats to validity. First, it is not possible to determine from the form or quality of situation-specific coping responses alone whether they are the products of a formal problem-solving process, or the outcome of some intuitive information processing system, such as emotional processing or automatic processing (Burns & D'Zurilla, 1999). Therefore, when an observer records and judges overt coping responses in real-life or role-played stress situations, one could not conclude that problem-solving ability is being measured unless it had been determined in advance, perhaps through self-report, that these situations were problematic for the particular subjects and actually prompted problem-solving activities. A second potential threat to validity with an observational approach is that actual solution outcomes might be confounded by the quality of the person's solution-implementation skills (e.g., assertiveness skills). In other words, a potentially good solution might have a poor outcome because the person has deficient solution implementation skills, which would reduce the validity of the outcome measure.

Because verbal and observational methods are not mutually exclusive, the most useful and valid assessment strategy might be one that integrates these two approaches. For example, verbal methods, such as interviews and questionnaires, might be employed first to identify critical problematic situations for a particular target population, and then observational methods could be used to assess the subjects' overt problem-solving performance in these situations. During or following these problem-solving events, other verbal methods (e.g., audiotape "think-aloud" recording devices, questionnaires) could be used to assess covert problem-solving processes, which would then be related to the observational measures.

Another possible integrative strategy that might be more cost-effective than the approach discussed previously is self-observation or *self-monitoring* (Barlow et al., 1984). In this method, the person identifies, observes, and records significant problematic situations and his or her responses as they occur in the real-life setting. The major appeal of this approach is that it capitalizes on some of the important advantages of both verbal and observational assessment (e.g., efficiency, specificity, cost-effectiveness, immediate recording of behavior), while avoiding some of their major limitations (e.g., reliance on memory, abstraction, high cost, inconvenience). A self-monitoring procedure that we have found useful in the practice of PST is the Problem-Solving Self-Monitoring (PSSM) method, which uses the following A-B-C-D format:

A: *Problem.* In this section, the person describes all of the relevant facts about the problematic situation, describes his/her goals or objectives in the situation, and identifies the obstacles that are interfering with goal attainment.

B: *Emotions.* Here the individual describes all feelings and emotions that were generated by the problematic situation and rates the intensity of his/her emotional distress.

C: *Solution.* In this section, the person describes how he/she attempted to cope with the situation, including all thoughts, words, and actions that were aimed at (a) changing the problematic situation, and/or (b) his/her emotional responses to it.

D: *Outcome:* After implementing the solution, the person rates the degree of improvement in (a) the problematic situation, and (b) his/her emotions. In addition, the individual also rates his/her satisfaction with the overall solution outcome.

In addition to assessing some aspects of problem definition and formulation (e.g., identification of relevant facts and information, identification of goals and obstacles), the PSSM method can also be modified to assess other process variables as well. For example, at "A" (problem), the person can be asked to describe his or her automatic thoughts about the problem in an attempt to identify problem orientation variables (e.g., perceived threat, self-efficacy expectancies, outcome expectancies). In addition, at "C" (solution), the person can be instructed to produce a list of possible solutions to assess the ability to generate alternative solutions. The person can then be asked to evaluate the list of solutions and choose the best or most preferred solution, thus providing an assessment of decision-making ability as well.

MAJOR SOCIAL PROBLEM-SOLVING MEASURES

Published studies on social problem solving and PST have used a number of different social problem-solving measures. Four of the most popular measures that have generated the most research data are described below.

Problem-Solving Inventory (PSI)

The PSI (Heppner & Petersen, 1982) is a 35-item, Likert-type inventory that is described by its authors as a measure of "problem-solving appraisal," or an individual's perceptions of his or her problem-solving behavior and attitudes (Heppner, 1988). This instrument is derived from an initial pool of 50 items that were generated to fit D'Zurilla and Goldfried's (1971) original five-stage social problem-solving model, that is, general orientation, problem definition and formulation, generation of alternatives, decision making, and verification. After a principal components factor analysis failed to provide support for a five-factor structure corresponding to the D'Zurilla and Goldfried model, Heppner and Petersen (1982) identified three factors which they labeled *problem-solving confidence* (11 items), *approach-avoidance style* (16 items), and *personal control* (5 items). According to Heppner (1988), problem-solving confidence is defined as self-assurance while engaging in problem-solving; approach-avoidance style refers to the general tendency to approach or avoid problem-solving activities; and personal control reflects the extent to which a person is in control of his or her emotions and behavior while solving problems. The most popular PSI measure has been a total score which is used as an overall index of social problem-solving ability. However, the three scale scores corresponding to the three factors have also been used. It should be noted that higher scores on the PSI indicate *less effective* problem-solving ability. Empirical findings on the reliability and validity of the PSI are reported in Heppner and Petersen (1982) and Heppner (1988).

Unfortunately, the three PSI factors identified by Heppner and Petersen (1982) describe social problem solving only in a global sense and are not linked to any specific components of the theoretical model from which the items were derived. In an attempt to bridge the gap between the empirical data on the PSI and current social problem-solving theory, A. M. Nezu and Perri (1989) and Elliott, Sherwin, Harkins, and Marmarosh (1995) have argued that the items of the problem-solving confidence and personal control scales are measuring *problem orientation,* whereas the items of the approach-avoidance scale are measuring *problem-solving skills.* Although the sampling representativeness of the PSI scales can be questioned when viewed as measures of these two problem-solving constructs, the aforementioned investigators have noted that, in general, the empirical findings on the PSI scales are consistent with predictions based on these theoretical constructs. Hence, the more recent studies by these investigators using the PSI scales (see chapter 7) have been interpreted in terms of the constructs of problem orientation and problem-solving skills.

Social Problem-Solving Inventory (SPSI)

The SPSI (D'Zurilla & Nezu, 1990) is a 70-item, Likert-type inventory that is linked to the social problem-solving model introduced by D'Zurilla and Goldfried (1971) and later expanded and refined by D'Zurilla and Nezu (1982, 1990). This model consists of two major components: (a) problem orientation, and (b) problem-solving proper—that is, the application of problem-solving skills. Problem orientation is the motivational part of the problem-solving process, consisting of cognitive, emotional, and behavioral (approach-avoidance) variables. The model identifies four major problem-solving skills: (1) problem definition and formulation, (2) generation of alternative solutions, (3) decision making, and (4) solution implementation and verification. On the basis of this general model, D'Zurilla and Nezu constructed a 30-item *Problem Orientation* scale and a 40-item *Problem-Solving Skills* scale, as well as 7 10-item subscales that assess the cognitive, emotional, and behavioral aspects of problem orientation and the four major problem-solving skills. A global problem-solving score can be calculated, as well as separate scores for each of the two major scales and the seven subscales. The SPSI has been estimated to have a 12th grade readability level (Frauenknecht, 1990). Data on the reliability and validity of the SPSI can be found in D'Zurilla and Nezu (1990), D'Zurilla and Sheedy (1991, 1992), and Sadowski and Kelley (1993).

Social Problem-Solving Inventory-Revised (SPSI-R)

The SPSI-R (D'Zurilla et al., 2002) is a 52-item, Likert-type inventory that is based on factor-analytic studies of the original theory-driven SPSI (Maydeu-Olivares & D'Zurilla, 1995, 1996). According to the results of these analyses, the SPSI is actually measuring two different, albeit related, problem orientation dimensions (positive and negative) and three partially independent problem-solving style dimensions (rational problem solving, impulsivity/carelessness style, and avoidance style). Hence, the SPSI-R consists of five major scales which measure these five problem-solving dimensions. The *Positive Problem Orientation* scale (5 items) taps a constructive problem-solving cognitive set (i.e., perceived challenge, self-efficacy, positive outcome expectancy), whereas the *Negative Problem Orientation* scale (10 items) reflects an inhibitive or disruptive cognitive-emotional orientation toward problems in living (i.e., perceived threat, self-inefficacy, negative outcome expectancies, low frustration tolerance). The *Rational Problem Solving* scale (20 items) measures a constructive problem-solving strategy that may be defined as the rational, deliberate, and systematic application of effective problem-solving skills. The *Impulsivity/Carelessness Style* scale (10 items) reflects a dysfunctional problem-solving style in which the person applies problem-solving techniques in a narrow, impulsive, careless, hurried, and incomplete manner. The *Avoidance Style* scale (7 items) taps another defective problem-solving style characterized by frequent procrastination (putting off problem solving), passivity or inaction (waiting for problems to resolve themselves), and dependency (shifting the responsibility for problem solving to others).

The items of the Rational Problem Solving scale can be divided into four subscales (each with five items) corresponding to the four problem-solving skills assessed by the SPSI. Although the factor analysis failed to distinguish among these four skills, continued research on these subscales is recommended to determine if any of these skills might have discriminant validity in some clinical populations. A 25-item short form of the SPSI-R is also available (the SPSI-R:S) which measures the five major dimensions but does not measure the specific skills within the rational problem-solving construct.

The five-dimensional model assessed by the SPSI-R was originally based on a large sample of 601 college students. This model was cross-validated in a second sample of 323 college students (Maydeu-Olivares & D'Zurilla, 1996). In addition, the model has also been cross-validated in a large sample of junior and senior high school students (Sadowski et al., 1994). Moreover, using translated versions of the SPSI-R, the five-dimensional model has been cross-validated in a Spanish sample (Maydeu-Olivares et al., 2000), a German sample (Graf, 2003), and a Chinese sample (Siu & Shek, 2005). Additional support for the reliability and validity of the SPSI-R can be found in D'Zurilla et al. (2002). The SPSI-R is appropriate for males and females 13 years of age and older.

Means-Ends Problem-Solving Procedure (MEPS)

The MEPS procedure (Platt & Spivack, 1975; Spivack et al., 1985) represents the operationalization of the following three hypothetical components of *means-ends thinking:* (a) the ability to conceptualize the sequenced steps or "means" that are necessary to achieve a particular problem-solving goal; (b) the ability to anticipate possible obstacles that may interfere with goal attainment; and (c) the ability to appreciate that successful problem solving takes time, or the fact that appropriate timing may be essential for effective solution implementation (Spivack et al., 1985). According to Spivack et al. (1976), means-ends thinking is one of the major cognitive abilities underlying the real-life interpersonal problem-solving process. From this viewpoint, the MEPS would be classified as a process measure. However, because the components of means-ends thinking represent a problem solution rather than the antecedent process that enables a person to find a solution, the MEPS is classified here as an outcome measure, or a problem-solving performance test.

The MEPS can be administered using either an interview or a pencil-and-paper format. Subjects are presented with a series of 10 hypothetical interpersonal problems or conflict situations consisting of incomplete stories that have only a beginning and an ending. In the beginning, the need or goal of the protagonist is specified, and at the end, the protagonist successfully satisfies the need or achieves the goal. The instructions present the instrument as a test of imagination. Subjects are asked to make up the middle part of the story that connects the beginning with the ending. As previously noted, the MEPS uses a quantitative scoring system that computes separate frequency scores for relevant means, obstacles, and time. Although the number of relevant means has been the most common MEPS score used in research, Spivack et al. (1985) have recommended a total score that sums the number of relevant means, obstacles, and time. Data on the reliability and validity of the MEPS can be found in Butler and Meichenbaum (1981), D'Zurilla and Maydeu-Olivares (1995), Marx et al. (1992), Platt and Spivack (1975), Schotte and Clum (1982, 1987), and Spivack et al. (1976).

OTHER PROBLEM-SOLVING MEASURES

In addition to the four instruments described previously, a number of other social problem-solving measures have been used in studies on social problem solving and PST. Some of these measures were designed to focus on a specific class of problems (e.g., diabetes-related problems) and/or a specific population of respondents (e.g., individuals with diabetes, schizophrenic patients). Unfortunately, many of these other social problem-solving measures have been presented with little or no information about their theoretical basis (if any), test construction, and/or data on their psychometric properties. In order to help researchers identify the most appropriate and useful measures for their studies, we briefly describe below some of the better or most promising instruments.

The English *Negative Problem Orientation Questionnaire* (NPOQ; Robichaud & Dugas, 2005a, 2005b) is an English translation of the 12-item French NPOQ (Gosselin, Pelletier, & Ladouceur, 2000, 2001), which was designed to measure a negative problem orientation construct that is similar to the construct measured by the 10-item Negative Problem Orientation (NPO) scale of the SPSI-R. However, whereas negative problem orientation as measured by the NPO is a cognitive-emotional construct, the NPOQ measures only the cognitive features of this construct—that is, perceived threat, self-inefficacy, and negative outcome expectancies. In addition to these cognitive features, the construct measured by the NPO scale also has an emotional element, namely, low frustration tolerance, or the tendency to easily get frustrated and upset when confronted with problems in living. Like the NPO scale, the English NPOQ has been found to have a unitary factor structure, good internal consistency, and good test-retest reliability (5 weeks). The NPOQ has been found to be highly correlated with the NPO (short form), and the two scales have similar correlations with criterion variables such as depression and anxiety (Robichaud & Dugas, 2005a, 2005b).

The *Social Problem-Solving Inventory for Adolescents* (*SPSI-A;* Frauenknecht & Black, 1995) is a 70-item modified version of the SPSI (D'Zurilla & Nezu, 1990) that was designed for an adolescent population at a 7th-grade level and higher. The instrument consists of three major scales: the Problem Orientation scale, the Problem-Solving Skills scale, and the Automatic Process scale. The Problem Orientation scale is subdivided into three subscales: Cognition, Emotion, and Behavior. Subsumed under the Problem-Solving Skills scale are four subscales: Problem Identification, Alternative Generation, Consequence Prediction, and Implementation/Evaluation/Reorganization. The Automatic Process scale was constructed by the investigators to assess an informal mode of problem solving that involves the recall of familiar coping strategies that have been successful in the past. Data on the reliability and validity of the SPSI-A are presented in Frauenknecht and Black (1995).

The *Modified Problem-Solving Inventory* (Maydeu-Olivares & D'Zurilla, 1997) is a reduced 16-item version of the PSI (Heppner & Petersen, 1982) consisting of two scales derived from an integration of theory and empirical data: the 7-item Problem-Solving Self-Efficacy (PSSE) scale and the 9-item Problem-Solving Skills (PSS) scale. Because Heppner and Petersen's (1982) interpretation of the 3-factor structure of the PSI is not clearly linked to any theory of social problem solving, Maydeu-Olivares and D'Zurilla (1997) conducted a content analysis of the PSI in an attempt to identify items that might be measuring components of our social problem-solving model. It was concluded that two meaningful problem-solving constructs could be extracted from 16 of the PSI items: (1) problem-solving self-efficacy (i.e., the belief that one is capable of solving problems effectively), which is an important aspect of positive problem orientation, and (2) problem-solving skills (e.g., problem definition and formulation, generation of alternative solutions, etc.). A maximum likelihood confirmatory factor analysis performed on this 16-item pool found support for a two-factor independent clusters solution corresponding to these two problem-solving constructs. The new PSSE and PSS scales were found to be highly correlated with the original Problem-Solving Confidence and Approach-Avoidance Style scales, respectively. Moreover, they were found to have similar relations with several criterion variables, including optimism, pessimism, and hopelessness. The advantages of the new scales are that they have fewer items without sacrificing reliability, they are more clearly linked to social problem-solving theory, and their scoring is more intuitive—that is, higher scores indicate greater problem-solving ability. More specific data on the psychometric properties of the PSSE and PSS scales can be found in Maydeu-Olivares and D'Zurilla (1997).

The *Perceived Modes of Processing Inventory* (PMPI; Burns & D'Zurilla, 1999) is a 32-item Likert-type self-report inventory consisting of a 12-item Rational Processing scale, a 10-item Emotional Processing scale, and a 10-item Automatic Processing scale. This instrument was originally designed to assess two different information processing styles in stress and coping situations based on Epstein's (1994) Cognitive-Experiential Self-Theory, namely, rational processing and experiential processing. However, exploratory and confirmatory factor analyses found that the instrument is actually measuring three different modes of processing—rational processing, emotional processing, and automatic processing. Individuals with high scores on rational processing report that they spend time and effort trying to figure out how to cope by using logical reasoning, creative thinking, and effective problem-solving skills. People with high scores on emotional processing report that they rely mainly on their feelings, emotions, hunches, and instincts when trying to decide how to cope. Individuals who score high on automatic processing report that they make coping decisions quickly and efficiently by relying on the recall of coping responses that have worked well in similar situations in the past. The Rational Processing scale is highly correlated with the Rational Problem Solving scale of the SPSI-R. Additional evidence supporting the reliability and validity of the PMPI scales is presented in Burns and D'Zurilla (1999).

The *Interpersonal Problem-Solving Assessment Technique* (IPSAT; Getter & Nowinski, 1981) is a 46-item, theory-driven, process/outcome test that was designed to assess interpersonal problem-solving competence in college students. The items and scoring system for the IPSAT are based on Rotter's (Rotter, Chance, & Phares, 1972) social learning theory and research on assertive behavior. The test uses a semistructured, pencil-and-paper format. Subjects are asked to (a) imagine being in each problematic situation at the present moment, (b) write down alternative ways of handling the situation, and (c) indicate which solution they would actually implement. Thus, in addition to assessing problem-solving outcomes, the IPSAT also assesses two process variables—the generation-of-alternative solutions and decision making. Chosen solutions are coded using the following qualitative categories: effective, avoidant, inappropriate, dependent, and unscorable, based on criteria provided in a detailed scoring manual. Data supporting the reliability and validity of the IPSAT are reported in Getter and Nowinski (1981).

The *Adolescent Problems Inventory* (API; Freedman et al., 1978) is a 44-item, empirically derived problem-solving performance test that was designed to assess personal and interpersonal problem-solving competence in adolescent boys. Test construction was based on Goldfried and D'Zurilla's (1969) behavioral-analytic model for assessing competence. Test items are presented via audiotape in individual testing sessions. Subjects are asked to imagine being in the situation and then to report into a second audiotape machine what they would say and do if they were really there. Test scores are based on independent competence ratings using criteria outlined in a rater's manual. Empirical support for the reliability and validity of the API can be found in Freedman et al. (1978), Hains and Herman (1989), and Simonian, Tarnowski, and Gibbs (1991).

The *Inventory of Decisions, Evaluations, and Actions* (IDEA; Goddard & McFall, 1992) is a 40-item, empirically derived problem-solving performance test that was designed to assess heterosexual problem-solving competence in college women. Test construction was based on a modified version of Goldfried and D'Zurilla's (1969) behavioral-analytic model. The targeted problem domain was the range of heterosexual problematic situations commonly faced by college women. The test instructions, testing format, and scoring system for the IDEA are basically the same as those used in the API. Data on the reliability and validity of the IDEA are presented in Goddard and McFall (1992).

The *Problem-Solving Task* (C. M. Nezu et al., 1991) was designed to measure the process and outcome of interpersonal problem solving in adults with mental retardation. Using an interview format, subjects are presented with interpersonal problematic situations that include a stated goal (e.g., to make a new friend). They are then asked a series of questions that attempt to assess several process variables (e.g., the ability to generate alternative solutions, the ability to anticipate consequences) in addition to outcome (i.e., ratings of solution quality). Interrater agreement has been found to be high ($r = 0.83$) and estimates of test-retest reliability indicate that responses are relatively stable over time ($r = 0.79$). In addition, the Problem-Solving Task has been found to be sensitive to the effects of problem-solving training (C. M. Nezu et al., 1991).

The *Diabetes Problem-Solving Scale-Self Report* (DPSS-SR; Hill-Briggs et al., 2005) is a 30-item self-report inventory that was designed to assess how adult patients approach and manage problems encountered in diabetes self-management. The inventory has seven subscales: Positive Motivation (two items); Negative Motivation (five items); Effective Problem Solving (six items); Impulsive Problem Solving (two items); Avoidant Problem Solving (three items); Positive Transfer/Learning (six items); and Negative Transfer/Learning (six items). The first five subscales are based on the five-dimensional social problem-solving model measured by the SPSI-R. The last two subscales measure the positive and negative transfer of past experiences with problematic situations to new problems. A total DPSS-SR can be derived as well as scores for each of the seven subscales. Higher scores indicate better self-reported problem solving. The DPSS-SR has been demonstrated to have good internal consistency. Construct validity is supported by relatively high correlations with the short form of the SPSI-R. With regard to criterion validity, in a sample of African Americans with type-2 diabetes, higher DPSS-SR scores were found to be associated with higher medication adherence, more frequent self-monitoring of blood glucose, and better glycemic control.

The *Social Problem Solving Assessment Battery* (SPSAB; Sayers & Bellack, 1995) was designed specifically to assess the functional ability of chronic psychiatric patients to solve interpersonal problems. The battery consists of three components: The Role Play Test (RPT), the Response Generation Test (RGT), and the Response Evaluation Test (RET). Using a role play procedure, the RPT measures the patient's ability to resolve interpersonal conflicts through conversation. The RGT measures the patient's ability to define interpersonal problems and generate realistic, appropriate solutions. The RET assesses the patient's ability to discriminate between effective and ineffective solutions to interpersonal problems. In support of the validity of the SPSAB, patients with schizophrenia, and patients with bipolar disorder have been found to perform worse than nonpatient controls on all three tests (Bellack, Sayers, Mueser, & Bennett, 1994).

SUMMARY

When considering measures of social problem-solving ability it is useful to distinguish between process measures and outcome measures. Process measures assess specific strengths and deficits in problem-solving attitudes and skills, whereas outcome measures assess problem-solving performance or the ability of individuals to apply their skills effectively to specific problems. Some problem-solving measures are designed to assess both process and outcome within a single format. It is also useful to distinguish between verbal measures and observational measures. Verbal measures are self-report measures that focus on a person's oral or written responses using a pencil-and-paper questionnaire or an interview format. Observational measures focus on the person's actual problem-solving behavior in the natural environment or some simulated problem-solving situation. Each type of measure has its own unique advantages and limitations. A major limitation of most outcome measures is that they are not based on any specific definitions of the major constructs in social problem-solving theory, namely, *problem, problem solving,* and *solution.* The most popular social problem-solving measures are described, as well as several other promising measures that have support for their reliability and validity.

CHAPTER FIVE

Role of Emotions in Social Problem Solving

Emotional factors play an important role in problem solving in the natural environment. Although a number of authors have discussed the effects of emotional arousal on social problem-solving performance (George, 1974; Janis, 1982; Janis & Mann, 1977; Mandler, 1982; Mechanic, 1970, 1974; Snyder, Bruck, & Sapin, 1962; Staats, 1975), the subject has received limited empirical attention to date. An adequate theory of social problem solving must account for the effects of emotional variables on real-life problem-solving performance, and PST programs must include methods for using and controlling emotions in order to maximize the efficiency and effectiveness of performance.

SOURCES OF EMOTIONAL AROUSAL

There are three major sources of emotional arousal in social problem solving: (a) the objective problematic situation, (b) problem orientation, and (c) problem-solving style—that is, the process by which the person attempts to find a solution to the problem. These emotional responses may be positive or negative—positive emotions are expected to facilitate performance, whereas negative emotions are expected to inhibit or disrupt performance.

The Objective Problematic Situation

In addition to setting the occasion for problem-solving behavior, the objective problematic situation may also elicit natural (unlearned) or learned emotional responses. Natural emotional responses are produced by stimulus conditions that are either aversive or pleasurable to most people independent of any prior learning experiences with those conditions. For example, problematic situations commonly include one or more of the following natural aversive conditions:

- Harmful or painful stimuli that threaten the homeostatic balance of the body, including various pathogens and any intense physical stimulus, for example, noise, heat, cold, or pressure (Selye, 1983).
- Conflict, such as competing stimulus demands, or interpersonal conflict (Epstein, 1982; Janis & Mann, 1977; Phillips, 1978).
- Frustration, or an obstacle preventing a goal response (Mather, 1970).
- Loss or deprivation of customary reinforcers (Mowrer, 1960).
- Uncontrollability and unpredictability of aversive events (Hamberger & Lohr, 1984).
- Ambiguity (Wrubel et al., 1981).
- Complexity or novelty that cannot be assimilated successfully with stored information or prior experience (McClelland & Clark, 1966; Hunt, 1963).

The following are "real-life" examples of such situations:

Jane lived alone and loved her pet parakeet very much. She liked to feed it, listen to it chirp, and walk around the apartment with it on her shoulder. One morning Jane woke up and went to feed her pet, but she found that it was dead and immediately got very upset (loss of customary reinforcer). After a few days, she was feeling even more upset because an image of the dead bird would often come to her mind, and she could not stop thinking about it (uncontrollability of an aversive event). It was particularly disturbing that the image could occur to her suddenly at anytime, in any place, without any warning (unpredictability of an aversive event).

Jim graduated from college with a degree in banking and finance. He took a job as an office worker with a small financial company. Because Jim was very ambitious and wanted to advance rapidly in his career, he applied after six months for a new job with much more responsibility in a major financial corporation. Prior to the job interview, Jim became somewhat anxious because the job description that was sent to him was very vague (ambiguity). After obtaining a more specific description, he became anxious when he learned that he lacked a particular skill that was important for the job (obstacle preventing a goal response). During his interview, he became even more anxious when he was asked several questions he could not adequately answer due to his lack of experience in the field (complexity or novelty that cannot be assimilated successfully with stored information or prior experience). After failing to get the job, Jim later became upset during a discussion with his wife because she urged him to stay in his present job for a few more years, whereas he wanted to continue applying for new jobs (conflict).

Learned emotional responses result from stimulus conditions in the problematic situation that have acquired the capacity to elicit emotional responses because they have been associated with emotional events or experiences in the past. These learned emotional responses are likely to vary greatly in subjective quality (positive versus negative) and intensity between individuals and across situations because of individual differences in past learning experiences. For example, a problematic situation involving negative evaluation may cause undue anxiety because negative evaluation was frequently associated with harsh punishment in the past. Consider the following example:

Mary's roommate, Beth, criticizes her occasionally because she forgets to clean the apartment when it is her turn. Although Mary believes that the criticism is justified, it provokes excessive anxiety in her because of past experiences in which negative evaluation was frequently followed by harsh physical punishment from her parents. Because of her extreme anxiety, Mary is having difficulty coping with this problem and usually tries to avoid Beth by staying out of the apartment as much as possible.

Although the emotions generated by objective problematic situations are often negative or unpleasant (e.g., anxiety, anger, depression), many situations include stimulus conditions and activities that produce learned or unlearned positive emotions as well. For example, a particular problematic situation may occur within a context that includes loved family members, supportive friends, enjoyable social activities, satisfying job activities, exciting sporting events, and pleasurable recreational activities. If these positive emotions are strong enough, they might function as buffers that serve to reduce, minimize, or even prevent negative emotions that the problematic situation might engender.

Problem Orientation

Problem orientation has been described as a generalized set of orient-ing variables that begin with problem recognition and also includes problem attribution, problem appraisal, perceived control, and time/effort commitment. By definition, problem recognition is associated with a state of unknowing or uncertainty concerning an effective or adaptive coping response for a particular situation, which is likely to be an aversive condition to most people. Problem recognition is likely to be even more disturbing if the person has a low tolerance for uncer-tainty or frustration (i.e., has the irrational belief that uncertainty or frustration cannot be tolerated; see Chang & D'Zurilla, 1996a). Depending on the nature of other problem-orientation variables (e.g., problem attribution, problem appraisal), a person's general problem orientation may produce positive emotions, negative emotions, or both. Specifically, positive emotions are likely to occur when an indi-vidual accepts problems as a normal part of living, appraises problems as a challenge or opportunity for benefit or gain, believes that they are capable of solving problems and implementing solutions effectively, believes that problems are solvable, understands that successful prob-lem solving often takes time and effort, and tolerates uncertainty and frustration until the problem is solved. In contrast, negative emotions are likely to occur when an individual blames themselves for problems, appraises problems as a significant threat to well-being, doubts their ability to solve problems or carry out solutions effectively, believes that problems are unsolvable, believes that a competent person should be able to solve problems quickly and effortlessly, and believes that uncertainty and frustration are intolerable. Consider the following examples:

The sales manager has informed John that he is expected to increase his sales performance next month by 50%. John is not immediately aware of how he can accomplish this goal, but he approaches the problem with feelings of hope and confidence. These positive feelings are the result of the way John thinks about problems in living and his own problem-solving ability. Instead of blaming himself for the problem and thinking that he is incompetent or inadequate, John realizes that problems such as this are a normal, inevitable part of life. In addition, he views the prob-lem as a challenge or opportunity to learn something new and improve himself. He believes in the philosophy that it is better to take on a chal-lenge and fail than to avoid the problem and not try to solve it at all. John also believes that there is a solution to the problem and that he is capable of finding it on his own if he tries hard enough. He realizes that solving the problem might take time, effort, and persistence, but he values independent problem solving and is willing to tolerate the frustration and uncertainty until the problem is solved.

Bob has also been informed by the sales manager that he is expected to increase his sales performance next month by 50%. Like John, Bob is not immediately aware of how he can accomplish this goal but, unlike John, he approaches the problem with feelings of anxiety, self-doubt, and hopelessness. These negative feelings are a result of the way Bob thinks about problems in living and his own problem-solving ability. Bob blames himself for the problem, thinking that he does not have the ability or the personality to be a successful salesman. Instead of viewing the problem as a challenge or opportunity for benefit or gain, he only sees it as a threat to his well-being. He doubts his ability to solve the problem on his own and even doubts that there is a solution for it. He believes that a competent person should be able to solve problems quickly and without much effort. Furthermore, he believes that frustration and uncertainty are intolerable. As a result, he gives up easily when he cannot find a solution quickly and, because he's afraid, he decides to quit the job and try to find some other kind of work.

Problem-Solving Style

As described in chapter 3, problem-solving style refers to the process by which a person attempts to find a solution to a problem. The most constructive problem-solving style is rational problem solving, which involves the deliberate, systematic, and effective application of four major problem-solving skills: (1) problem definition and formulation; (2) generation of alternative solutions; (3) decision making (judging, comparing, and choosing a solution); and (4) solution implementation and verification (evaluating the actual solution outcome). Each skill has been described as a specific goal-directed task that has a unique purpose or function in the problem-solving process. Positive or negative emotions may occur during any of these tasks, depending on the quality of the person's skills and how effectively they are implemented. The deliberate, effective and timely application of problem-solving skills (i.e., a rational problem-solving style) contributes to positive problem-solving outcomes which, in turn, are likely to produce positive emotions. On the other hand, dysfunctional problem-solving styles, such as impulsivity/ carelessness (i.e., inadequate application of problem-solving skills) and avoidance (e.g., putting off or avoiding problem solving), are likely to result in negative outcomes that tend to produce frustration and negative emotions.

In addition to the emotional effects of successful versus unsuccessful problem-solving outcomes, other emotional responses may be generated during each of the aforementioned problem-solving tasks. When attempting to define and formulate the problem, certain cognitive distortions may cause emotional distress (e.g., exaggerated appraisals of harm or loss). While generating alternative solutions, specific solution ideas may elicit conditioned emotional responses based on past emotional experiences with those particular solutions. During decision making, anticipation of the positive or negative consequences of different solution alternatives may produce positive or negative emotions, respectively. During solution implementation and verification, the performance of specific solutions may elicit conditioned emotional responses based on past emotional experiences with those solutions.

EFFECTS OF EMOTIONS ON PROBLEM SOLVING

Emotions from all three sources described in the previous paragraphs can either facilitate or inhibit problem-solving performance, depending on such variables as the subjective quality (positive versus negative), intensity, and duration of the emotional responses, as well as the ability of problem solvers to use and control their emotions in a constructive manner. Specifically, these emotions may influence (a) problem recognition, (b) motivation for problem solving, (c) goal setting, (d) solution preferences, (e) evaluation of solution outcomes, (f) the likelihood of future problem-solving behavior, and (g) the efficiency of problem-solving performance.

Problem Recognition

Emotional responses elicited by the objective problematic situation might facilitate problem solving if individuals use them as cues to monitor their transactions with the environment and correctly identify the problematic situation that is causing them. On the other hand, if they dwell on their negative emotions instead of focusing on the life situation that is producing them, people might mislabel the problem as an *emotional* problem, rather than a *situational* problem (e.g., a marital problem or a job problem), which is likely to inhibit effective problem solving.

Motivation for Problem Solving

Emotional responses produced by the objective problematic situation and the person's problem orientation might generate approach or avoidance motivation, depending on the nature and intensity of these responses. Positive emotions and mild or moderate negative emotions are most likely to motivate the person to confront the problem "head on" and attempt to solve it, whereas strong negative emotions are more likely to motivate the person to avoid problem solving by ignoring or denying the problem, putting off problem solving until a later time, waiting for the problem to resolve itself, or shifting the responsibility for solving the problem to someone else. Moreover, the amount of effort, persistence, and tolerance of frustration and uncertainty that the person shows during problem solving is likely to be influenced by these emotions as well as any new emotions that are generated by the four problem-solving tasks (e.g., problem definition and formulation, generation of alternative solutions, etc.).

Goal Setting

Emotions from the objective problematic situation and the person's problem orientation are also likely to influence the problem-solving goals that are set during problem definition and formulation. When strong negative emotions threaten to disrupt problem solving aimed at problem-focused goals, the problem-solver might first set a goal of reducing or controlling these disruptive emotions. In addition, when a problematic situation is perceived as unchangeable or only partially changeable, the most realistic and valuable problem-solving goal might be to reduce, minimize, control, or tolerate the emotions that are generated by the situation.

Solution Preferences

Emotions linked to specific solution alternatives and their anticipated consequences are likely to have a significant effect on solution preferences and choices. In chapter 8, emotional well-being (i.e., anticipated emotional consequences) is identified as an important criterion to consider when judging and comparing possible solutions. Decision-making research has also suggested that people tend to prefer solutions that avoid or minimize negative emotional outcomes more than solutions that maximize positive emotions (Kahnemann & Tversky, 1979; Tversky & Kahnemann, 1981).

Evaluation of Solution Outcomes

The emotional consequences of solution implementation are important criteria to consider when evaluating solution outcomes. Positive emotional consequences may contribute to a *satisfactory* judgment and a decision to terminate the problem-solving process. Negative emotions, on the other hand, are more likely to contribute to an *unsatisfactory* judgment, which may set the occasion for *troubleshooting* and *recycling* in an attempt to find a better solution to the problem.

Likelihood of Future Problem-Solving Behavior

Based on Mowrer's (1960) learning theory, there are four types of solution consequences that elicit four kinds of emotions that can influence future problem solving: (a) something desirable happens (e.g., hope); (2) something noxious or undesirable is escaped from or avoided (e.g., relief); (c) something undesirable happens (e.g., anxiety); and (d) something desirable fails to occur or is lost (e.g., disappointment). Hope and relief are likely to reinforce future problem-solving behavior, whereas anxiety and disappointment are likely to decrease or discourage future problem solving.

Efficiency of Problem-Solving Performance

Emotional arousal from all three sources can combine to have a significant, generalized effect on performance efficiency throughout the problem-solving process. The variables that influence the relationship between emotional arousal and problem-solving performance efficiency have not yet been clearly established, but they are likely to include the subjective quality, intensity, and duration of emotional arousal. In general, positive emotions are likely to facilitate performance, whereas negative emotions are likely to inhibit performance. In addition, however, the effects of emotions on performance may also depend to a considerable extent on the intensity of arousal. If we apply the Yerkes-Dodson Law to social problem solving, we might expect an inverted U relationship between emotional arousal and performance efficiency (Yerkes & Dodson, 1908). When arousal is low, performance efficiency should be poor, but as arousal increases, performance should also increase to an optimal level, after which a further increase in arousal should result in a deterioration in performance. The intensity of arousal is also likely to influence the subjective quality of the emotional experience. Arousal levels above the optimal point are likely to be experienced as negative affect, whereas arousal below the optimal level may be experienced as either positive or negative affect, depending on the person's interpretations and appraisals of the specific cues in the situation.

Whereas the inverted U model has much common-sense appeal, its generality has been seriously questioned (Hockey & Hamilton, 1983; Mandler, 1982). According to Hockey and Hamilton (1983), there is general support for the positive part of the curve, but less unambiguous direct support for the detrimental effects of *excessive* arousal. Studies have produced conflicting results. One possible reason is that the measures of arousal have varied widely. Moreover, Lacey (1967) has argued that there is no single unitary and useful concept of arousal. Another explanation more relevant here is related to the cue utilization hypothesis of Easterbrook (1959). According to this view, as emotional arousal increases, a narrowing or restriction in attention occurs, reducing the number of cues attended to. Easterbrook points out that in some cases, a narrowing of attention may result in an improvement in performance. For example, when the excluded cues are irrelevant to the task, performance might improve because of the activating effects of arousal. However, on complex tasks, which require attention to a wider range of cues, as is often the case in problem solving, a narrowing of attention is more likely to reduce performance efficiency.

It has often been observed that individuals attempting to perform under stress frequently focus their attention on task-irrelevant dues, such as their own autonomic activity and their own threatening interpretations and appraisals (Mandler, 1982; Sarason, 1980). Sarason calls the latter cognitions "self-preoccupying thoughts," which include catastrophizing, blaming oneself, unproductive worries, and helplessness thoughts. After reviewing several studies on the narrowing of attention under stress, Mandler (1982) concluded that stress reduces attentional capacity and narrows it to central cues—that is, the cues that are initially maximally attended to in the stress situation. The task-irrelevant cues described previously are often central for a problem solver under stress because they are threatening, and thus, considered to be highly significant for well-being (Baddeley, 1972). However, if a problem solver perceives the target problem-solving task as central, then problem-solving performance could very well improve under stress.

According to Mandler (1982), the narrowing of thought processes under high stress may affect the generation of alternatives and decision making in such a way that only obvious solution alternatives and outcomes are considered, thus severely limiting the range of available solutions and the range of outcomes affecting solution choice. In a similar vein, Janis (1982, 1983) points out that high stress is likely to result in cognitive deficiencies which include narrowing the range of perceived alternatives, overlooking long-term consequences, seeking inefficient information, erroneously evaluating expected outcomes, and using oversimplified decision rules that fail to take into account the full range of values relevant to the choice.

Janis and Mann (1977) have identified two maladaptive decision-making patterns that result from high stress: (a) defensive avoidance; and (b) hypervigilance. Defensive avoidance is characterized by procrastination and by attempts to shift responsibility for decision making to someone else. Hypervigilance is a panic-like state in which the decision maker searches frantically for a solution, rapidly shifting back and forth between alternatives, and impulsively seizing upon a hastily contrived solution that seems to promise immediate relief.

Thus far, our discussion has focused on the effects of the intensity and subjective quality of emotional arousal on performance efficiency. Another variable that may influence these effects is the duration of emotional stress. Prolonged emotional stress may result from frequent exposure to difficult life problems, emotional oversensitivity to problems, and/or the inability to solve problems effectively, resulting in frequent punishment (i.e., aversive consequences, loss of reinforcement) and a perception of uncontrollability.

What are the possible effects of repeated or prolonged exposure to stressful problems on performance efficiency? Although this question has not yet been adequately studied, stress research by Hans Selye (1983) has provided some clues. Working with both animals and human subjects, Selye found that a nonspecific pattern of biochemical responses occurs when an organism is continuously exposed to any *stressor* or strong demand for adjustment. This nonspecific response pattern, called the general adaptation syndrome, evolves over time through three stages: (1) the alarm reaction, (2) the stage of resistance, and (3) the stage of exhaustion. The alarm reaction is the organism's initial reaction to the occurrence of a strong demand for adjustment. This reaction has two phases—shock and countershock. In the shock phase, there are physical symptoms, such as tachycardia, loss of muscle tone, decreased temperature, and decreased blood pressure. In the countershock phase, there is a rebound reaction marked by a mobilization of the body's defenses, involving an increase in blood pressure, enlargement of the adrenal cortex, and secretion of corticoid hormones.

According to Selye, most of the acute stress diseases correspond to the two phases of the alarm reaction. It appears that this reaction is associated with high levels of autonomic arousal and negative affect, which are likely to reduce performance efficiency and increase vulnerability to additional problems or stressors, as well as contribute to or exacerbate negative physical symptoms. With continued exposure to the stressor, the body's hormonal defenses allow the alarm reaction to give way to the stage of resistance, when full adaptation to the stressor occurs, including an improvement in, or disappearance of, the physical symptoms. During this stage, autonomic arousal seems to decrease somewhat, but it still remains relatively high. The affective experience is still likely to be negative, but less unpleasant. Therefore, performance efficiency is likely to improve during this stage, but this improvement is very tenuous, as the person still remains more vulnerable to an increase in the intensity of the stressor or the occurrence of new problems.

If the stressor is intense and prolonged enough, the hormonal reserves eventually become depleted, and the organism enters the stage of exhaustion when physical symptoms reappear and there is decreased ability to resist either the original stressor or other new stressors. During this stage, arousal level drops and the individual is likely to experience a sensation of fatigue and an affective experience of apathy or depression, with a consequent reduction in performance efficiency. The clinical implications of this stage tend to be clear— when a depressed client has a history of ineffective problem solving, the depression may not simply be a result of lack of reinforcement or negative self-evaluations. Instead, a major contributing factor may be prolonged emotional stress, which may or may not involve a deficit in stress-resisting hormones.

When excessive or prolonged emotional distress appears to be a disruptive factor in problem solving, PST programs should include training in various stress- and anxiety-management techniques (see A. M. Nezu, Nezu, & Lombardo, 2003, 2004). Potentially useful methods include cognitive restructuring (Beck, Rush, Shaw, & Emery, 1979; Ellis & Dryden, 1997; Goldfried, Decenteceo, & Weinberg, 1974), self-instruction methods (Janis, 1983; Meichenbaum & Cameron, 1983), and relaxation/desensitization techniques (Bernstein & Borkovec, 1973; Woolfolk & Lehrer, 1984). Cognitive restructuring methods, such as decatastrophizing, help to reduce anxiety resulting from irrational beliefs and exaggerated threatening appraisals. Self-instruction methods help the problem solver learn to focus on task-relevant cues and on beliefs and expectations that are likely to facilitate problem-solving performance. Finally, relaxation and desensitization techniques help the problem solver maintain an optimal level of arousal for effective problem solving. These techniques might include progressive muscle relaxation, meditation, the use of *relaxation breaks* during difficult or extended problem solving, and the use of imaginal rehearsal, where problem solving under emotional conditions is practiced in the imagination. The latter procedure may be used to *desensitize* an individual to problem-solving situations, or to provide practice in the use of relaxation as an active coping skill in such situations.

SUMMARY

Emotional factors play a major role in problem solving in the real-life setting. There are three sources of emotional arousal in social problem solving: (a) the objective problematic situation, (b) problem orientation, and (c) problem-solving style—that is, the application of problem-solving skills. Emotions from all three sources may either facilitate or inhibit problem-solving performance, depending on such variables as the subjective quality (positive versus negative), intensity, and duration of emotional responses, as well as the ability of the problem solver to use and control his or her emotions in a constructive manner. Specifically, emotional variables may influence (a) problem recognition, (b) motivation for problem solving, (c) goal setting, (d) solution preferences, (e) evaluation of solution outcomes, (f) the likelihood of future problem-solving behavior, and (g) the efficiency of problem-solving performance.

Awareness and control of emotional responses is important for efficient and effective problem-solving performance. When excessive or prolonged emotional distress appears to be a disruptive factor in problem solving, the PST program should include training in various stress and anxiety management techniques, such as cognitive restructuring (decatastrophizing, correcting misconceptions) self-instruction methods (coping self-directions, positive self-talk) and relaxation/desensitization techniques.

CHAPTER SIX

A Relational/Problem-Solving Model of Stress

The major assumption underlying the use of PST is that much of what we view as "psychopathology" can be understood as ineffective or maladaptive coping behavior and its consequences, where individuals are unable to resolve certain stressful problems in their lives and their inadequate attempts to do so engender negative effects, such as anxiety, depression, anger, physical symptoms, and the creation of new problems (D'Zurilla & Goldfried, 1971). Given this basic assumption, the theory of PST is based on two conceptual models: (a) the social problem-solving model described in chapters 2 and 3 of this volume, and (b) the relational/problem-solving model of stress. The present chapter focuses on the latter model.

In the relational/problem-solving model of stress, the concept of social problem solving is given a central role as a general coping strategy that increases adaptive coping and psychological-physical wellness which, in turn, reduces and prevents the negative effects of daily stress on psychological and physical well-being (D'Zurilla, 1986, 1990; A. M. Nezu, 1987; A. M. Nezu & D'Zurilla, 1989; A. M. Nezu & Ronan, 1985). This model integrates Richard Lazarus's relational model of stress (Lazarus, 1981, 1999; Lazarus & Folkman, 1984) with the social problem-solving model presented here. An integration between these two models is possible because the concepts of *stress, cognitive appraisal,* and *coping* in relational stress theory overlap considerably with the concepts of *problem, problem solving,* and *solution* in social problem-solving theory.

LAZARUS'S RELATIONAL MODEL

Lazarus's relational model is based on a view of humans as thinking, active, problem-solving organisms that *interact* with their environment, as opposed to the radical behavioristic conception of people as passive organisms that simply *react* passively to environmental stimuli. In the relational model, stress is neither a characteristic of the environment alone, nor is it a characteristic of the person alone. Instead, stress is viewed as a particular type of relationship between a person and his or her environment in which demands are appraised as taxing or exceeding available coping resources and endangering well-being (Lazarus & Folkman, 1989). In addition to Lazarus, a number of other prominent stress theorists have endorsed this relational view of stress, including Joseph McGrath (1970, 1976) and Wolfgang Schönpflug and Peter Schulz (Schönpflug, 1983; Schulz & Schönpflug, 1982).

According to Lazarus, a person in a stressful situation significantly influences both the quality and intensity of stress responses through two major processes: (a) cognitive appraisal, and (b) coping.

Cognitive appraisal is the process by which a person determines the meaning or personal significance of a specific stressful encounter with the environment. Two important kinds of cognitive appraisal are primary appraisal and secondary appraisal. *Primary appraisal* refers to the person's evaluation of the relevance (actual or potential) of the encounter for physical, social, or psychological well-being. *Secondary appraisal* involves the person's evaluation of his or her coping resources and options with respect to the particular stressful encounter. Both of these appraisals can influence the subjective quality and intensity of stress responses. Negative primary appraisals (e.g., harm, loss, threat) and negative secondary appraisals (e.g., uncertainty, perceived uncontrollability) are likely to produce negative stress responses, whereas positive primary appraisals (e.g., perceived challenge or opportunity for benefit) and positive secondary appraisals (e.g., perceived control) are likely to prevent or minimize negative stress effects and may even produce positive responses, such as feelings of hope and exhilaration. In social problem-solving theory, generalized cognitive appraisals are included within the problem-orientation component of the problem-solving process, and situation-specific appraisals are included within the problem definition and formulation component.

In Lazarus's model, the term *coping* refers to the various cognitive and behavioral activities by which the person attempts to manage stressful situational demands, as well as the emotions that they generate. Two major types of coping are problem-focused coping and emotion-focused coping. *Problem-focused coping* is directed at changing the stressful situation for the better (i.e., meeting, changing, or controlling situational demands). *Emotion-focused coping,* on the other hand, is aimed at managing the emotions that are generated by the stressful situation. Research has shown that, in general, problem-focused coping predominates when stressful conditions are appraised as changeable or controllable, whereas emotion-focused coping predominates when these conditions are appraised as unchangeable or uncontrollable (see Lazarus, 1999). Although both strategies can be effective in reducing stress when conditions are appropriate, problem-focused coping is generally considered to be the more useful and adaptive form of coping. In support of this view, Bandura (1997) has noted that there are few stressful situations in life where there is absolutely nothing that people can do to improve the situation. Hence, the emotional impact of what is uncontrollable in particular problematic situations can often be diminished by attempting to identify and change those aspects of the situation that are controllable.

Lazarus and Folkman (1984; Folkman & Lazarus, 1980) have defined problem solving as a form of problem-focused coping, which means that problem-solving goals are equated with mastery goals, or control of the environment. In this view, problem solving is futile and maladaptive when stressful conditions are unchangeable. In social problem-solving theory, problem solving is conceived as a more versatile coping strategy, as will be described later in this chapter.

THE RELATIONAL/PROBLEM-SOLVING MODEL

The relational/problem-solving model retains the basic assumptions and essential features of Lazarus's relational model of stress. However, these features are cast within a general social problem-solving framework, and problem solving is given an expanded and more important role as a general coping strategy. Within this model, stress is viewed as a function of the reciprocal relations among three major variables: (a) stressful life events, (b) emotional stress responses, and (c) problem-solving coping.

Stressful Life Events

Stressful life events are life experiences that present a person with strong demands for personal, social, or biological readjustment (Bloom, 1985). Two important types of stressful life events that affect most people are major negative events and daily problems. A *major negative event* is a broad event or happening, such as a major negative life change, that calls for sweeping readjustments in a person's life (e.g., divorce, death of a loved one, job loss, major illness, or injury). A *daily problem* (or problematic situation) is a more narrow and specific life event characterized by a perceived discrepancy between adaptive demands and available coping responses. In Lazarus's model, a situation is stressful if (a) the person perceives an imbalance or discrepancy between demands and available coping resources, and (b) this discrepancy is appraised as a threat to well-being. Comparing the definitions of a daily problem and a stressful situation, it is clear that a daily problem is likely to be stressful if it is at all significant for well-being. This comparison also suggests that problem solving might be a very important strategy for coping with stress in daily living. A daily problem may be a single, time-limited event (e.g., getting stuck in traffic when you have an important appointment), a series of similar or related events (e.g., repeated disputes with one's spouse about the sharing of domestic responsibilities), or a continuous, ongoing situation (e.g., chronic pain, periods of boredom or loneliness).

In the present model, major negative events and daily problems are assumed to influence each other. A major negative event, such as a major life change or loss, often creates many new daily problems with which the person must cope. For example, the death of one's spouse might result in such problems as loneliness, reduced income, increased domestic responsibilities, and child-care problems. It should be noted, however, that daily problems may also develop independently from major negative events as a normal part of everyday living. Moreover, an accumulation of unresolved daily problems in a particular area of living may eventually result in a major negative event which, in turn, may produce more daily problems. For example, frequent problems at work may eventually result in getting fired (a major negative event), which may lead to new problems, such as having enough money to pay bills, finding another job, finding a new place to live, and trying to maintain self-esteem.

Although daily problems are less dramatic than major negative events, research suggests that the frequency of these problems may have a greater impact on psychological and physical well-being than major negative events (Burks & Martin, 1985; DeLongis, Coyne, Dakof, Folkman, & Lazarus, 1982; Kanner, Coyne, Schaefer, & Lazarus, 1981; A. M. Nezu, 1986a; A. M. Nezu & Ronan, 1985; Weinberger, Hiner, & Tierney, 1987). Hence, the relational/problem-solving model of stress focuses on coping with daily problems. When major negative events occur, they are broken down into more manageable subproblems (i.e., current and anticipated daily problems) that are solved one at a time.

Emotional Stress Responses

The concept of emotional stress refers to the immediate emotional responses of a person to a stressful life event, as modified or transformed by appraisal and coping processes (Lazarus, 1999). These stress emotions include perceived autonomic activity and other physiological reactions, along with the subjective affective experiences that accompany them (Mandler, 1982). Although emotional stress responses are often negative, including such feelings as anxiety, anger, disappointment, and depression, they can also be positive in nature (e.g., hope, relief, exhilaration). Negative emotions are likely to predominate when the person (a) appraises a problem as harmful or threatening to well-being, (b) doubts his or her ability to cope with the situation effectively, and (c) makes ineffective or maladaptive coping responses. On the other hand, positive emotions may be experienced when the person (a) appraises the stress situation as a challenge or opportunity for benefit, (b) believes that he or she is capable of coping with the situation effectively, and (c) makes coping responses that are effective in reducing harmful or threatening conditions or the negative emotions that are generated by them. Negative emotional stress is harmful because of its negative impact on adaptive functioning (including problem solving) and psychological-physical well-being. Hence, one of the most important goals of coping is to minimize negative emotions and maximize positive emotions during stressful encounters with problematic situations.

Problem-Solving Coping

The third and most important concept in the relational/problem-solving model is *problem-solving coping,* which integrates all cognitive appraisal and coping activities within a general social problem-solving framework. A person who applies the problem-solving coping strategy (a) perceives a stressful situation as a "problem-to-be-solved," (b) believes that he or she is capable of resolving the problem successfully, (c) generates a variety of alternative "solutions" (i.e., potentially effective coping responses), (d) chooses the "best" solution, (e) implements that solution effectively, and (f) carefully observes and evaluates the outcome. Positive outcomes are expected to *reduce* emotional distress, whereas negative outcomes are expected to *increase* distress. Negative outcomes may result from deficiencies in problem orientation, problem-solving skills, solution implementation skills, or any combination of these factors. Hence, problem-solving coping is conceived as an important mediator of the relationship between stressful life events and emotional stress, which ultimately impacts a person's well-being (psychological, social, and physical).

In contrast with Lazarus's view of problem solving as a form of problem-focused coping, problem solving is conceived within our model as a broader, more versatile coping strategy in that *problem-solving goals are not limited to mastery goals.* The goals may include problem-focused goals, emotion-focused goals, or both, depending on the nature of the particular problematic situation and how it is defined and appraised. When the situation or major aspects of it are appraised as changeable or controllable, then problem-focused goals would be emphasized, although the person might also set an emotion-focused goal if emotional distress is extremely high. On the other hand, if the situation is largely unchangeable or uncontrollable, then emotion-focused goals would be emphasized. These goals may be changed at some point during the problem-solving process. For example, if the person initially attempts to find a problem-focused solution only to discover later that nothing works, he or she may then switch to an emotion-focused goal. *Regardless of what goals are set, the ultimate expected outcome of problem solving is to reduce and minimize the negative effects of stressful life events on well-being.*

In addition to increasing the likelihood of positive coping outcomes in specific stress situations, problem-solving coping has several additional advantages that contribute to well-being. First, a positive problem orientation includes cognitive variables that have been found to act as stress moderators or buffers, including *self-efficacy* (belief in one's own problem-solving ability; Bandura, 1997), *optimism* (i.e., positive outcome expectancies; Scheier & Carver, 1985), and *hardiness* (i.e., challenge, perceived control, and commitment; see Kobasa, Maddi, & Kahn, 1980). Second, problem solving is a versatile coping strategy that can be applied across a wide range of problematic stress situations, which should result in more generalized stress reduction. Third, problem solving gives a person more coping options to choose from in stressful situations, which should result in more generalized satisfaction with coping outcomes. Finally, problem solving is a self-control method that enables a person to cope more independently with stressful situations, which should increase his or her self-efficacy and sense of mastery and control.

The hypothesized relationships between the three major components of the relational/problem-solving model of stress and well-being (psychological, social, physical) are summarized in Figure 6.1. As the figure shows, the two types of stressful life events, major negative events and daily problems, can influence each other. Major negative events, such as a divorce, can result in many new daily problems for an individual (e.g., insufficient finances, difficulty meeting people). Conversely, an accumulation of unresolved daily problems, such as an increasing number of unresolved conflicts with one's spouse, can eventually result in a major negative event, such as a divorce. In addition to influencing each other, the figure also depicts that both types of stressful life events can affect well-being directly, as well as indirectly via problem-solving coping. If problem-solving coping is effective, the effect on well-being is expected to be positive (e.g., less emotional distress, positive affect, feelings of mastery and control). On the other hand, if problem-solving coping is ineffective, the effect on well-being is expected to be negative (e.g., anxiety, anger, depression, psychological and physical symptoms). There are two reasons why problem-solving coping may be ineffective. First, the person

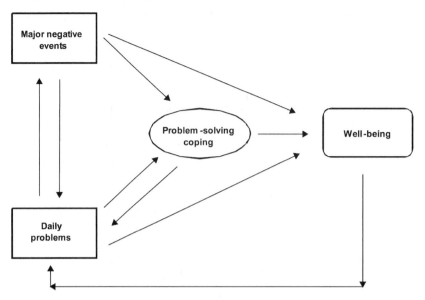

FIGURE 6.1   Hypothesized relationships between the major components of the relational/problem-solving model of stress and well-being.

may have deficits in constructive problem-solving attitudes and skills. Second, if the magnitude of stress is high enough (e.g., a major traumatic event, many daily problems), the impact on problem solving may be negative (i.e., a disruption or inhibition in problem-solving performance), resulting in negative coping outcomes.

In addition, Figure 6.1 suggests that the relationship between daily problems and problem solving is reciprocal. Specifically, in addition to stressful problems impacting on well-being indirectly via problem-solving coping, problem solving can have a direct impact on daily problems as well (i.e., ineffective coping leads to additional problems; effective problem solving leads to a decrease in daily problems). Further, the relationship between stressful events and well-being is also reciprocal. For example, decrements in well-being can lead to increases in both major events and daily problems, whereas improvements in well-being can engender decreases in the intensity and frequency of stressful events.

CLINICAL ASSESSMENT

In addition to providing a theoretical rationale for PST, the relational/problem-solving model of stress also provides a useful cognitive-behavioral framework for assessing emotional and behavioral disorders prior to treatment, in order to determine if PST might be a useful intervention. To conduct this assessment, the therapist first identifies and pinpoints major negative events, current daily problems, negative emotional stress responses, and maladaptive coping responses. Then, using an assessment instrument such as the Social Problem-Solving Inventory-Revised (SPSI-R), the therapist assesses problem orientation (positive and negative) and problem-solving styles (rational problem solving, impulsivity/carelessness style, and avoidance style). Based on the results of this assessment, PST can then be applied to achieve one or more of the following goals:

- Increase positive problem orientation
- Reduce negative problem orientation
- Improve rational problem solving (i.e., effective problem-solving skills)
- Reduce impulsive-careless problem solving
- Prevent avoidance of problem solving
- Improve solution implementation skills

The successful achievement of these goals is expected to increase adaptive situational coping, general competence, and psychological-physical wellness which, in turn, is expected to reduce and prevent the negative impact of stress on personal-social functioning—such as, maladaptive, self-defeating coping behavior; excessive psychological distress; and negative physical symptoms.

EMPIRICAL SUPPORT FOR THE RELATIONAL/ PROBLEM-SOLVING MODEL

Over the past two decades, a large number of studies on the relations between social problem solving and adjustment have provided support for the major assumptions of the relational/problem-solving model. A representative sample of these studies will be presented in the next chapter. Although all of these studies support the view that social problem solving plays an important role in adjustment, the strongest support for the relational/problem-solving model comes from a subset of studies that have demonstrated that problem solving mediates the relationship between stressful life events and personal-social functioning, or moderates the negative impact of stress on psychological well-being and adaptive functioning. Hence, we will highlight these studies in the following paragraphs.

Folkman and Lazarus (1988) studied coping as a mediator of emotion in two samples of community residents—a middle-aged sample and an elderly sample. Once each month for 6 months they interviewed these residents about how they coped with the most stressful situations that occurred during the previous week. Emotions were assessed at the beginning of a stressful encounter, during the encounter, and at the end of the encounter. In both samples, the results showed that planful problem solving was the only coping strategy that was consistently associated with less negative emotions and more positive emotions. In their interpretation of these results, the investigators speculated that problem solving may have both a direct and an indirect effect on emotions in stress situations. The direct effect is that people are likely to feel better when they make an attempt to solve the problem that is causing distress. The indirect effect is that problem solving, when effective, can change the problematic situation for the better, which in turn, has positive emotional outcomes.

A. M. Nezu and his associates conducted several studies that were designed to evaluate the role of social problem-solving ability as a moderator or buffer of the negative effects of major negative life events on psychological well-being. In one study that employed a college student sample and depression as the dependent variable, A. M. Nezu, Nezu, Saraydarian, Kalmar, and Ronan (1986) found a significant interaction between major negative life events and problem-solving ability, which indicated that the relationship between major negative events and depression varied with the level of problem-solving ability. Specifically, the relationship was significantly weaker for individuals with good problem-solving ability than for those with poor problem-solving ability. These findings were replicated by A. M. Nezu, Perri, Nezu, and Mahoney (1987) in a sample of subjects diagnosed with major depression. In another study focusing on college students, A. M. Nezu (1986b) found that social problem-solving ability also moderated the impact of major negative events on state and trait anxiety. In a study focusing on cancer patients, social problem-solving ability was found to moderate the negative effects of cancer-related stress (A. M. Nezu, Nezu, Faddis, DelliCarpini, & Houts, 1995). Specifically, under similar levels of cancer-related stress, individuals with poor problem-solving ability reported higher levels of depression and anxiety than those with better problem-solving ability.

Because the aforementioned studies are all cross-sectional in nature, rival hypotheses regarding the possible influence of emotional distress on problem-solving ability cannot be ruled out. Therefore, A. M. Nezu and Ronan (1988) conducted a prospective study with college students that attempted to predict depressive symptoms at Time 2, while statistically controlling for the level of depression at Time 1. The results confirmed that problem-solving ability moderates the impact of major negative events on later depressive symptoms even after controlling for the prior level of depression.

Two additional studies examined the role of social problem solving as a mediator of the relationship between daily problems and psychological distress. In one study using path-analytic methods, A. M. Nezu and Ronan (1985) tested a model in a college student sample that incorporated major negative life events, daily problems, problem-solving ability, and depressive symptoms. The results provided support for the following causal hypothesized relations: (a) major negative life events increase the number of daily problems, (b) more daily problems result in more depression, and (c) problem solving mediates the relation between daily problems and depression. In other words, the magnitude of the relation between daily problems and depression is at least partly accounted for by problem-solving ability. These results were replicated in a subsequent study by A. M. Nezu, Perri, and Nezu (1987), which employed clinically depressed subjects.

In the other study, Kant, D'Zurilla, and Maydeu-Olivares (1997) examined the role of social problem solving as a mediator of the relations between daily problems and depression and anxiety in middle-aged and elderly community residents. A significant mediating effect was found in both samples, which indicates that problem solving reduces the relation between daily problems and both forms of emotional distress. Further analyses indicated that negative problem orientation contributed most to this mediational effect. Social problem-solving ability was found to account for approximately 20% of the relation between daily problems and depression and about 34% of the variance between daily problems and anxiety in both age groups. Overall, the prediction model consisting of daily problems and social problem-solving ability accounted for 50% of the variance in depression and 50% of the variance in anxiety in both age samples.

In a recent study, Londahl, Tverskoy, and D'Zurilla (2005) examined the role of interpersonal problem solving as a moderator of the relationship between interpersonal conflicts and anxiety in college students. The measure of interpersonal problem solving was a modified form of the Social Problem-Solving Inventory: Short Form (SPSI-R:S; D'Zurilla et al., 2002). The SPSI-R:S was modified to focus on *interpersonal conflicts* (i.e., disagreements or disputes between two people in a relationship) rather than problems *in general*. The results showed that negative problem orientation was a highly significant moderator of the relationship between romantic partner conflicts and anxiety symptoms. Specifically, the relationship between conflicts and anxiety was weaker when negative problem orientation was low rather than high.

SUMMARY

The theory of PST is based on two conceptual models: (a) the social problem-solving model described in chapters 2 and 3 of this volume, and (b) the relational/problem-solving model of stress. The present chapter focused on the latter model, which integrates Lazarus's relational model of stress with the social problem-solving model. Within this model, stress is viewed as a function of the reciprocal relations among three major variables: (a) stressful life events, which include major negative events and daily problems, (b) emotional stress responses, and (c) problem-solving coping. Problem-solving coping is assumed to be an important mediator of the relations between stressful life events and personal-social functioning, as well as a moderator of the impact of stress on psychological well-being and adaptive functioning. Empirical results are presented that provide support for these assumptions. The relational/problem-solving model of stress suggests that PST is likely to be an effective stress-management strategy and clinical intervention for psychological and behavioral disorders that are caused or exacerbated by stressful life events, negative cognitive appraisals, and coping skill deficits.

CHAPTER SEVEN

Social Problem Solving and Adjustment

According to the theory on which PST is based, social problem solving is an important overall coping process that fosters adaptive situational coping and behavioral competence. This in turn reduces and prevents the negative effects of stressful life events with regard to both psychological and physical well-being. If this set of assumptions are valid, then social problem-solving ability should be related to a wide range of adaptive and maladaptive reactions and consequences. In this chapter, we provide a brief review of the research regarding the relationship between problem-solving ability and adaptive functioning and well-being. The purpose of this overview is to provide the reader with an appreciation of the wide range of adaptive outcomes that have been found to be empirically linked to problem-solving ability.

SITUATIONAL COPING AND BEHAVIORAL COMPETENCE

Using the Problem Solving Inventory (PSI; Heppner & Peterson, 1982) as the measure of problem solving, Larson, Piersel, Imao, and Allen (1990) found that more effective problem solving was associated with increased use of active problem-engagement coping strategies and less disengagement coping behaviors (see chapter 4 for a description of the PSI). McNair and Elliott (1992) further found that positive problem orientation and problem-solving skills measured by the Problem-Solving Confidence and Approach-Avoidance Style scales of the PSI, respectively, were significantly associated with the use of problem-focused coping, whereas negative problem orientation (i.e., the Personal Control Scale of the PSI) was related to the use of emotion-focused coping. In a study using the Social Problem-Solving Inventory-Revised (SPSI-R; D'Zurilla et al., 2002), D'Zurilla and Chang (1995) reported that the Positive Problem Orientation (PPO) and Rational Problem Solving (RPS) scales prospectively predicted the use of active problem-engagement coping, whereas the remaining three SPSI-R scales, Negative Problem Orientation (NPO), Impulsivity/Carelessness Style (ICS), and Avoidance Style (AS), were related to the use of disengagement coping (see chapter 4 for a description of the SPSI-R and its five scales). In a partial replication of this study using only the problem orientation scales, Chang and D'Zurilla (1996b) reported that PPO predicted active problem-engagement coping even after controlling for optimism and positive trait affectivity. Finally, in a study using the Perceived Modes of Processing Inventory, Burns and D'Zurilla (1999) found that the use of rational processing (which includes the use of effective problem-solving skills) in stressful situations was related to the use of more adaptive problem-engagement coping.

In addition to facilitating adaptive situational coping, effective social problem solving is expected to increase competent performance in general, including social performance, academic performance, and job performance. Using the Problem-Solving Confidence and Approach-Avoidance Style scales of the PSI, Elliott, Godshall, Herrick, Witty, and Spruell (1991) found both constructive problem-solving dimensions to be related to a greater likelihood of assertive behavior in patients with spinal cord injuries. Burns and D'Zurilla (1994; reported in D'Zurilla et al., 2002) studied the relationship between interpersonal problem-solving ability and social competence using a modified version of the SPSI-R in which the instructions asked subjects to focus only on *inter-personal* problems. They found that PPO and RPS were related to a self-report measure of social adjustment, as well as peer ratings of interpersonal competence. In addition, PPO was found to be related to extraversion. Moreover, NPO was found to be negatively related to all three of these measures. ICS was negatively related to social adjustment and interpersonal competence, whereas the AS scale was negatively correlated to social adjustment and extraversion. In a study using the SPSI-R that focused on junior and senior high school students, Sadowski et al. (1994) reported that PPO and RPS were both positively related to a measure of social skills, whereas NPO, ICS, and AS were negatively related to such skills.

Elliott, Godshall, Shrout, and Witty (1990) reported that PSI scores were significantly related to the use of more adaptive study habits and attitudes in college students enrolled in a developmental course for academically unprepared students. Moreover, they found that problem-solving ability also predicted students' semester grade point average. In a study using the SPSI, D'Zurilla and Nezu (1990) found that both problem orientation and problem-solving skills predicted semester grade point average among a college student sample. D'Zurilla and Sheedy (1991) found that only problem-solving skills predicted the academic year grade point average after controlling for the level of academic aptitude. These data were later reanalyzed by D'Zurilla et al. (2002) using SPSI-R scores obtained from the original SPSI item scores. The results suggested that the significant relationship between problem-solving skills and grade point average found in these two studies can be accounted for by an impulsive/careless problem-solving style.

There is also evidence that suggests social problem-solving ability is related to parenting and caregiving effectiveness. In one study, Azar, Robinson, Hekimian, and Twentyman (1984) found that a group of abusive and neglectful mothers showed significantly poorer problem-solving skills on a problem-solving performance test as compared to a group of nonabusive mothers. Robinson, Drotar, and Boutry (2001) investigated maternal problem-solving abilities as they relate to specific child-rearing situations among a sample of mothers of infants diagnosed with failure to thrive (FTT). Results indicated that in contrast to a matched group of comparison mothers, mothers of infants with FTT generated poorer quality solutions to hypothetical problem situations related to parenting. These authors concluded that limited maternal problem solving may contribute to FTT by interfering directly with the quality of nurturance, feeding, and caloric intake the child receives.

In a study focusing on family caregivers of persons with recent-onset physical disability, Elliott, Shewchuk, and Richards (2001) reported that the ICS scale of the SPSI-R significantly predicted acceptance of disability in the family member at discharge from a rehabilitation program, as well as pressure sore diagnosis after one year.

POSITIVE PSYCHOLOGICAL FUNCTIONING

Social problem solving is also expected to have both a direct and an indirect link to positive psychological well-being and functioning. The direct link involves the overlap between problem orientation and positive psychological (cognitive and emotional) constructs such as perceived internal control, optimism, and positive affectivity. The indirect link is that effective social problem solving facilitates adaptive coping and general competence, which in turn, is likely to enhance positive psychological conditions, including positive affectivity, a sense of mastery and control, self-esteem, and life satisfaction. Positive well-being is an important correlate of social problem solving, because it acts as a buffer against the negative effects of stress and can attenuate or prevent symptoms of psychopathology.

Using the Problem-Solving Confidence scale of the PSI to measure positive problem orientation, Elliott and his associates have found that a positive problem orientation is related to positive mood states in routine and stressful situations, as well as more positive trait affectivity overall (Elliott, Herrick, MacNair, & Harkins, 1994; Elliott, Sherwin, Harkins, & Marmarosh, 1995). Similarly, in a study using the SPSI-R, Chang and D'Zurilla (1996b) reported that the PPO scale was significantly related to positive trait affectivity and optimism. Other studies using the SPSI and the SPSI-R have also found PPO to be related to an internal locus of control (D'Zurilla & Nezu, 1990; D'Zurilla et al., 2002). Positive problem orientation and problem-solving skills, measured by the PSI, were also found to be linked to an internal locus of control (Heppner & Petersen, 1982). Using the total PSI score, Heppner, Reeder, and Larson (1983) found that social problem-solving ability was also related to self-esteem. In addition to these findings, positive problem orientation and rational problem solving measured by the SPSI-R have both been found to be related to self-esteem and life satisfaction (D'Zurilla et al., 2002). Consistent with these results, rational processing measured by the PMPI has also been found to be related to self-esteem and life satisfaction (Burns & D'Zurilla, 1999).

Focusing on the construct of hope, Chang (2003) recently reported that among a sample of middle-aged men and women, total SPSI-R scores were found to be significantly correlated with life satisfaction. In addition, results from a similar study by Chang, Sanna, and Edwards (2003) suggests that greater life satisfaction may involve the use of more effective problem-solving skills, more care and attention when attempting to solve problems in living, and a greater willingness to address problems directly when they occur.

A series of more recent studies by Elliott and his colleagues provide further support for the existence of a significant relationship between social problem solving and subjective well-being. These include a study focusing on adult caregivers of individuals who suffered a stroke (Grant, Elliott, Giger, & Bartolucci, 2001), a sample of adults with diabetes (Elliott, Shewchuk, Miller, & Richards, 2001), and a sample of college students (Elliott et al., 1995).

Last, Chang (as reported in Chang, Downey, and Salata, 2004) found significant relationships between each of the five SPSI-R scales and a measure of positive well-being among a sample of 238 college students. Based on a series of regression analyses, he concluded that our model of social problem solving appeared to be particularly relevant to an understanding of subjective well-being. More interestingly, he found that NPO was not a robust predictor of positive psychological functioning, which is in contrast to the ubiquitous finding that NPO is a major predictor of psychological maladjustment (A. M. Nezu, 2004).

GENERAL PSYCHOLOGICAL DISTRESS

Several investigations have found strong links between social problem solving and general emotional distress. For example, deficits in problem-solving ability, as measured by the PSI, have been found to be related to general psychological symptom severity (Heppner, Kampa, & Brunning, 1987) and general maladjustment (Heppner & Anderson, 1985). In addition, Elliott and his associates found that a negative problem orientation is associated with more negative emotions in routine and stressful situations, as well as more negative trait affectivity (Elliott et al., 1994). Using the SPSI-R, Chang and D'Zurilla (1996b) reported that a negative problem orientation is related to negative trait affectivity and pessimism. In a prospective study using the SPSI, D'Zurilla and Sheedy (1991) found that a negative problem orientation predicted later psychological stress in college students even after controlling for prior levels of psychological stress and self-reported frequency of daily problems. In a study focusing on nurses working in physical rehabilitation units, Elliott, Shewchuk, Hagglund, Rybarczyk, and Harkins (1996) found that a negative problem orientation was associated with more occupational burnout.

Because significant correlations have been found between NPO and both pessimism and negative trait affectivity (Chang & D'Zurilla, 1996b; Elliott et al., 1994, 1995), a question can be raised concerning whether the latter cognitive and emotional constructs might account for the significant relations between NPO and general symptom severity reported in the previous investigations. This hypothesis was rejected by Chang and D'Zurilla (1996b), who found that NPO was significantly related to symptom severity even after controlling for pessimism and negative trait affectivity. Hence, it can be concluded that NPO contributes significant incremental validity to the prediction of general symptom severity above and beyond the contributions of pessimism and negative trait affectivity.

DEPRESSION

Problem-solving deficits have been hypothesized to be a core etiological variable regarding depression (A. M. Nezu, 1987). A large number of investigations have supported this hypothesis, in part, by identifying a strong association between problem-solving deficits and depression using various problem-solving measures and across a variety of subject samples. For example, using problem-solving performance measures that were developed and validated in previous investigations (D'Zurilla & Nezu, 1980; A. M. Nezu & D'Zurilla, 1979, 1981a, 1981b), A. M. Nezu and Ronan (1987) found that depressed college students produced fewer and less effective solutions to hypothetical interpersonal problems than their nondepressed counterparts. Moreover, a different sample of depressed college students was found to choose less effective solutions than nondepressed participants when given a list of alternative solutions to hypothetical interpersonal problems.

Using a measure of impersonal problem solving, Dobson and Dobson (1981) found that depressed, versus nondepressed, college students evidenced various problem-solving deficits and an overall conservative problem-solving style. Goodman, Gravitt, and Kaslow (1995), using a measure that addresses one's ability to generate effective solutions in response to three hypothetical peer conflict situations, found that children providing less effective alternative solutions also reported higher levels of depressive symptoms.

Several investigators have used the Means-End Problem-Solving procedure (MEPS; Platt & Spivack, 1975) as the measure of problem-solving performance to investigate the association between depression and social problem solving (see chapter 4 for a description of the MEPS). For example, Gotlib and Asarnow (1979) found significant depression-related problem-solving deficits when comparing both depressed and nondepressed college students enrolled in introductory courses, as well as depressed and nondepressed students in treatment for depression at the university counseling center. Similar results were identified by Marx and Schulze (1991), as well as A. M. Nezu and Ronan (1988), regarding various college student samples; by Marx, Williams, and Claridge (1992) concerning adult patients diagnosed with major depressive disorder; and by Sacco and Graves (1984) who focused on elementary school children. However, Blankstein, Flett, and Johnston (1992) found no differences between depressed and nondepressed college undergraduates on a college student version of the MEPS, although they did find that depressed students had more negative expectations and appraisals of their problem-solving abilities as compared to their nondepressed student counterparts.

Investigations using the PSI provide additional substantial evidence of a significant relationship between problem solving and depression or negative affectivity. These cut across various populations, including American college undergraduates (e.g., Elliott et al., 1995; A. M. Nezu,

1985, 1986a; A. M. Nezu & Nezu, 1987; A. M. Nezu et al., 1986; A. M. Nezu & Ronan, 1985, 1988), Chinese college students (Cheng, 2001), French adolescents (Gosselin & Marcotte, 1997), patients with spinal cord injuries (Elliott et al., 1991), graduate students (Miner & Dowd, 1996), clinically depressed adults (A. M. Nezu, 1986a; A. M. Nezu et al., 1987), and South African undergraduates (Pretorius & Diedricks, 1994). In addition, the PSI was found to predict recovery from a depressive episode (Dixon, 2000), as well as demonstrate that problem-solving deficits are both an antecedent and a consequence of depression (Dixon, Heppner, Burnett, Anderson, & Wood, 1993). In other words, poor problem solving was found to serve not only as a vulnerability factor for depression, but it also was found to be a consequence of depression (i.e., negative affect leads to impaired problem solving).

Both the SPSI and SPSI-R have also been used to study the relationship between social problem-solving ability and depression or negative affectivity. This set of findings also cuts across a variety of sample populations, including college undergraduates (e.g., Chang, 2002a; Chang & D'Zurilla, 1996), adult psychiatric inpatients (D'Zurilla, Chang, Nottingham, & Faccini, 1998; Garland, Harrington, House, & Scott, 2000), adolescent psychiatric inpatients (Reinecke, DuBois, & Schultz, 2001), family caregivers of patients with spinal cord injuries (Elliott, Shewchuk, & Richards, 1999; Elliott, et al., 2001; Elliott & Shewchuk, 2003), caregivers of patients with Alzheimer's Disease (Rothenberg, Nezu, & Nezu, 1995), caregivers of family members living with congestive heart failure (Kurylo, Elliott, DeVivo, & Dreer, 2004), adolescent girls (Frye & Goodman, 2000), adult community residents (Kant, D'Zurilla, & Maydeu-Olivares, 1997), adult cancer patients (C. M. Nezu et al., 1999), and high school students (Sadowski et al., 1994). However, among these studies, there appears to be an inconsistency with regard to *which* SPSI-R scales are related to depression scores. For example, among two different samples (college undergraduates and psychiatric inpatients), D'Zurilla et al. (1998) found all SPSI-R scales to be highly correlated with a measure of depression with the exception of RPS. A similar pattern of results also was evident across four assessment points within a year regarding a sample of family caregivers of patients with spinal cord injuries (Elliott et al., 2001). Among a sample of adolescent girls, only the NPO, AS, and ICS scales were significantly correlated with depression scores (Frye & Goodman, 2000). Haaga, Fine, Terrill, Stewart, and Beck (1995), focusing on a college student sample, also found depression scores to be related to only problem orientation, and not problem-solving skills per se. Further, McCabe, Blankstein, and Mills (1999) and Reinecke et al. (2001) found depression scores to be significantly related to all SPSI-R scales *except* RPS. On the other hand, in a sample of middle-aged community residents, Kant et al. (1997) found all SPSI-R scales, including RPS, to be correlated with depressive severity, this being similar to the results of two separate studies by C. M. Nezu et al. (1999) conducted with adult cancer patients.

ANXIETY

Similar to the research regarding depression, researchers have used a variety of measures of social problem solving when investigating its relationship to anxiety. However, it appears that the MEPS was employed much less frequently in these anxiety studies as compared to the research addressing depression. One study by Davey (1994) that used the MEPS (as well as the PSI), failed to identify anxiety-related deficits in problem-solving performance among a group of college undergraduates, but did find that worry was associated with lowered problem-solving confidence and perceived self-control. In contrast to this study regarding problem-solving performance deficits are the findings from Brodbeck and Michelson (1987). Focusing on a population of women diagnosed with agoraphobia and panic attacks, these researchers found that, compared to normal controls, these individuals evidenced lowered performance on a measure requiring respondents to generate alternatives and make decisions concerning a series of hypothetical real-life problems.

Studies using the PSI further provide evidence of a significant association between problem solving and anxiety or worry. Although the majority of these investigations include college undergraduates as the sample population (e.g., Davey & Levy, 1999; A. M. Nezu, 1986d; Zebb & Beck, 1998), two studies were identified that did include clinical samples. A. M. Nezu and Carnevale (1987) evaluated the relationship between posttraumatic stress disorder (PTSD) and problem solving among a sample of Vietnam veterans who fell into one of the following four categories: (a) combat veterans reliably diagnosed with PTSD; (b) combat veterans with significant adjustment problems (AP) but not PTSD diagnosable; (c) combat veterans who were well adjusted (WA); and (d) veterans with little or no combat exposure who served during the Vietnam era (ERA). Results indicated that the PTSD group reported poorer problem solving than all three other groups, whereas the AP had higher total PSI scores (indicating poorer problem solving) than the WA and ERA participants.

Ladouceur, Blais, Freeston, and Dugas (1998) focused on patients diagnosed with generalized anxiety disorder and found such individuals, as compared to "moderate worriers," to endorse a more negative problem orientation as measured by scales of both the PSI and SPSI, although no differences were identified regarding the problem-solving skills scale.

Investigators seeking to assess the relationship between problem solving and anxiety have also employed the SPSI or SPSI-R. Of these studies, four have found *all* SPSI-R scales to be strongly associated with measures of state and trait anxiety across samples of college undergraduates (Belzer, D'Zurilla, & Maydeu-Olivares, 2002), adults living in the community (Bond, Lyle, Tappe, Seehafer, & D'Zurilla, 2002; Kant et al., 1997), and adult cancer patients (C. M. Nezu et al., 1999). In addition, Belzer et al. (2002) found the AS and ICS scales of the SPSI-R to be associated with measures of worry. Using a hierarchical regression analysis, Belzer and D'Zurilla (1998) found support for a mediational model indicating that negative problem orientation has both a direct and an indirect effect on anxiety. The indirect effect is that negative problem orientation increases worrying, which in turn, increases anxiety.

SUICIDE

A link has also been established between social problem-solving ability and hopelessness and suicidality. Using the MEPS, Schotte and Clum (1982), for example, found that the combination of high stress and poor problem-solving ability predicted hopelessness and suicidal intent in a sample of college students with suicidal ideation. In another study, Schotte and Clum (1987) compared suicidal psychiatric patients with nonsuicidal patients on a modified version of the MEPS. They found that the suicidal patients generated less alternative solutions to problems and reported more potential negative consequences than did the nonsuicidal group. In a study with suicidal psychiatric inpatients, Linehan et al. (1987) scored the MEPS for active versus passive relevant means. They found that psychiatric inpatients admitted following a parasuicide (i.e., deliberate, self-inflicted injury) generated less active relevant means than those admitted for suicidal ideation without parasuicide. Additional investigations using the MEPS provide further support for a strong link between social problem solving and suicide and parasuicide (Biggham & Power, 1998, 1999; Evans, Williams, O'Loughlin, & Howells, 1992; Hawton, Kingsbury, Steinhardt, James, & Fagg, 1999; Pollock & Williams, 2001; Sidley, Whitaker, Calam, & Wells, 1997).

Using the total score of the PSI, Bonner and Rich (1988) found that problem-solving ability was related to hopelessness in college students even after controlling for depression. They also found that problem-solving ability moderated the impact of major negative life events on hopelessness. Dixon, Heppner, and Anderson (1991) found that positive problem orientation, measured by the Problem Solving Confidence scale of the PSI, was negatively related to both hopelessness and suicidal ideation in college students. In another study, using the PSI in a sample of young adults in an outpatient program targeting suicidal behavior and/or ideation, Dixon, Heppner, and Rudd (1994) found support for a mediational model in which problem-solving deficits increased hopelessness, which in turn, increased suicidal ideation. In addition, studies have found the problem-solving confidence factor of the PSI to be particularly linked to suicidality (Clum & Febbraro, 1994; Rudd, Rajeb, & Dahm, 1994). However, when controlling for depression, Clum et al. (1997) found the problem orientation score of the PSI to be unrelated to suicidal ideation. Yet, a tendency toward avoiding, rather than approaching problems, was noted in this study, suggesting that it is problem-solving skill deficits, rather than orientation variables, that uniquely predicted suicidality. Based on findings from the same research team (Clum, Yang, & Febbraro, 1996), Clum et al. (1997) suggested that problem-orientation deficits exert their influence on suicidality in an indirect manner via their effects on depression.

In a study using the SPSI, Sadowski and Kelly (1993) compared adolescent suicide attempters with psychiatric and normal controls. They found that the suicide attempters had lower problem-solving ability than both control groups. Moreover, psychiatric controls had less effective problem-solving ability than normal controls. More specific analyses indicated that negative problem orientation was primarily responsible for the difference between the suicide attempters and the psychiatric controls. Both clinical groups were found to have poorer problem-solving skills than the normal controls, but they did not differ from each other on this measure.

Using the SPSI-R, D'Zurilla et al. (1998) reported that positive and negative problem orientation were most strongly related to hopelessness and suicidal ideation in college students and general psychiatric inpatients, whereas all five problem-solving dimensions were highly correlated with both of these variables among suicidal inpatients. In another study using the SPSI-R, Chang (1998) found that social problem-solving ability predicted suicidal probability in college students even after controlling for ethnic status (Caucasian versus Asian) and maladaptive perfectionism. Further, Chang (2002a) found evidence to support the hypothesis that general problem-solving deficits mediate the relationship between stress and suicidal ideation. In addition, Chang (2002b) found that problem-solving deficits also mediate the relationship between perfectionism and suicidal ideation. Using the PSI, Yang and Clum (2000) provide further support for the mediating role of social problem solving, where confidence in one's problem-solving ability was found to be an important mediator of the relationship between early life stress and suicidal behavior.

SCHIZOPHRENIA

Problem-solving training programs have been cited as a potentially effective mental health intervention for major mental disorders, including schizophrenia (Faloon, 2000). This is in part based on research that has examined the relationship between social problem-solving deficits and severe psychopathology. Using the MEPS, for example, Platt, Spivack, and their associates have found deficits in problem-solving performance in adolescent psychiatric patients (Platt, Spivack, Altman, Altman, & Peizer, 1974) and adult psychiatric patients (Platt & Spivack, 1972a, 1973). In addition, two further studies found MEPS performance to be related to the level of social competence *within* patient groups. In one study, lower MEPS performance was found to be associated with a lower level of premorbid social competence in adult psychiatric patients (Platt & Spivack, 1972b). In the second investigation, male psychiatric patients who obtained low scores on the MEPS were found to have Minnesota Multiphasic Personality Inventory (MMPI) profiles that were more clearly psychotic than those of patients who had high MEPS scores (Platt & Siegel, 1976).

Using a social problem-solving assessment test battery, Bellack et al. (1994) compared the problem-solving performance of schizophrenic inpatients, a sample of inpatients with bipolar disorder, and matched nonpatient controls. The test battery was designed to assess the ability to generate solutions to problems, the ability to evaluate the effectiveness of solutions, and the ability to implement solutions in a role-play format. Substantial deficits were found on all three tests among the two patient groups as compared to the nonpatient controls, but no significant differences were found between the two patient samples. These authors concluded that problem-solving deficits may be more of a general characteristic of severe psychopathology and not necessarily unique to schizophrenia.

The Assessment of Interpersonal Problem-Solving Skills (AIPSS; Donahoe et al., 1990) was used to evaluate differences between schizophrenic and nonschizophrenic subjects by several investigators (Bowen et al., 1994; Donahoe et al., 1990; Toomey, Wallace, Corrigan, Schuldberg, & Green, 1997). The AIPSS involves the viewing of videotapes regarding various social problems. Subjects are asked to identify the problem, generate solutions, chose an alternative, and role play the solution with an examiner. In all three studies, patients with schizophrenia were found to perform worse than nonpatients on all scales of the AIPSS. However, it is unclear as to whether such differences could be attributable to group differences in age or intellectual ability (Morris, Bellack, & Tenhula, 2004).

ADDICTIVE DISORDERS AND SUBSTANCE ABUSE

Research in this area has found a link between social problem-solving ability and substance use and abuse. In a study using the PSI, Williams and Kleinfelter (1987) found that college students with a lower positive problem orientation reported a greater use of alcohol to cope with negative emotions and escape from responsibilities. In two additional investigations, college students classified as being ineffective problem solvers were also found to report more alcohol use than effective problem solvers. In addition, Godshall and Elliott (1997) found that greater avoidant tendencies in college students were associated with greater daily alcohol consumption over a two-week period. Elliott, Johnson, and Jackson (1997) found that a lowered positive problem orientation and a greater negative problem orientation were also associated with more substance risk taking (e.g., driving after drinking) among male college students. In studies using the MEPS, deficits in problem-solving performance have been found in adult alcoholics (Nixon, Tivis, & Parsons, 1992) and in heroin addicts (Platt, Scura, & Hannon, 1973), as compared to matched controls. Further, Appel and Kaestner (1979) found less effective MEPS performance in a group of narcotic drug abusers judged to be in *poor* standing in an outpatient rehabilitation program as compared to a group judged to be in *good* standing.

In a recent study, Jaffee and D'Zurilla (2006) examined the role of social problem solving in the relationship between personality and substance use in adolescents. The study focused on four personality dimensions that had previously been found to be implicated in substance abuse: anxiety sensitivity, hopelessness, impulsivity, and sensation seeking (Woicik, Conrod, & Pihl, 2002). The SPSI-R was used to assess social problem-solving ability. Analyses focused on each of the five problem-solving dimensions. The results showed that rational problem solving (i.e., effective problem solving skills) added significant incremental validity to the prediction of substance use (lifetime alcohol and marijuana use) beyond that of personality. Moreover, rational problem solving was also found to be a significant mediator of the relationship between hopelessness and lifetime alcohol and marijuana use as well as the relationship between impulsivity and lifetime marijuana use.

Borsoi and Toneatto (2003) used the PSI to study problem solving among three groups of gamblers, as categorized by DSM-IV scores—asymptomatic, problem, and pathological. Results indicated that pathological gamblers were less confident and felt less in control than the other two groups while engaging in problem-solving activities. Problem gamblers tended to engage in more negative self-appraisals of control than asymptomatic gamblers. In addition, negative appraisal scores were found to be a significant predictor of DSM-IV scores for pathological gambling.

OFFENDING BEHAVIOR

In an attempt to better understand the role of social cognitive factors in the development and maintenance of offending behavior such as crime and aggression, researchers have addressed the relations between these behaviors and social problem solving (e.g., Antonowicz & Ross, 2005; Ross & Hilborn, 2005). An early example is a study by Platt et al. (1973) that found young prisoners addicted to heroin performed less effectively on the MEPS as compared to a sample of nonaddicted controls. Leadbeater, Hellner, Allen, and Aber (1989) found social problem-solving skills to be correlated with problem behaviors, such as delinquency, among groups of high-risk youth. Individuals who were court-ordered to attend treatment because they were caught stealing were compared to a sample of high school student controls in a study by Greening (1997). The criminal youth were found to generate less effective solutions to hypothetical problems contained in the MEPS, and also showed a tendency to become frustrated by the length of time needed to achieve a problem-solving goal.

Using the SPSI-R, Jaffe and D'Zurilla (2003) assessed the relationship between social problem solving of adolescents and their parents and aggression and delinquency. Results initially indicated that adolescents in general were characterized by less effective problem solving as compared to their parents. In addition, with specific regard to the adolescent group, avoidance style was found to be linked to both aggression and delinquency, whereas a negative problem orientation was found to be associated with aggression. Last, an impulsive/careless problem-solving style was correlated with delinquency.

Also using the SPSI-R, McMurran, Egan, Blair, and Richardson (2001) examined the relationship between social problem solving and personality in a sample of 52 mentally disordered offenders. Results indicated that high neuroticism was associated with poor problem solving. Moreover, poor problem solving appeared to mediate the relationship between personality and criminal behavior.

Various social problem-solving dimensions were also found to be related to aggression among a sample of undergraduates in the United Kingdom. Specifically, McMurran, Blair, and Egan (2002) found that a higher level of impulsivity was related to poorer problem-solving, and poorer problem solving was related to greater aggression. But by combining impulsivity and problem solving, it was found that less effective problem solving, not impulsivity, appeared to exert the major influence over aggression in this sample.

In a related study, Basquill, Nezu, Nezu, and Klein (2004) investigated attributional bias and social problem-solving deficits in two groups (aggressive versus nonaggressive) of adult males with mild mental retardation. When presented with vignettes depicting various problem situations, aggressive participants were less accurate in correctly identifying interpersonal intent, were characterized by more problem-solving deficits, and generated higher numbers of aggressive solutions to resolve problems, as compared to their nonaggressive counterparts.

Using the SPSI-R, D'Zurilla, Chang, and Sanna (2003) examined the relations between self-esteem, social problem solving, and aggression in college students. Self-esteem and social problem-solving ability were each found to be significantly related to aggression. In addition, social problem-solving ability was found to be a significant mediator of the relationship between self-esteem and aggression. Further analyses of the five problem-solving dimensions showed that negative problem orientation contributed most to this mediational effect.

Focusing on a sample of child molesters, C. M. Nezu, Nezu, Dudek, Peacock, and Stoll (2005) used the SPSI-R to assess the relationship between various problem-solving dimensions and sexual deviance. In order to minimize the influence of biased self-reports regarding their behavior, these researchers used a lie scale on one of the dependent measures, the Multiphasic Sex Inventory (MSI; Nichols & Molinder, 1984), as a criterion score. More specifically, as previous research indicated that offenders who score greater than seven on this lie scale are likely to be dishonest when reporting information about their sexual interests, all participants who obtained such a score were excluded from further consideration regarding data analysis. This led to a reduction of an original sample size of 124 incarcerated child molesters to 68 participants.

In general, results indicated that as compared to normative data, this group of sexual offenders was characterized as significantly different than the general population with regard to two problem-solving dimensions—negative problem orientation and impulsivity/carelessness. In addition, results from hierarchical regression analyses revealed that with regard to self-reported sexual deviance, after controlling for various demographic characteristics and prior abuse as a child, two problem-solving dimensions were found to significantly add to the overall amount of variance explained—impulsivity/carelessness and negative problem orientation. In predicting a measure of clinician-rated sexual aggression, also after controlling for demographics and prior abuse, only the avoidance scale of the SPSI-R was found to significantly add to the accounted variance. Of particular interest is the lack of any association between the rational problem-solving scale and measures of sexual deviance. Parenthetically, this suggests that treatment programs that only target these specific rational problem-solving skills, as compared to the full array of maladaptive problem-solving styles, may likely fail as these do not appear to be influential mechanisms of action (A. M. Nezu, 2004; C. M. Nezu, D'Zurilla, & Nezu, 2005).

MEDICAL POPULATIONS AND HEALTH BEHAVIORS

Several investigators have focused on the relationship between social problem solving and various health problems and health-related behaviors. In two studies using the PSI, college students identified as ineffective problem solvers were found to report more health problems and physical symptoms than effective problem solvers (Elliott and Marmarosh, 1994; Tracey, Sherry, & Keitel, 1986). In another study using the PSI, Godshall and Elliott (1997) found that a negative problem orientation was associated with negative perceptions of health among college students. In addition, these researchers also found that less effective problem-solving skills were related to more sedentary leisure activities. Using the SPSI-R, Elliott et al. (1997) found that a positive problem orientation was associated with more accident prevention in college students, whereas an avoidant problem-solving style was related to more traffic risk taking. In addition, these investigators also found that rational problem solving (use of effective problem-solving skills) was related to more accident prevention in men, whereas the same measure was related to more wellness behavior in women.

Researchers have also been interested in the relationships between of social problem solving, emotional distress, and other health-related variables among various medical patient populations. For example, Elliott and his colleagues have conducted several studies focusing on individuals who suffered a spinal cord injury (SCI). For example, Elliott et al. (1991) found that SCI patients were more likely to report greater depression and psychosocial disability if they were also characterized by negative appraisals regarding their problem-solving ability. Herrick, Elliott, and Crow (1994) further found that less effective problem-solving skills were linked to a greater incidence of pressure sores and urinary tract infections among persons with a SCI. In addition, Elliott (1998), using the SPSI, found that problem orientation (positive and negative problem orientation) and problem-solving skills (rational problem solving, impulsivity/carelessness style, and avoidance style) each contributed to the prediction of self-reported adjustment after discharge from a medical rehabilitation program for recent-onset physical disability, even after controlling for the level of depressive behavior at admission. More specific analyses indicated that positive problem orientation and rational problem solving were both associated with greater acceptance of disability, whereas negative problem orientation and an impulsive/careless problem-solving style were both associated with a diminished acceptance of one's disability.

With regard to adult cancer patients, A. M. Nezu, Nezu, Faddis, DelliCarpini, and Houts (1995) found poorer problem solving, as measured by the SPSI-R, to be predictive of higher levels of both depressive and anxiety symptomatology. In addition, C. M. Nezu et al. (1999) reported two studies that further confirmed a link between social problem solving and emotional distress among cancer patients. The first study focused on a group of 105 patients who recently had been diagnosed with cancer. A canonical correlational analysis indicated that study participants who were characterized by less effective problem solving also reported higher levels of anxiety and depressive symptomatology, as well as greater numbers of cancer-related problems. The second study focused on the predictive relationship of problem solving and cancer-related distress among a sample of 64 women who had successfully undergone surgery for breast cancer from 1 to 13.3 years prior to their participation in this investigation. To control for the effects of recent stressors, negative life events served as a covariate in a series of multiple regression analyses. Social problem solving, as measured by the SPSI-R, was found to be a significant predictor of psychological distress, whereas time since surgery was not associated with cancer-related distress symptomatology. Collectively, these two studies provide strong support for the existence of an important relationship between social problem solving and cancer-related distress (see also A. M. Nezu, Nezu, Houts, Friedman, & Faddis, 1999).

Using the SPSI-R, Hill-Briggs et al. (2006) found that both the impulsive/careless and avoidant problem-solving styles were significantly associated with glycemic control among a sample of adults with Type II diabetes. More recently, these same researchers developed a measure of problem solving specific to populations of adults with diabetes (Hill-Briggs et al., 2005). This measure, the Diabetes Problem-Solving Scale Self-Report (DPSS-SR), specifically assesses how adult patients approach and manage problems encountered in diabetes self-management. Initial findings indicate that better problem solving, as measured by the DPSS-SR, was associated with higher levels of medication adherence, more frequent self-monitoring of blood glucose, and lowered levels of hemoglobin A1c (a measure of glycemic control).

Elliott et al. (2001) conducted a cluster analysis of SPSI-R scores with regard to a population of adults living with diabetes in order to determine the possibility of differential profiles of problem-solving abilities. Results indicated that distinct profiles did occur and that these groupings were distinguished by their different patterns of adjustment. Specifically, four different profiles were identified: distressed and unskilled (e.g., highest level of distress, low levels of positive orientation, high levels of negative orientation); pessimistic and frustrated (e.g., second highest level of distress, second highest positive orientation, but also second-highest negative orientation); low-key and managing (e.g., second highest level of optimal functioning, second lowest average scores on both orientation scales); and ideal problem solvers (e.g., optimal level of adjustment, overall profile consistent with an ideal problem-solving approach). Interestingly, these authors also suggest that these differing profiles point to the idea that an elevated negative orientation may override the beneficial attributes of more adaptive problem-solving abilities.

Recently, Dreer, Elliott, Fletcher, and Swanson (2005) assessed the relationship between SPSI-R scores and distress, depression, well-being, and impairment among a sample of persons participating in a low vision rehabilitation program. Results of their investigation indicated that a negative problem orientation significantly predicted both depressive symptoms and emotional distress, whereas the rational problem-solving scale predicted life satisfaction.

Researchers have also addressed the role of social problem solving and pain. For example, Elliott (1992) found that a diminished sense of control when solving problems was significantly linked to premenstrual and menstrual pain complaints of college women regardless of oral contraception usage. Witty, Heppner, Bernard, and Thoreson (2001) found problem solving to predict psychosocial impairment and distress among a sample of patients entering a pain rehabilitation program. Social problem solving was also identified to be a significant predictor of functional impairment among adults experiencing chronic low back pain (Shaw, Feuerstein, Haufler, Berkowitz, & Lopez, 2001; van den Hout, Vlaeyen, Heuts, Stillen, & Willen, 2001). Kerns, Rosenberg, and Otis (2002) found that lower self-appraised problem-solving confidence, as measured by the PSI, was related to increased pain, depression, and disability among a sample of 234 chronic pain patients. In their current work in behavioral cardiology, A. M. Nezu and his associates have found total SPSI-R scores to be significantly related to measures of emotional distress and pain severity among individuals undergoing chest pain (A. M. Nezu, Nezu, & Jain, 2005).

SUMMARY AND CONCLUSIONS

We began this chapter by reiterating a basic assumption underlying PST, that is, social problem solving is an important general coping strategy that increases adaptive situational coping and behavioral competence, which in turn, reduces or prevents the negative effects of stressful life events both on psychological and physical well-being. An overview of the literature during the past three decades provides substantial support of this basic hypothesis. In other words, social problem solving, as measured by various instruments and measures, has been consistently found to be related to a wide range of adaptive and maladaptive responses. However, caution is required when interpreting the results of many of these studies, as the majority are cross-sectional in nature, and thus provide only tentative results regarding the direction of causality. Although a reasonable interpretation of these findings is that they do support our basic hypothesis that problem-solving deficits cause or contribute to psychopathology, other alternative explanations do exist. For example, it cannot be ruled out that psychopathology itself has a negative effect on problem-solving ability and performance (Mitchell & Madigan, 1984; Schotte, Cools, & Payvar, 1990; see also chapter 4). In addition, a third interpretation is possible, whereby a reciprocal relationship exists between social problem-solving ability and various forms of psychopathology (Bandura, 1977; Mitchell & Madigan, 1984; A. M. Nezu, 1987, 2004). In a reciprocal causal model, problem-solving deficits can lead to psychological distress and other maladaptive responses, which in turn, can cause more deficits in problem-solving ability and performance (and so forth). This is consistent with the study by Dixon et al. (1993) which found that poor problem solving was not only a vulnerability factor for depression, but was also a consequence of being depressed. Further, it is possible that psychological distress and symptoms from other causes may also contribute to problem-solving deficits. Regardless of the direction of the relationship between problem-solving deficits and psychopathology, PST has been found to be an efficacious treatment approach for a variety of psychological disorders and problems (see chapter 10). In addition, some support for our hypothesized causal relationship between problem-solving deficits and psychopathology emanates from those studies that used prospective designs, where prior levels of psychological distress and symptomatology are controlled when predicting subsequent distress and symptoms (e.g., A. M. Nezu & Ronan, 1988). These studies reduce the possibility that the dependent variable (distress and symptoms) is influencing the predictor variable (problem-solving ability) instead of the alternative explanation.

In reviewing this literature, several trends across studies become apparent. First, social problem-solving deficits appear to be general to psychopathology—there is little evidence that deficits in social problem-solving ability are specific to a particular form of maladaptive behavior or psychological disorder. In fact, it is more likely that problem solving interacts in combination with other psychosocial variables (e.g., type of stressor, personality characteristics) to produce the varying types of disorders and distress symptomatology (A. M. Nezu, 2004; A. M. Nezu & D'Zurilla, 1989).

A second trend involves differences across studies regarding the relations between distress and the problem orientation and problem-solving skills dimensions. Overall, across several different population samples of both clinical (e.g., depressed patients, veterans diagnosed with PTSD) and nonclinical (e.g., college students, community residents) groups, and using various types of measures (e.g., PSI, SPSI-R, MEPS), a large body of studies have identified strong associations between various social problem-solving variables and negative affect, such as depression, anxiety, and worry. In particular, a negative problem orientation appears to be an especially strong predictor of depression and anxiety across various samples and measures of problem solving. However, somewhat contradictory findings exist concerning problem-solving skills. The Rational Problem-Solving scale of the SPSI-R is comprised of items specifically related to four major problem-solving skills: *problem definition, generation of alternatives, decision making,* and *solution implementation and verification.* Although several studies that used the SPSI-R did find a relationship between these problem-solving skills with negative affect, several others failed to find a significant association between rational problem solving and measures of distress. Only focusing on this latter group of studies would suggest that the crucial problem-solving variables actually involve more cognitive-affective processes (i.e., orientation variables), rather than the rational problem-solving tasks themselves. However, the majority of studies that employed the MEPS or other performance-based measures of problem solving found otherwise. More specifically, actual problem-solving skills deficits were associated with higher levels of both depression (e.g., Goodman et al., 1995; A. M. Nezu & Ronan, 1987) and anxiety (Brodbeck & Michelson, 1987). Why such inconsistent discrepancies?

A significant part of a negative orientation involves lowered self-evaluations regarding one's ability to competently solve problems in living. Therefore, it is surprising that depressed or anxious individuals in certain investigations (e.g., Haaga et al., 1995) who did endorse a strong negative problem orientation did not also judge their actual problem-solving skills as less effective than nondepressed or nonanxious people, especially when other studies did find such a depression-associated deficit, for example, in generating alternative solutions or making decisions (e.g., A. M. Nezu & Ronan, 1987). Future research, then, needs to conduct more fine-tuned analyses to better understand such contradictions. For example, studies evaluating differences in social problem solving between depressed and nondepressed individuals should incorporate a variety of problem-solving measures in the same investigation, where differences on a performance measure can be compared to differences (or lack of) regarding self-evaluations of one's orientation and rational problem-solving.

Another trend we identified is that the two constructive problem-solving dimensions (positive problem orientation and effective problem-solving skills) tend to facilitate *positive* adaptation and well-being (e.g., adaptive coping, social competence, positive health behaviors, optimism, self-esteem, life satisfaction), whereas the three dysfunctional dimensions (negative problem orientation, impulsive/careless problem solving, and problem-solving avoidance) are more likely to lead to *negative* behavioral and psychological outcomes (e.g., maladaptive coping, psychological symptoms, health-compromising behavior).

In conclusion, these three patterns across studies are consistent with expectations based on social problem-solving theory. Therefore, it would appear that the empirical literature reported in this chapter does provide strong support for the theory on which PST is based.

SECTION II

Clinical Applications

CHAPTER EIGHT

Problem-Solving
Training Manual

In this chapter, we offer recommendations to therapists and clinical researchers regarding how to effectively conduct problem-solving therapy (PST). However, rather than provide a single training manual that may only be appropriate for a minority of the large number of possible applications for which PST has been found to be effective (see chapter 10), both in terms of target patient problems (e.g., depression, anxiety, health-related difficulties) and modes of implementation (e.g., individual face-to-face therapy, telephone counseling), we have broken down PST into differing modules that represent various training activities and exercises geared to address specific problem-solving objectives (e.g., to enhance one's positive problem orientation, to improve decision-making ability). In that manner, the reader can develop his or her own unique PST "manual" for a specific patient or research project. In a clinical setting, the choice of which modules to implement should be based on the goals of therapy (e.g., reducing depressive symptoms, overcoming obstacles to adhering to prescribed medical regimens) as well as a comprehensive and individualized assessment of the patient's problem-solving strengths and weaknesses. In a research setting, the modules would be based on the specific research questions or objectives (e.g., to evaluate the efficacy of the entire PST package, to evaluate the efficacy of specific components of PST).

Before we continue, we wish to underscore an important caveat. PST should be defined as a grouping of clinical intervention strategies that are implemented in order to reach a particular goal. As such, we emphasize the notion of focusing on *behavior change principles*, rather than equating effective PST exclusively with the specific training exercises or activities contained in this manual. For example, there may be several differing ways to help a patient reverse a negative problem orientation other than the modules we offer (e.g., "formal" cognitive restructuring training, "formal" rational emotive therapy, bibliotherapy, psychoeducation). In other words, we provide such a module as one possible example of how to reach important treatment objectives (i.e., improving problem orientation) and suggest that it represents various important therapeutic *principles* (e.g., increasing one's ability to recognize problems when they occur; minimizing the likelihood that one wishes to avoid a problem instead of confronting it), rather than how PST *must be* delivered. In fact, we hope that clinicians use their own brainstorming capabilities in order to be creative in the clinical setting, focusing primarily on attaining important treatment objectives, rather than simply implementing what might be perceived as our only "prescription." Whereas we do delineate various treatment *strategies* that comprise effective PST, we emphasize that there are many *tactics* that can be identified that can achieve various PST goals, both in terms of differential treatment activities and modes of implementation. On the other hand, we can state with a large degree of certainty, based on our collective research and clinical experience, that the suggestions, exercises, and activities we include in this chapter have been found to be very effective in reaching the objectives. Therefore, for those interested in conducting PST outcome research, we also provide recommendations regarding the construction of standardized PST manuals that can be used in well-controlled research protocols.

PATIENT MANUAL

To accompany the therapists' manual described in this chapter, we have developed a self-help problem-solving training guidebook written for the layperson entitled *Solving Life's Problems: A 5-Step Guide to Enhanced Well-Being* (A. M. Nezu, Nezu, & D'Zurilla, 2007). To a large degree, this self-help manual mirrors our recommendations for the clinician or researcher presented in this chapter. Because social problem solving helps individuals to adapt more successfully to their environments, the manual uses the acronym *ADAPT*, as described below, to remind the reader to engage in the five problem-solving steps of our model.

A = *Attitude*. Suggests that before attempting to solve the problem, individuals should adopt a positive, optimistic *attitude* (i.e., problem orientation) toward the problem and their problem-solving ability.

D = *Define*. After adopting a positive attitude, this step recommends that individuals *define* the problem by obtaining relevant facts, identifying obstacles that inhibit goal achievement, and specifying a realistic goal.

A = *Alternatives*. Based upon a well-defined problem, persons are directed to next generate a variety of different *alternatives* for overcoming the identified obstacles and achieving the problem-solving goal.

P = *Predict*. After generating a list of alternatives, people are directed to *predict* both the positive and negative consequences of each alternative in order to choose the one(s) that has the highest probability of achieving the problem-solving goal, while additionally minimizing costs and maximizing benefits.

T = *Try out*. When individuals have chosen a solution, they are then asked to *try out* the solution in real-life and monitor its effects. If they are satisfied with the results, the problem is solved and they should engage in self-reinforcement. On the other hand, if they are not satisfied, they are then directed to go back to the A step and *try again* in order to find a more effective solution.

This self-help manual also contains multiple exercises, many of which parallel those included in this chapter, that are geared to successfully accomplish these five problem-solving steps. Many of these can be used for homework assignments as well. The guidebook is written in a language that is more user-friendly, thus providing examples to therapists or counselors of how to explain the various problem-solving concepts to patients. It is strongly recommended that a patient, client, or research subject receiving PST should use this self-help manual in tandem with therapist-led treatment. However, in cases where bibliotherapy is viewed as a potentially effective treatment or preventive strategy by itself, or as an initial stage in treatment before implementing a more formal intervention package, this manual is self-contained such that individuals will be able to assess their problem-solving deficits and enhance their overall problem-solving ability and performance on their own. It even includes a self-directed method of assessing one's own problem-solving strengths and weaknesses.

IMPORTANT CLINICAL CONSIDERATIONS

Similar to many other directive forms of psychotherapy or counseling, in particular those under a cognitive-behavioral umbrella, the success of PST to a large degree depends on the effectiveness of the manner in which it is actually implemented. Therefore, in this section, we offer suggestions regarding how to (a) use various instructional or training techniques to effectively conduct PST, (b) enhance the therapeutic relationship, and (c) assess a patient's problem-solving abilities and skills to help guide treatment planning. We finish this section with a list of PST "Do's and Don'ts."

Training Strategies

Didactic methods. PST involves imparting substantial psychoeducational knowledge, using verbal instructions and written materials, while also making use of the Socratic approach to instruction, which emphasizes questions and discussions that encourage individuals to think for themselves and formulate their own conclusions, deductions, and elaborations. Such instruction is consistent with the PST goal of facilitating independent productive thinking.

Coaching primarily involves verbal prompting, such as leading questions, suggestions, and instructions. For example, during initial brainstorming sessions, the problem-solving therapist can prompt the participant to begin the process of generating alternative solutions.

Modeling includes written and verbal problem-solving examples and demonstrations conducted by the therapist (or group members if conducting PST in a group format), using hypothetical problems, as well as real problems presented by the participant(s). This can be done in vivo, through filmed or pictorial presentation, or through role-plays. To facilitate learning and to help individuals discriminate more effectively, it is important at times to model both correct *and* incorrect ways of applying various problem-solving principles.

Shaping involves specific training in the problem-solving process in progressive steps, with each new step being contingent on successful performance in the previous step. In addition, it can be useful to develop a hierarchy of a patient's problems, based on the dimensions of severity or complexity, such that less intense or difficult problems can then be used as relevant examples early in training. Once the patient (or group) has mastered certain prerequisite problem-solving skills, more difficult problems can then be addressed.

Rehearsal involves problem-solving practice exercises and homework assignments. In addition to written exercises and assignments, rehearsal may involve role-playing, practice in imagination (covert rehearsal), and practice with real-life problematic situations. Homework assignments are a particularly important feature of any skill acquisition. Without practice, the ability to actually implement problem-solving skills in real life can be compromised.

Performance feedback should be provided to patients directly, as well as via self-monitoring and self-evaluation using various procedures, including the Problem-Solving Self-Monitoring (PSSM) method (see chapter 4) or other homework or practice forms (see the "Problem-Solving Test" worksheet in the *Solving Life's Problems* self-help guidebook).

Positive reinforcement includes the therapist's praise, as well as social reinforcement by other members if implemented in a group format, as well as the natural reinforcement of successful problem-solving performance in the real-life setting.

Building a Positive Therapeutic Relationship

In order to maximize training effectiveness, it is important to conduct problem-solving training within the context of a positive, collaborative, therapeutic relationship with the participant(s). Below are some general guidelines for therapists to help develop such a relationship.

Be Warm, Empathic, and Genuine. Three major therapist characteristics that contribute to a positive therapeutic relationship are warmth, empathy, and genuineness. Express warmth by smiling and being friendly, kind, and gentle and showing that you care about the well-being of the participant(s). Express empathy by listening carefully when the participants describe their problems and concerns, recognizing their feelings, and communicating your understanding by paraphrasing their thoughts and reflecting their feelings. Show genuineness by being a *real person* in the relationship, using self-disclosure if and when appropriate (i.e., your own successful problem-solving experiences), and answering the participants' questions and concerns honestly and respectfully without being patronizing or condescending.

Be Enthusiastic and Optimistic. Maximize feelings of hope and expectations of benefit in the participant(s) by emphasizing the *relevance* and *effectiveness* of problem-solving training for their personal lives. Explain that problem solving will help them cope more effectively with stressful daily problems and reduce the negative impact of stress on their emotional and physical well-being. Point out that training is *not* just for people who are poor problem solvers. Emphasize the fact that it helps good problem solvers become even *better* problem solvers, as well as better teachers of problem solving (for example, teaching their children to be better problem solvers), and that it helps people learn how to apply their old problem-solving skills (e.g., those applied at work) effectively to new problems (e.g., those required to improve a relationship).

Encourage Participation. Conduct problem-solving training in an interactive manner that encourages as much participation by the individuals as possible. The major training methods for encouraging participation are *rehearsal* and *homework assignments*. Rehearsal involves guided practice in solving hypothetical and real problems in the training sessions, and homework assignments involve supervised practice in applying problem solving to real, current problems in the natural environment. Remember the old Chinese adage regarding the most effective teaching approach—*Tell me, and I will probably forget; Show me, and I might remember; Involve me, and I will understand.*

Assessment of Problem-Solving Strengths and Weaknesses

In research settings, we strongly advocate using a psychometrically sound measure of social problem solving, such as the SPSI-R (D'Zurilla et al., 2002), that can provide for a valid measure of the status of one's problem-solving strengths and weaknesses at baseline, as well as a reliable measure of changes in problem solving as a function of treatment. As noted in chapter 4, the SPSI-R provides scores in five major scales—positive problem orientation, negative problem orientation, rational problem solving, impulsivity/carelessness style, and avoidance style. A long version (52 items), as well as a short version (25 items) exists, both of which are available in English and Spanish.

In clinical settings, the SPSI-R can also be very useful, especially as the test manual provides for normative data categorized by age and gender, as well as across various patient and nonpatient populations. In that manner, it is possible to obtain a sense of an individual client's relative strengths and weaknesses across the five dimensions in order to determine which modules to include or emphasize in training. In addition, in the 52-item version, the rational problem-solving scale provides for scores in the following four subscales—problem definition and formulation, generation of alternatives, decision making, and solution implementation and verification.

For the *Solving Life's Problems* self-help guidebook, we developed the "Problem-Solving Test," a self-assessment inventory for patients themselves to complete in order to engage in Step 1 of the process— that is, self-assessment. Whether engaging in a self-directed approach to improving one's problem solving, or in tandem with therapist-led PST, this procedure can provide valuable information to the individual in order to obtain a better appreciation of one's own problem-solving skills. Note that this test should be used only as a *qualitative* clinical tool, as it has not been evaluated regarding its psychometric properties.

The PSSM method, as described in chapter 4, can also be used early in treatment in order to determine how successful a patient's attempts were at solving or coping with a recently experienced stressful problem. This approach can also serve as a useful springboard during interview sessions to obtain multiple details about the client's problem-solving thinking, emotional reactions, behavioral attempts at carrying out a solution plan, and self-ratings of success or failure.

Last, we recommend a form titled the "Problem-Solving Worksheet" in the *Solving Life's Problems* self-help guidebook as another example of a problem-solving self-monitoring procedure. This form was based on the "Record of Coping Attempts" worksheets that we have previously used in our outcome research (e.g., A. M. Nezu, Nezu, Friedman, Faddis, & Houts, 1998; A. M. Nezu, Nezu, Felgoise, McClure, & Houts, 2003), and requests that an individual, when attempting to solve a problem or cope with a stressful event, complete this form to document various thoughts, feelings, behaviors, and self-ratings regarding the problem.

PST Pitfalls to Avoid

The following list of PST *Do's* and *Don'ts* are offered as important clinical considerations based on our experience both in clinical and research settings regarding the effective conduct of PST (see also A. M. Nezu et al., 1998).

1. *DO NOT present PST in a mechanistic manner*—PST should not be conducted in a rote-like manner, devoid of a therapeutic atmosphere. Training in problem-solving skills should be as interactive as possible.

2. *DO make PST relevant to a particular client or group*—training examples should be specific and relevant to the people at hand. The therapist needs to adapt PST to the specific needs of a patient or group. Do not deliver a *canned* treatment that does not incorporate relevant life experiences of a given individual or group.

3. *DO include homework assignments*—as mentioned previously, practice is an important component of PST. Clients should be encouraged to practice as much as possible between PST sessions.

4. *DO focus on the patient, as well as the treatment*—although correctly implementing PST is important to ensure its effectiveness, the patient should always be the primary focus of attention. Consistently demonstrate respect for the patient's feelings and foster the idea that he or she can use these negative emotions as important information (i.e., that a problem exists).

5. *DO NOT focus only on superficial problems*—the therapist needs to use his or her own clinical decision-making skills to assess whether the problems being discussed are in fact the most crucial for a given client, otherwise, the effectiveness of treatment will be limited. For example, a superficial problem might involve helping a patient to "get more dates," when the more important or core issue might entail coping with the fear of committing to an intimate relationship.

6. *DO focus on solution implementation*—the client or group should be encouraged to implement as many solutions as possible during training in order to obtain the best feedback possible (i.e., problem resolution).

7. *DO NOT equate problem-focused coping with problem-solving coping*—as described in chapter 6, we define problem-solving coping as the more general process of dealing with stressful situations. Problem-solving coping entails *both* problem-focused coping (i.e., strategies to change the nature of the situation), as well as emotion-focused coping (i.e., strategies geared to minimize emotional distress related to the problem). As such, the therapist needs to convey to clients that both forms of coping are advisable, depending upon the nature of the situation. For instance, if a problem situation is perceived as *unchangeable* (e.g., the other person involved in an interpersonal problem is unwilling to change), then a potentially viable and effective solution alternative might be acceptance that the situation will not change.

8. *DO use handouts as adjuncts to training*—written handouts help clients to remember and practice the skills between sessions. Often it may be useful to encourage the participants to purchase a looseleaf-type notebook to store the handouts in for current and future reference. Again, it would be important to adapt such handouts to be relevant to a given target population. We decided to develop the *Solving Life's Problems* self-help guidebook because we have found handouts to be an extremely useful and effective training tool in our research (A. M. Nezu & Perri, 1989; A. M. Nezu et al., 2003; C. M. Nezu et al., 1991).

9. *Do conduct an adequate assessment of an individual's problem-solving strengths and weaknesses*—do not assume that all patients are equal, and conduct PST accordingly (unless if required as part of a controlled clinical research study).

MODULES

The following are a list of possible modules that comprise PST. As repeatedly mentioned throughout, the choice of which modules to implement should be based on both the nature and purpose of the program (e.g., clinical versus research; individual versus group; number of sessions), as well as a comprehensive and individualized assessment of a patient's problem-solving abilities. For examples of detailed PST treatment manuals, the reader is directed to A. M. Nezu, Nezu, & Perri (1989) with regard to the treatment of depression and A. M. Nezu et al. (1998) concerning PST for cancer patients.

With regard to well-controlled outcome investigations, we suggest that a sole PST intervention at a minimum should contain training in aspects of modules 1 through 13. Depending on the population, training can proceed in one of three ways after conducting an initial introductory session: (a) each subsequent session is devoted to a specific problem-solving dimension (e.g., training in problem orientation is provided in session 2, PDF training in session 3, GOA training in session 4, and so forth; see A. M. Nezu & Perri, 1989, and A. M. Nezu et al., 2003, for examples of outcome investigations that used this approach); (b) training in problem orientation is conducted in the next one (or two) sessions, followed by a session devoted to all four rational problem-solving skills, followed by multiple sessions devoted to guided practice; and (c) If research findings identify a given population as being particularly in need of training in problem orientation (see A. M. Nezu, 2004), several sessions are devoted to such training before focusing on problem-solving skills.

Finally, we highly recommend that the *Solving Life's Problems* self-help guidebook be consulted for examples of user-friendly language to explain various concepts, as well as to recommend that the patient read the book in conjunction with therapist-led PST.

Module 1. Initial Structuring
Module 2. Problem-Solving Assessment
Module 3. Obstacles to Effective Problem Solving: Limited Capacity of
    the Conscious Mind
Module 4: Problem Orientation: Introduction and Fostering Self-Efficacy
    Beliefs
Module 5: Problem Orientation: Problem Recognition
Module 6: Problem Orientation: Viewing Problems as Challenges
Module 7: Problem Orientation: Use and Control of Emotions in Problem
    Solving
Module 8: Problem Orientation: STOP and THINK!
Module 9: Problem Definition and Formulation (PDF)
Module 10: Generation of Alternative Solutions (GOA)
Module 11: Decision Making (DM)
Module 12: Solution Implementation and Verification (SIV)
Module 13: Guided Practice
Module 14: Rapid Problem Solving
Module 15: Communication Skills and Interpersonal Problem Solving

Module 1. Initial Structuring

The purpose of this introductory module is to provide an overview of, and rationale for, PST, as well as to establish a positive therapeutic relationship. It should set the pace for the remainder of the training. The therapist should refer to chapters 2, 3, and 6 in this volume for explanations regarding the various concepts to be presented in this module, as well as chapters 1 and 2 in the *Solving Life's Problems* self-help guidebook. If you are using the self-help guide as part of an overall PST package, the client should be directed to read these two chapters.

Key Objectives and Training Activities

Establish a positive therapeutic relationship (see previous suggestions).

Present PST rationale and overarching training goals (i.e., to help individuals adopt a more positive problem orientation and to learn to apply a set of rational problem-solving skills that can increase their overall personal-social competence and to reduce, minimize, control, and prevent stress in daily living). This general problem-solving goal should be directly linked to a particular client's own treatment goals, such as to reduce depression, improve interpersonal relationships, adhere better to a difficult medical regimen in order to improve health, or decrease obsessive worrying.

Discuss reasons for initially seeking treatment. Encourage individual or group members to discuss why they are participating in the program. One training tip involves having patients treat this request as "a problem-to-be-solved." In other words, they should ask themselves the question (i.e., "problem statement")—"What should I tell the therapist (or group) about myself at this time?" They are then asked to close their eyes and imagine alternative self-introductions. Following the actual self-introductions, individuals are asked to describe their thoughts and feelings when the request was first made, while they were imagining alternative self-introductions and trying to decide what to say about themselves, and during their actual self-introductions. Regardless of whether or not people reveal all their true thoughts and feelings at this time, this experience can be used by the PST therapist as a concrete example to help illustrate some important points about problem recognition, other problem-orientation variables (e.g., problem attribution, problem appraisal), the nature of stress, the role of emotions in problem solving, and the use of specific problem-solving skills or principles (e.g., problem definition and formulation, generation of alternative solutions, and so forth).

Explain concepts of "stress," "problems," "effective coping," and so on, where relevant. Ask individual or group members to provide personal examples of each of these concepts.

Describe the problem-solving model of stress. Explain how effective problem solving can mitigate against the negative effects of stress. Depending on the initial referral question, explain how stress relates to that problem (e.g., stressful events can lead to depression; stressful problems can serve as major obstacles to effective behavior change, such as adherence to a medical regimen).

Briefly describe specific PST objectives. Link these to actual content of future sessions (i.e., various didactics, exercises, and activities will be provided to reach these objectives during future training sessions): (a) enhance positive problem orientation, (b) decrease negative problem orientation, (c) enhance rational problem-solving skills, (d) minimize tendency to be impulsive or careless, and (e) minimize tendency to avoid problems.

Compare PST training to learning other skills (e.g., management skills, sports, music). Liken the process with regard to (a) the need to *break down* various skills into exercises and activities, and (b) the need for practice "in order to get really good."

Delineate the actual structure of the intended PST program. Explain how many sessions will be involved, the length of each session, the inclusion of homework, and so forth. Explain also various ground rules and therapy expectations (i.e., therapist and patient responsibilities).

Encourage optimism. Highlight the efficacy of PST across many patient problems and populations (see chapter 10 for examples), and communicate the client's potential for competence and actual change. With regard to this latter point, one tip is to ask individuals to state one skill (e.g., playing a musical instrument or sport; artistic ability) of which they are proud. This can be used to delineate the process of how time and effort were involved to achieve this skill. It can also be used later in treatment as a reference to recognize competency or to help motivate the patient to continue to use problem solving.

Module 2. Problem-Solving Assessment

An assessment of the individual's problem-solving strengths and weaknesses should be conducted early in treatment (or prior to conducting a controlled outcome study). The results of this assessment should help guide module selection and emphasis. Feedback to the patient would be important, especially if he or she has certain strengths (i.e., this will help to foster a sense of competence and self-efficacy).

In addition to a semistructured interview geared to obtain detailed information about how a person handled a recent stressful problem, we advocate one or more of the "formal" methods of problem-solving assessment: the SPSI-R, the Problem-Solving Test, the PSSM method, or the "Problem-Solving Worksheet".

SPSI-R

As described previously (see chapter 4), the SPSI-R is a self-report measure of problem solving that captures information across the two differing problem orientation dimensions (positive, negative), as well as the three differing problem-solving styles (rational problem solving, impulsivity/carelessness, avoidance). Because of the normative data available across various ages and patient populations (D'Zurilla et al., 2002), it is possible to obtain an understanding of how a given individual's scores compare to the *norm*. Such information might be particularly helpful to determine the intensity of one's *strengths* and *weaknesses*. Further, because the SPSI-R also has been found to be sensitive to the effects of PST training, it can be a psychometrically sound method of assessing the presence or absence of improvements in problem solving.

Problem-Solving Test

This test is contained in chapter 3 of the *Solving Life's Problems* guidebook. Individuals are directed to take this test as a means of completing a self-assessment of their problem-solving abilities. This can be both an entertaining and educational means for individuals to learn more about themselves with regard to their current problem-solving abilities. It can also be used as a means of assessing improvement.

PSSM Method

Described in chapter 4, the Problem-Solving Self-Monitoring (PSSM) method provides for a self-monitoring approach to problem-solving assessment. This can be used throughout the training, both as a method of gathering daily or weekly information concerning a person's actual attempts, as well as to monitor improvement.

As an example, the following is a PSSM record (excluding the ratings) that was produced early in treatment by a 40-year-old woman with a problem involving the loss of a relationship through divorce. Note that it reflects an unsuccessful attempt at coping.

Problem

I have not been able to meet any stable, respectable, single men who are interested in a serious, long-term relationship. Most interesting men that I meet are either married or they are just interested in a "one-night stand." I am beginning to believe that I will never have an intimate long-term relationship with a man again and that I will be alone for the rest of my life.

Emotions

I have been feeling lonely and depressed most of the time. I am losing my self-confidence and feeling very inadequate as a woman. I am feeling increasingly anxious and fearful about the future.

Solution

I decided to join Parents Without Partners. I thought that this choice would make me feel the least uncomfortable and would involve the least financial cost.

Outcome

I went to several Parents Without Partners meetings and social activities. I felt only slightly uncomfortable initially. However, I did not meet any interesting or likeable men. I was bored most of the time. This experience has made me feel even more discouraged and depressed.

As training progresses, it is expected that improvements in problem-solving ability will be reflected in the PSSM records, with individuals reporting better problem-solving skills and more successful solution outcomes.

Problem-Solving Worksheet

The "Problem-Solving Worksheet" is another example of a problem-solving self-monitoring procedure and is contained in chapter 3 of the *Solving Life's Problems* self-help guidebook. This can also be used throughout a PST program, both as a method of gathering daily or weekly information concerning a person's actual attempts at problem resolution, as well as to monitor improvement. Essentially, it asks individuals to provide the following information: (a) brief description of the problem; (b) thoughts that occurred before, during, and after the problem; (c) feelings that occurred before, during, and after the problem; (d) actual behaviors engaged in when attempting to improve the problem situation; and (e) a rating, from 1 ("not at all") to 10 ("very much"), concerning "how pleased are you with what you did to improve the problem situation?"

Homework

- Direct the client to use either the PSSM method or "Problem-Solving Worksheet" between sessions to self-monitor problem-solving activities. For example, these protocols can be used to (a) list problems that occur in daily living during the week, and (b) record two or three of the most difficult and significant problems.
- Provide feedback during subsequent sessions. This can be repeated on a regular weekly basis throughout counseling.

Module 3. Obstacles to Effective Problem Solving: Limited Capacity of the Conscious Mind

Describe Human Limits to Multitask Effectively

Research in cognitive psychology during the past several decades has shown that the conscious mind is remarkably limited in the amount of activity that it can perform efficiently at any one time. According to Levine (1988), the conscious mind engages in three important activities during problem solving: (a) receives information from the environment (external and internal) and interprets it; (b) "displays" information when needed (remembering); and (c) manipulates information that is remembered and attempts to comprehend it (e.g., combines information, adds and subtracts information).

However, the capacity of the conscious mind is limited in that it cannot perform all three activities efficiently at the same time, especially when the quantity or complexity of the information is great. Often, one activity interferes with another. For example, attempting to remember all the important information about a problem may, under certain conditions, interfere with the manipulation of information that is involved in the comprehension or understanding of the problem.

As a training activity, the PST therapist cannot only explain these concepts to patients, but also engage in discussions and demonstrations of the three principles using information about personally relevant problems either gleaned from PSSM or "Problem-Solving Worksheet" forms, or during a previous discussion.

Ways to Facilitate Problem-Solving Multitasking

Three rules that are particularly useful for enhancing the process of problem solving include externalization, visualization, and simplification (Levine, 1988).

Externalization involves the display of information externally as often as possible (e.g., writing it down, drawing diagrams to show relationships), including information about the nature of the problem, alternative solutions, and solution outcomes. This procedure relieves the conscious mind from having to actively display information being remembered, which allows one to concentrate more on other activities, such as interpretation and comprehension of information.

Visualization emphasizes the use of vision and visual imagery whenever possible during the problem-solving process. To apply this rule, one should directly observe all aspects of the problematic situation, rehearse alternative solutions using role-playing, and actively test different solution options in the real problematic situation. When these procedures are not feasible or practical, an individual can use his or her imagination to visualize the problematic situation and test or rehearse solution alternatives. Research has demonstrated convincingly that visualization is a powerful tool that facilitates remembering, as well as the comprehension of verbal information (i.e., grasping the logic, perceiving relationships between bits of information).

Simplification involves attempting to "break down" or simplify the problem in order to make it more manageable. To apply this rule, one should attempt to focus only on the most relevant information, break down complex problems into more manageable subproblems, and translate complex, vague, and abstract concepts into more simple, specific, and concrete terms.

Homework

- Direct the patient to practice these three methods when attempting to complete one of the problem-solving self-monitoring protocols.
- Provide feedback and added practice during subsequent sessions.

Module 4. Problem Orientation: Introduction and Fostering Self-Efficacy Beliefs

This introductory module to problem orientation involves describing and emphasizing the importance of focusing on one's problem orientation. The superordinate point is to highlight the notion that the way in which people focus attention, predict, think about, and interpret problems they experience will have a great impact on their emotional and behavioral reactions. In addition, it is important to begin to enhance a patient's sense of self-efficacy regarding his or her ability to effectively cope with such problems. Refer to chapter 3 in this book for explanations of these concepts and to chapter 3 in *Solving Life's Problems*. If you are using this self-help guidebook in conjunction with therapist-led PST, assign the relevant reading and exercises in chapter 3. When discussing the various aspects of each type of orientation, it is helpful to encourage the client to identify which aspects of each are particularly personally relevant, especially as previously identified during the self-assessment step.

Key Training Objectives and Activities

Describe and discuss problem orientation. Define problem orientation as an individual's general awareness, beliefs, assumptions, and expectations concerning life's daily problems and his or her ability to solve them. Emphasize the fact that one's orientation greatly influences the way he or she actually copes with such difficulties, as well as the amount of stress experienced in the process. This orientation can be described as the "set of glasses we wear when we are confronted by problems in living."

Describe and discuss aspects of a negative or maladaptive problem orientation (see Table 8.1 for detailed description).

Describe and discuss aspects of a positive or adaptive problem orientation (see Table 8.2 for detailed description).

Foster a patient's sense of positive self-efficacy. Engage in a visualization exercise (different from the one described in module 3). This exercise is particularly helpful to those individuals who tend to have doubts about their ability to effectively solve most of life's problems (i.e., one aspect of a negative orientation). For them, the technique of *visualization* may be useful to help restructure their image of themselves from being helpless or ineffective, to one of competent persons who can solve personal problems. With this strategy, the therapist's goal is to help patients create the experience of the success in their minds eye, and vicariously experience the potential reinforcement to be gained.

This technique involves having patients close their eyes and imagine that they have successfully solved a current problem. Even if the patient

TABLE 8.1   Characteristics of a Negative Problem Orientation

1. Such individuals tend to blame themselves for *causing* the problem. As such, they believe that there is something wrong with themselves (e.g., they are "abnormal," "incompetent," "stupid," "bad," or "unlucky").

2. People with this orientation tend to perceive the problem as a significant threat to their well-being that should be avoided or attacked immediately without any plan. They minimize the possible benefits of solving the problem successfully and instead exaggerate the harm or loss that might result from failure to solve the problem successfully.

3. Individuals characterized by a negative orientation have low expectations of coping with the problem effectively, either because they perceive the problem as unsolvable, or because they do not believe that they are capable of solving the problem successfully. As a result, they avoid the problem or attempt to get someone else to solve it.

4. Such persons believe that a competent individual should be able to solve the problem quickly, without much effort. They believe that their failure to do so is a sign of inadequacy or incompetence. In addition, they do not place a high value on independent, effortful, problem-solving activity. They prefer to have someone else solve the problem.

TABLE 8.2   Characteristics of a Positive Problem Orientation

1. Individuals characterized with a positive orientation perceive problems in general as normal, ordinary, inevitable events in life. They realize that problems are not necessarily an indication that something is wrong with themselves. They recognize when a problem is caused by environmental circumstances or transient personal factors (e.g., lack of experience, uncertainty), rather than by global and stable personal defects or abnormalities. They believe that when a problem is a result of some personal deficit or inadequacy, this indicates only that they are human and not perfect.

2. Instead of appraising the problem primarily as a *threat-to-be-avoided,* such individuals perceive the problem as a *challenge* or opportunity for personal growth or self-improvement (e.g., learning something new, changing one's life for the better, feeling better about oneself). They do not view failure as a catastrophe, but instead, view it as a potential corrective learning experience. In addition, they believe in the philosophy that "it is better to take on a problem or a challenge and fail, than not to try to solve it at all."

3. Such individuals believe that there is a solution to the problem and that they are capable of finding this solution on their own. They understand that the more people believe that they can cope with problems successfully, the better they will actually be able to cope with them.

4. Persons with a positive orientation realize that solving the problem is often likely to take time and effort. They resist the temptation to respond to the problem impulsively. They further understand that the first impulse and ideas are not usually the best as they tend to be influenced more by negative feelings than by reasoning. They value independent, effortful problem solving, and are prepared to be persistent if a solution is not quickly discovered. Such individuals also realize that even the best problem solvers need time to think in order to solve difficult problems effectively. However, they also understand that if they have tried their best and still cannot succeed, then they must either accept the problem as unchangeable in its present form and try to view it from a different perspective (e.g., acceptance, reducing personal distress, seeking a compromise) or go get help with it.

indicates that it is not possible at present, the therapist can remind him or her to try to create an imaginary scene. The instructions should include a visualization of the end point (i.e., successful resolution of the problem). It is important to convey to the patient that, "It doesn't matter how you are actually able to do it—just that a difficult problem is solved." To facilitate this process, the therapist can ask, "Did you solve the problem?" "How would your life be different with this problem solved?" "How would you be feeling?" "What would you be doing?" "How would you feel about yourself that is different than how you were feeling moments ago?" If the patient experiences difficulty imagining they've solved the problem, the therapist can suggest visualizing role models (e.g., famous figures, persons whom the patient admires) solving the same or a similar problem.

As the patient begins to visualize successful resolution to a problem, it is important for the therapist to listen carefully for the positive moments that the patient reports or experiences and reflect these statements back to the individual (e.g., "I feel relieved," "It must feel really good to experience relief").

The central goal of this strategy is to have people create their own positive consequences to solving a difficult problem as a motivational step toward self-efficacy. Therefore, it is also important to pay close attention and actually record positive statements to recap later for the patient (e.g., "It sounds like one of the benefits to increase your problem-solving skills is being able to feel more in control of your relationships and unafraid of the future"). By asking patients to describe likely positive consequences, they will provide their own intrinsic reasons why problem solving may be important and effective for them.

Module 5. Problem Orientation: Problem Recognition

This module continues with training in problem orientation with specific regard to enhancing a person's ability to recognize problems when they occur. Refer to chapter 3 in this book and chapter 3 in *Solving Life's Problems*. If you are using this self-help guidebook in conjunction with therapist-led PST, assign the relevant reading and exercises in chapter 3.

Key Training Objectives and Activities

Describe and discuss the concept of problem recognition. Convey to the patient that problems may not always be easy to recognize. They are often embedded within a social context that contains many problem-*irrelevant* aspects. The relevant information about a problem is often vague, ambiguous, or not immediately available. In addition, because many problems are stressful, people often tend to avoid them to protect themselves from threat and anxiety. This is often self-defeating because people experience the negative consequences of the unsolved problem (i.e., emotional distress, ineffective performance) and tend to label these consequences as "the problem" without recognizing the *real* problem.

Describe, discuss, and demonstrate the following aids to increase one's ability to recognize problems when they occur.

1. *Using one's feelings as a cue that a problem exists.* Instead of labeling one's negative feelings as the *problem,* individuals should be directed to use these feelings as a signal that a problem exists and then to observe their environment and monitor their behavior in an attempt to recognize the *real* problem that is causing these feelings. Common emotional consequences of stressful problems are anxiety, uncertainty, depression, anger, dissatisfaction, disappointment, confusion, guilt, feelings of inadequacy, and feelings of helplessness. Explain that *feelings* in this context not only refers to emotional states (e.g., "I feel sad"), but also to concomitant physiological states (e.g., "I feel like there are butterflies in my stomach," "My head hurts just thinking about this," "I feel so shaky and jittery").

2. *Using one's ineffective behavior as a signal that a problem exists.* Negative emotions may not always be sufficient cues for accurate problem recognition. It may be only after people continue to make mistakes and fail to respond effectively that they will realize that a problem exists. Instead of having patients focus on their ineffective behavior and label it as the problem, direct them to use such actions as a signal to seek out and identify the problematic situation (both personal factors and environmental factors) that they are not coping with effectively.

3. *Using certain thoughts as cues that a problem exists.* In addition to negative emotions or ineffective behavior, certain thoughts may be indicators that a problem exists. Thoughts such as "I *should* have gotten a perfect score on that test, now I'll never get into medical school," "The bills seem to be piling high this month, I'll just forget about them for now "cause they just make me upset," "I *should* ask Sally to marry me even though I'm, not sure—it's my 'gut feeling' and I should go with that" should signal that a problem exists.

4. *Use a "problem checklist."* Once negative feelings, ineffective behavior, or certain thoughts prompt the recognition that a problem exists, a checklist can often serve as a means to better pinpoint specific problems. Examples of a work-related problem checklist and a general problem checklist are contained in Tables 8.3 and 8.4, respectively. A comprehensive problem checklist for use in problem-recognition training is the Mooney Problem Checklist (Mooney & Gordon, 1950). Depending on the focus of the group, other checklists may exist or be developed that provide for common problems that many of the group members may have experienced. For example, Table 8.5 is an adapted list

TABLE 8.3   Work-Related Problem Checklist

Job-finding problem?

Not enough job autonomy?

Job interview problem?

Limited opportunity for advancement?

Inadequate job performance?

Absenteeism or tardiness?

Unsafe practices?

Poor communication with superiors?

Too much work?

Too little work?

Work not challenging enough?

Poor communication with subordinates?

Work too difficult or complex?

Ambiguous job demands?

Poor relationships with peers?

Ambiguous job goals?

Interpersonal disputes?

Conflicting job demands?

Ineffective delegation or lack of assertiveness?

Too much responsibility?

Too little responsibility?

Lack of recognition?

Lack of opportunity to participate in decision-making which affects my job?

Aversive or unhealthy work environment?

Inadequate pay or benefits?

Procrastination?

Poor job security?

Unproductive meetings?

Commuting problems?

Wasting time?

Too much traveling in the job?

TABLE 8.4 General Problem Checklist

Job or career problem?

Drug problem?

Marriage problem?

Time-management problem?

Problem with children or adolescents?

Self-discipline problem?

Low self-esteem?

Academic problem?

Emotional problem?

Conflict between job and family responsibilities?

Moral conflict?

Religious problem?

Conflict between academic and family responsibilities?

Legal problem?

Lack of recreation or leisure activities?

Housekeeping or home maintenance problem?

Transportation problem?

Problem with parents or other relatives?

Concern about the neighborhood?

Concern about the community?

Lack of social relationships?

Concern about the environment?

Interpersonal conflicts?

Problems with business products or services?

Sexual problem?

Sleep problem?

Problem with professional services?

Financial problem?

Illness or disability problem?

Problem with social or government services?

Lack of exercise?

Weight problem?

Concern about world problems?

Drinking problem?

TABLE 8.5   Cancer-Related Problem Checklist

Physical

I have trouble walking

I have difficulty with household chores

I can't engage in recreational activities anymore

I'm losing weight

I'm having problems working

I have lots of pain

Psychological Distress

I'm ashamed of the way my body looks

I worry more than ever now

I can't seem to think straight

I have problems making decisions

I have difficulty talking to my friends

Most of my friends shun me

I feel sad all the time

I have trouble sleeping

Marital and Family

We aren't talking a lot lately

There is too little affection between us

My family won't leave me alone

There is a change in family roles

Interactions with Health Care Team

I can't get the information I want

I can't seem to communicate with the medical team

I don't like feeling out of control

I get nervous asking questions

I get very angry waiting for so long to talk to the doctor for just a few minutes

I feel like I'm just a patient, not a real person

Sexual

I lost interest in sex

Sex is difficult for me

My partner doesn't want to have sex with me anymore

I feel so unattractive

Sex is now very painful

I can't let my husband see my surgical scars

from our work with distressed cancer patients (e.g., A. M. Nezu et al., 1998; A. M. Nezu et al., 2003). If working in a group format, these types of lists can be helpful to facilitate members' awareness and relief that others may be experiencing similar types of difficulties (i.e., "normalizing and validating" the experience of such problems).

Homework

- Direct individuals to look over various checklists in order to note which problems they are currently experiencing.
- Have clients continue to self-monitor various problem-solving attempts (i.e., PSSM or "Problem-Solving Worksheets"); have them focus on their feelings, thoughts, or behavior to determine if they represent signals that a problem exists.

Module 6. Problem Orientation: Viewing Problems as Challenges

This module is geared to help individuals adopt that part of a positive problem-solving orientation that highlights the belief that problems in living are generally *challenges,* or opportunities for personal growth, mastery, or achievement, instead of thinking of them only in negative terms, such as threats, conflicts, frustrations, or hassles. Refer to chapter 3 in this book and chapter 3 in *Solving Life's Problems.* If you are using this self-help guidebook in conjunction with therapist-led PST, assign the relevant reading and exercises in chapter 3.

Key Training Activities

Encourage patients to think of what can be gained, instead of lost, by experiencing a problem. Direct patients to: (a) think of all the *normal* or ordinary problems they have experienced recently (problems that do not signify abnormality or deviance); and (b) think of all the problems they have experienced recently that can be viewed as challenges or opportunities to learn something worthwhile or to improve themselves in some way. Direct them to develop lists of such problems.

If individuals have difficulty generating ordinary problems and challenges, the PST therapist can act as a model and present hypothetical examples or ones from various problem checklists or PSSM/"Problem-Solving Worksheet" records. This exercise can also be modified by asking patients to recognize the ordinary problems and challenges from problem checklists presented to them (see module 5).

Engage the patient in "Reversed Advocacy Role-Play." If the patient continues to espouse negative self-statements, he or she may benefit from this role-play procedure, which is based on various cognitive therapy strategies developed by Beck (1967) and Ellis (Ellis & Dryden, 1997) and is aimed to help patients change their maladaptive beliefs and distorted perceptions of external stimuli (see also A. M. Nezu et al., 1998). In this exercise, any or all maladaptive and irrational attitudes toward problems-in-living are to be temporarily adopted by the PST counselor using a role-play format. Examples of such attitudes are contained in Table 8.6. The role of the therapist is to attempt to provide reasons or arguments for the statement being incorrect, maladaptive, or dysfunctional. In this manner, the patient begins to actually verbalize those aspects of a positive problem orientation. The process of identifying a more appropriate set of beliefs toward problems and providing justification for the validity of these attitudes helps the individual to begin to actually personally adopt this orientation. This strategy also lends itself well to a group setting, whereby different members of the group can take turns playing both sides of the statement (i.e., maladaptive versus adaptive).

Homework

- Direct individuals to look over various checklists in order to note which problems they are currently experiencing.

TABLE 8.6   Dysfunctional Attitudes

1. Most people do *not* have similar kinds of problems—no one else has difficulty coping with _____ (unless they are psychologically weak).

2. *All* of my problems are *entirely* caused by me.

3. It is best to avoid facing problems or making decisions. Most problems disappear on their own.

4. The *first* solution that comes to mind is the best. I should *always* operate on instincts.

5. There is a *right* and *perfect* solution to most problems. I just have to keep on trying to get that perfect solution no matter how long it takes.

6. Only someone who is experiencing the *exact* same problem as me can be helpful—*no* one else can understand.

7. People can't change. The way I am is the way I'll *always* be! You can't teach old dogs new tricks!

8. Average people *cannot* solve most of life's problems on their own.

- Have clients continue to self-monitor various problem-solving attempts (i.e., PSSM or "Problem-Solving Worksheets"); have them focus on their feelings, thoughts, or behavior to determine if they represent signals that a problem exists.

Module 7. Problem Orientation: Use and Control of Emotions in Problem Solving

The major objectives for this module involve discussing the role of emotions in problem solving, as well as teaching patients how to (a) use such emotions to facilitate problem-solving success, and (b) control disruptive emotions. Refer to chapter 5 in this volume and chapter 3 in *Solving Life's Problems*. If you are using this self-help guidebook in conjunction with therapist-led PST, assign the relevant reading and exercises in chapter 3.

Key Training Activities

Explain and discuss the role of emotions in problem solving. Emphasize the notion that negative emotions can inhibit or limit subsequent problem-solving effectiveness (i.e., high levels of negative emotions are likely to *reduce* performance efficiency by causing a narrowing of attention to task-irrelevant cues, such as unproductive worries, negative self-judgments, threatening problem appraisals, and one's own disturbing physiological responses). Alternatively, positive emotions (e.g., hope, relief), which are often generated by perceiving problems as challenges, are likely to *facilitate* problem-solving effectiveness.

Explain and discuss how emotions can be used to facilitate problem-solving effectiveness. The following are ways that people can use their emotional responses in order to enhance problem-solving success:

1. *As a cue for problem recognition.* When individuals experience a negative emotional response, direct them to look for the antecedent problematic situation that may be producing it.
2. *To facilitate motivation for problem solving.* This can be done by adopting the positive problem-solving orientation that was discussed earlier (e.g., viewing a problem as a *challenge* rather than a *threat*).
3. *As a problem-solving goal.* It is often adaptive to set a problem-solving goal of increasing positive affect (e.g., feelings of self-worth, sexual pleasure) or reducing negative affect (e.g., anxiety, anger). For example, when a stressful situation is relatively stable or unchangeable, the only realistic problem-solving goals may

be to accept the reality of a situation and then to minimize emotional distress and maintain or increase feelings of self-worth.

4. *As a possible consequence to consider when anticipating solution outcomes during decision making.* The possible effects of a solution alternative on feelings of emotional well-being is an important criterion to consider when evaluating these alternatives.

5. *As a criterion for evaluating the solution outcome following solution implementation.* The actual emotional outcome is an important criterion to consider when evaluating the effectiveness of the solution in the actual problematic situation.

6. *To reinforce effective problem-solving behavior.* The careful application of effective problem-solving rules and principles can facilitate successful problem-solving performance, which in turn, can produce positive emotions (e.g., hope, relief). These emotions help to reinforce effective problem-solving behavior.

Teach individuals to control disruptive emotions via the ABC method of constructive thinking. The rationale for this strategy can be explained as focusing on the thoughts that people say to themselves, their expectations of situations, and their understanding of how the world operates. Explanations frequently employed in other cognitive therapies of the strong connection between how one thinks and feels (Beck, Rush, Shaw, & Emory, 1979; Beck, 1995) are similarly useful here when presenting a rationale to the patient. As such, the *ABC Model of Constructive Thinking* is presented with the explanation that how one thinks about a situation can have a *direct* impact on one's emotional state. This analysis uses the following components in order to break down a person's internal reactions to an event: *A* = Activating event; *B* = What you believe or say to yourself about *A;* and *C* = Emotional consequences.

The therapist then personalizes the strategy by asking the individual to identify beliefs and attitudes that trigger an emotional reaction. Using an example of a current troubling experience, the procedure can be used to diagnose nonconstructive or negative *self-talk* or thoughts that are likely to lead to unpleasant emotions. These include: (a) highly evaluative words (e.g., should, must), (b) catastrophizing words when *not* pertaining to life and death circumstances (e.g., "It's awful that I was so angry, I'm terrible to be so selfish"), and (c) overgeneralizing terms (e.g., "*Nobody* can possibly understand").

Patients are directed to look at their own self-talk, whereby both therapist and patient can engage in separating between constructive and realistic statements (e.g., "I wish," "I would have preferred") and nonadaptive talk (e.g., "I was stupid not to," "I should have"). Methods for disputing negative self-talk that can be taught to patients include:

- Argue against negative self-talk with realistic statements
- Argue against words such as "should" and "ought" with the phrase—"why should I?"
- Question catastrophic words and assess *real* damage potential of situation
- Challenge overgeneralizations
- Use challenging positive self-statements (see Table 8.7 for a list of positive self-statements).

Many of these techniques can be modeled by the PST counselor within the context of the Reversed Advocacy Role-Play strategy described in module 6.

Teach individuals to control disruptive emotions via various stress management strategies. Effective strategies for controlling disruptive

TABLE 8.7   Positive Self-Statements

I can solve this problem!
I'm okay—feeling sad is normal under these circumstances.
I can't direct the wind, but I can adjust the sails.
I don't have to please everyone.
I can replace my fears with faith.
It's okay to please myself.
There will be an end to this difficulty.
If I try, I can do it!
I can get help from _____ if I need it.
It's easier, once I get started.
I just need to relax.
I can cope with this!
I can reduce my fears.
I just need to stay on track.
I can't let the worries creep in.
Prayer helps me.
I'm proud of myself!
I can hang in there!

emotions include relaxation training, deep breathing, autogenic training, guided imagery, or meditation (see Gramling & Auerbach, 1998 or A. M. Nezu et al., 2005, for self-help books that provide instruction in these types of emotion-focused coping strategies). Additional strategies to lessen emotional arousal may include distraction, exercise, engaging in various pleasant activities (e.g., movies, reading), hobbies, or prayer.

Homework

- Use PSSM method or "Problem-Solving Test" worksheets to have the patient engage in the ABC approach to understanding emotional reactions and to determine whether they are appropriate or dysfunctional.
- Encourage the patient to practice the differing ways to combat negative thinking.

Module 8. Problem Orientation: STOP and THINK!

Becoming more sensitive to cues that a problem exists can often lead certain people to avoid problems and others to jump in and attempt to solve them immediately, especially when desirous of feeling better quickly (i.e., reduce fear, sadness). The purpose of this module is to teach patients to use the "STOP and THINK" strategy as a means of inhibiting the tendency to react in either manner automatically. Refer to chapter 3 in this volume and chapter 3 in *Solving Life's Problems*. If you are using this self-help guidebook in conjunction with therapist-led PST, assign the relevant reading and exercises in chapter 3.

Key Training Activities

Describe and discuss impulsive/careless and avoidant problem-solving styles. Discuss the personal relevance of these types of styles; focus on the likelihood of negative consequences occurring when one engages in these types of behaviors.

Teach STOP and THINK technique. Direct the patient to *visualize* a STOP sign or red traffic light and engage in a rehearsed self-statement to *STOP and THINK* when confronting a problem or experiencing a negative emotion. Familiar phrases such as "Look before you leap" may also be useful to include in the self-cueing procedure, especially in terms of not impulsively trying to solve the problem *prior* to knowing what the problem actually is, considering a range of possible alternatives, and so forth. In addition, as many individuals are familiar with the theory of "fight or flight" during times of stress, some patients have found the following rationale to be useful—that when under stress, human beings have a third choice, they can "fight, flight, or *think*" in response to problematic internal and external experiences. This particular phrase has been useful in helping patients understand the importance of learning to *STOP* the descending spiral of negative emotions and to *THINK* in order to understand what the problem is and then focus attention on extending efforts to solve it. In addition, this visual red light can *STOP* the tendency to avoid the problem or to *STOP* the tendency to act impulsively or carelessly.

Homework

- Provide a handout or poster (or direct patients to develop one themselves) that displays both a red stop sign and a lightbulb to signal the phrase *STOP and THINK.*
- Have the patient place the poster in a prominent place at home (e.g., refrigerator, bathroom mirror).
- Develop and carry cue cards that state *STOP and THINK.*
- Practice visualizing a stressful situation and immediately engage in developing a visual image of a large red stop sign.

Module 9. Problem Definition and Formulation (PDF)

Problem Definition and Formulation (PDF) represents the first of four rational problem-solving skills. The overarching goal of training in PDF is to help individuals better understand the nature of a problem and to set realistic goals. It is perhaps this skill that sets the tone for the likelihood of successful problem-solving attempts. Without an accurate understanding of the problem or goal to be achieved, people's attempts at generating, selecting, and implementing alternative solutions are likely to be misguided and unsuccessful. As the old adage by John Dewey suggests—*a problem well-defined is half solved.* Refer to chapter 3 in this volume and chapter 4 in *Solving Life's Problems*. If you are using this self-help guidebook in conjunction with therapist-led PST, assign the relevant reading and exercises in chapter 4.

A training tip is to conceptualize the process of solving problems as developing a road map. Hence the problem solver becomes a traveler. As such, the first major goal is to identify one's destination (i.e., problem-solving goal). Although the shortest route between two points is a straight line, rarely in reality does one travel in such a manner, whether by walking, train, plane, or car. Therefore, part of defining a problem is to identify various obstacles present in reaching one's travel destination in order to eventually be able to identify means to overcome these obstacles.

Using such an analogy can provide a context in which to explain the various concepts and objectives involved in PDF.

Objectives and Key Training Activities

1. To gather relevant and factual information about the problem
2. To understand the nature of the problem
3. To set a realistic problem-solving goal
4. To reappraise the significance of the problem for personal-social well-being

Gathering Information

Often times, information about a problem is not immediately available to the individual. This can limit his or her ability to adequately define the problem. This aspect of PDF involves directing individuals to gather relevant, factual information about the problematic situation. To facilitate this task, the following types of questions can be helpful:

1. Who is involved?
2. What happened (or did not happen) that bothers you?
3. Where did it happen?
4. When did it happen?
5. Why did it happen? (i.e., known causes or reasons for the problem).
6. What was your response to the situation? (i.e., actions, thoughts, and feelings).

In keeping with the *simplification* rule (see module 3), direct individuals to describe such information in specific, concrete terms. This helps to distinguish more easily between relevant and irrelevant information, as well as between objective facts and unsubstantiated assumptions, inferences, and interpretations. For example, if the relevant information one is seeking concerns the behavior of another person, it is important that the information describes what that person actually *said* or *did*. The description, "John is too lazy," is too general and vague. Instead, "John does not start working until an hour after he punches in," is a more concrete description of John's problem behavior that is likely to result in a better understanding of the problem.

As another aid, individuals should be directed, based on the *externalization* rule (module 3), to write down as much of this information as possible.

With regard to fostering one's ability to distinguish between *facts* and *assumptions,* we have found it useful to have ready a somewhat ambiguous photograph or picture to use as a stimulus to prompt a discussion (i.e., a magazine advertisement with the descriptive product information cut off, a flower arrangement, a picture in the clinician's office). The patient is asked to focus on the object or picture for about a minute and then report what he or she observed. Either the therapist or patient should record these observations for the purpose of discussion later in the session. After the patient has completed the description, which usually entails inaccurate evaluations, misperceptions, and inferences, the therapist provides the rationale for the exercise and for attending to the facts versus assumptions in daily problem-solving activities. Upon completion of this presentation, the therapist should guide the patient in reviewing the recorded observations and to practice differentiating the factual information from one's opinions, judgments, or inferences (i.e., what the individual assumed was in the picture versus what was actually in the picture).

Relevant information about the problem may include information about environmental events (e.g., task requirements, the behavior and expectations of other people), personal events (i.e., one's own thoughts, goals, feelings, physical sensations, behavior, and relationships), or interactions between both types. A useful *visualization* technique (see module 3) to facilitate the identification of relevant information in these categories is the *imaginal role-play technique.* The following is an example of possible directions for patients:

Close your eyes and reconstruct in your imagination a recent experience that was an instance of a recurring problem or part of a current, ongoing problematic situation. First, imagine that you are in the situation (not viewing it as an observer), and experience it imaginally as it actually happened. As you are experiencing the situation, ask yourself, "What am I thinking and feeling?" Next, repeat the experience, but this time as an observer, as if watching a movie or videotape of the situation. Play it in slow motion and ask yourself, "What is happening? What is the other person(s) saying, doing, and feeling? What am I saying, doing, and feeling?" This technique can also be used to anticipate and pinpoint possible future problems.

Another strategy to help gather information in an objective manner is to direct individuals to pretend that they are investigative reporters or detectives who have the task of gaining information about an event in an unbiased manner. A reporter would ask the questions listed in the previous paragraph in an objective way in order to find out the facts of a story. He or she would have the ethical responsibility to relay all the facts of a story as they are obtained from reliable sources. For a detective to report back to headquarters, "who," "what," "when," "where," and "how" questions would have to be answered in a thorough and objective manner to allow for an uninformed person to understand what actually happened based on the details conveyed. In these contexts, taking on such a role can often help guide the process of gathering objective facts concerning a problem.

Understanding the Nature of the Problem

Training in this aspect of PDF focuses on two issues:

1. Correcting any distortions or misconceptions that can interfere with an accurate problem definition
2. Identifying *why* a given situation is a problem

Correcting Distortions and Misconceptions. After obtaining relevant facts about the problem, individuals are directed to structure or *process* (i.e., interpret, appraise) this information in order to begin to better understand the nature of the problem. At times, subjective factors, such as feelings and values, can influence this process and result in distortions. Distorted information can result in an inaccurate understanding of the problem, which can then lead to ineffective problem solving.

Table 8.8 contains some common types of distortions that can occur when processing social information (Beck et al., 1979). The PST therapist should explain these concepts, as well as provide feedback when and if an individual actually engages in any of them.

Note that if an individual displays significant distortions during this phase of training, it may be important to go back to module 6 and engage him or her in the reversed advocacy role-play exercise as a means of overcoming such distortions.

Identifying Why This Is a Problem. A problem can be understood as an imbalance or discrepancy between *what is* (i.e., present conditions) and *what should be* (i.e., conditions that are demanded or desired), together with certain obstacles that limit the availability of an effective response for reducing this discrepancy. When enough relevant factual information about the problem has been obtained, individuals are next directed to specify:

1. What present conditions are unacceptable (*what is*)
2. What changes or additions are demanded or desired (*what should be*)

TABLE 8.8   Common Distortions That Can Impede Accurate Problem Definition

1. *Arbitrary Inference.* A person draws a conclusion without sufficient facts to support it or rule out alternative interpretations. For example, a woman turns down a request for a date, and the man automatically concludes that the woman does not like him.

2. *Selective Abstraction.* A person attends to certain selected information or cues in a situation and makes an assumption or draws a conclusion based on this information while ignoring other important information that contradicts this assumption or conclusion. For example, a man participating as a member of a team in an athletic contest concludes that his mistake cost the team a victory, while ignoring the fact that several other team members made more serious errors.

3. *Overgeneralization.* A person makes assumptions about the general characteristics of people or situations within a given class on the basis of a single event. For example, a worker makes a single mistake, and the boss concludes that he or she is incompetent.

4. *Magnification or Minimization.* Magnification occurs when an individual exaggerates the value, intensity, or significance of an event. Minimization refers to the opposite distortion, that of inappropriately devaluing or reducing the significance of an event. An example of magnification is exaggerating the possible threat or risks associated with meeting new people at a party. An example of minimization would be inappropriately minimizing the danger of leaving one's car unlocked in an unfamiliar neighborhood at night.

5. *Misattribution.* This refers to the tendency to be extreme when incorrectly attributing or identifying the cause of the problem to be oneself (e.g., "It's always my fault") or others (e.g., "It's not my fault, it's always the other guy").

---

3. What obstacle(s) exist that limit one's ability to go from A to B (i.e., what makes it a problem?).

The conditions targeted for change and the obstacles preventing change may both include environmental events, personal events, and interactions between the two. Environmental events can include physical conditions, task characteristics, the behavior of other people, and various structures, such as rules, systems, and relations, including relationships between people. Personal events include one's own behavior, physical condition, values, beliefs, and expectations, as well as various negative emotions, such as anxiety or anger. The demands for change may originate in the environment (e.g., job demands) or within the individual person (i.e., one's personal goals, values, and commitments). In most cases, both sources influence the demands for change.

The obstacles to reaching goals are likely to include the following:

- novelty or unfamiliarity
- complexity
- conflicting goals
- skill deficits
- lack of resources
- uncertainty
- emotional difficulties

Note that, as with most real-life complex problems, it is often likely that *multiple factors* exist that serve to make the situation a problem, whether they are numerous obstacles, multiple conflicting goals, a variety of reduced resources, or any combination of such factors. As such, part of the task during this phase of problem solving would be to break large problems into smaller ones. Moreover, when setting goals, it is important to delineate several subgoals or steps toward reaching larger goals. In addition, when choosing among solutions during the decision-making phase and developing an overall solution plan, it is generally the case where multiple solution ideas need to be combined in order to address these multiple factors, either simultaneously or sequentially. In other words, certain parts of an overall solution plan would be geared to address certain subgoals, whereas other strategies would be included in order to reach other objectives.

Continuing to use the "problem solver as traveler" analogy, the question to ask now is, "What is preventing me from getting from A (i.e., where I am now) to B (i.e., where I want to go)?" During this training, it would be advisable to use problems already described in previously completed PSSM or "Problem-Solving Test" worksheet forms as personally relevant examples to use for practice in identifying obstacles.

Getting at the Real Problem

At times, a person may not focus on the basic, primary, or most important problem. In some cases, a specific problem may be only part of a more important, broader problem that the person does not recognize. By focusing only on a specific (or superficial) problem, people limit their alternatives for dealing with the broader problem. In other cases, the problem might actually be a consequence or effect of a more important antecedent problem in a cause-effect problem chain. As such, attempts to solve the secondary problem might not be successful without solving the primary (antecedent) problem first. A useful technique for getting at the basic or primary problem is to have the patient state the problem-solving goal for the problem and then ask the question, "Why?" The answer might help to suggest a broader, more basic problem, or a more important primary problem.

Dealing With a Complex Problem

At times, problems may be too complex to deal with as a whole. In that case, according to the *simplification rule* (module 6), the problem should be broken down into more manageable subproblems in order to solve them one at a time in some predetermined order based on importance or priority. For example, in the case of a cause-effect problem chain, it would be more important to focus on the first problem in the chain, if possible. If the problem is unchangeable, then the individual can be directed to address the secondary problems that can be solved.

Setting Goals

The two most important rules in goal-setting are to (a) state the goals in specific, concrete terms, and (b) avoid stating goals that are unrealistic or unlikely to be attained. Stating goals in specific, concrete terms helps one to identify relevant, appropriate solutions and facilitates decision-making effectiveness. Unrealistic goals would change the problem from one that is solvable to an insoluble one, where it would be impossible to find a satisfactory solution. This can lead to increased frustration and stress.

The general problem-solving goal is to reduce the discrepancy between *what is* and *what should be*. For a particular problem, the specific goal(s) may focus on: (a) meeting the demands or expectations for change in the present conditions; (b) overcoming a specific obstacle to meeting these demands; (c) reducing or changing the demands; (d) accepting that the problem situation, in fact, is actually unchangeable, or (e) some combination of these. The goals are stated in the form of a "How" or "What" question, such as, "How can I meet more men?" "What can I do to reduce the frequency of interruptions when I am trying to work?" "What can I do to reduce my boss's unreasonable demands?" "How can I accept that my marriage is really over?"

Reappraising the Problem

Once the problem has been clearly defined, it may no longer be as threatening as it appeared to be when it was still vague and undefined. Therefore, it may be helpful to encourage patients to reappraise the problem at this time. This can be accomplished through a simple cost-benefit analysis. Direct individuals here to consider both the benefits and costs involved in solving the problem, as compared to not solving the problem. They should consider possible *immediate* benefits and costs, possible *long-term* benefits and costs, as well as benefits and costs to *themselves* and to *significant others.*

This exercise can be enhanced if patients are directed to write these benefits and costs down on paper. For example, individuals could make two columns on a page, listing potential benefits and costs associated with *not* solving the problem in a left-hand column, and listing possible benefits and costs associated if a given goal *is obtained* in the right-hand column. They can then compare such consequences and use this cost-benefit analysis to reappraise the problem in terms of what impact addressing it will have on their well-being. What is listed can also serve as an assessment regarding the person's ability to identify and predict various consequences based on a given action, a skill that is essential to effective decision making later in the process.

Note that if individuals tend to emphasize more possible costs involved, they will likely continue to perceive the problem as a threat. If so, a discussion can ensue based on the following questions: "Where's the threat?" and "What's the worst thing that can happen?" Conversely, if people emphasize the benefits that may result from solving the problem, they will probably perceive the problem as a challenge, which would help to reduce threat and anxiety and provide increased incentives to continue the problem-solving process.

Homework

Complete PDF worksheet(s) that contains the following questions before the next session:

- What is the problem? (Describe the facts, and remember to use concrete and unambiguous language.)
- How is this a problem for you?
- What are your goals? (Be sure to state realistic ones.)
- What are the major obstacles present in reaching your goal(s)?

Module 10. Generation of Alternative Solutions (GOA)

The basic idea behind the Generation of Alternative Solutions (GOA) task is to think of as many alternative solutions (coping options) as possible, in order to maximize the likelihood that the best solution will be among them. Refer to chapter 3 in this volume and chapter 5 in *Solving Life's Problems.* If you are using this self-help guidebook in conjunction with therapist-led PST, assign the relevant reading and exercises in chapter 5.

In this module, individuals are taught to:

1. Overcome major blocks to being creative
2. Use brainstorming techniques to generate ideas
3. Generate relevant solutions
4. Think of both strategies and tactics

Major Blocks to the Creative Generation of Solutions

Major blocks to the creative generation of solutions include habit and convention. Although such habits can be helpful and adaptive in many situations, including those that require problem solving (i.e., when solutions learned in past situations can be applied successfully to new, but similar problems), they can also hinder problem solving when people respond automatically to new problems with previously learned habits without questioning their appropriateness or applicability in the new problematic situation. Therefore, training in GOA involves teaching individuals to use brainstorming principles to help overcome blocks to creativity.

Brainstorming Principles for Generating Alternative Solutions

The three basic principles of brainstorming include: (a) the quantity principle, (b) the deferment-of-judgment principle, and (c) the variety principle.

Quantity Principle. According to the quantity principle, the more alternative solutions that are produced, the more good-quality solution ideas will be made available. To apply this principle, individuals should be instructed to "think of as many alternative solutions as possible without limiting your search to conventional solutions, ordinary solutions, or solutions that have worked well in the past. Do not give up the search too soon. If you 'block' and can't think of any more ideas, take a break, if possible, and return to the task later."

Deferment-of-Judgment Principle. The deferment-of-judgment principle states that more good quality solution ideas will be generated when one suspends judgment or critical evaluation of solution ideas until later in the problem-solving process (i.e., during the decision-making task). Individuals are instructed to "let your imagination 'run loose' and try to produce an abundance of original ideas without filtering them through any evaluative screens, such as appropriateness, conventionality, practicality, feasibility, or utility. Don't worry about wasting time thinking of 'silly' or 'ridiculous' ideas. A 'ridiculous' idea can often be toned down or modified to produce a very good, realistic solution which may not have been discovered otherwise." As an example, indicate that the solution to "hire a housekeeper" may not be a feasible solution for some people experiencing a conflict between domestic and career responsibilities, but this idea may suggest the following more practical idea—"Hire someone to come in a few hours a week to do the ironing."

Variety Principle. According to the variety principle, the greater the range or variety of solution alternatives generated, the more good quality ideas will be made available. When generating specific solution alternatives, individuals often develop a *set* to produce ideas that reflect only one strategy or general approach to the problem. This narrow set may occur even when the quantity and deferment-of-judgment principles are being applied effectively. To change such a perspective, individuals are directed to peruse their list of solution alternatives after using the quantity and deferment-of-judgment principles and to identify all the different strategies that are represented. In essence, this is a classification task, that is, grouping solution alternatives according to some common theme.

If any of the strategies have very few specific solutions, individuals should attempt to think of more specific solution alternatives for that particular strategy. They can then try to think of new strategies that are not yet represented by any of the available solutions and generate additional specific solution ideas for those strategies.

Generating Relevant Solution Alternatives

Although the generation of alternatives is a creative process that emphasizes imagination and originality, it is not free association. Rather, the emphasis is on the generation of *relevant*, goal-oriented solutions. A goal-oriented solution is a coping response(s) aimed at achieving the problem-solving goal(s). The relevant solutions for a particular problem may vary depending on how the goals are stated. Therefore, individuals should consider alternative goal statements when generating alternative solutions (e.g., meeting task demands versus reducing task demands, or changing an objective situation versus changing one's personal reactions to it). More relevant, potentially effective solutions may be available for one goal statement than for another. Further, most complex problems involve multiple obstacles, thus requiring multiple goals and multiple solutions.

Problem-Focused Versus Emotion-Focused Solutions

As indicated earlier, we emphasize the notion that problem-solving coping actually entails both *problem-focused* goals (i.e., objectives involving changing the problematic nature of the situation itself) and *emotion-focused* goals (i.e., those goals that are relevant for situations that are not changeable or controllable). An example of the latter type of goal involves a situation where one's marriage in highly unlikely to remain intact because the spouse is adamant about getting a divorce. If so, one may need to define the goal as "how can I be more accepting of the end of my marriage?" as compared to "how can I get my spouse to love me again and come back?" (see case 2 in chapter 9). As such, if one is focusing on *emotion-focused goals,* it is important to foster the generation of more *emotion-focused solutions* (e.g., increased acceptance or tolerance), rather than only problem-focused ones.

Generating Specific Solutions

Solutions may be generated at different levels of specificity. At the most general level is a solution *strategy,* which is the statement of an objective with the means to the objective being left unspecified or stated only in vague, general terms. At the most specific level is a *tactic* or concrete course of action, which describes in behavioral terms the means required to reach an objective. A strategy-level solution would be difficult to evaluate later in the decision-making process because it is too far removed from the actual behavior. Instead of a specific course of action, it is actually a *class* of coping responses, which may vary considerably in effectiveness. Therefore, when people break down solution strategies into more specific courses of action, they not only facilitate the decision-making process, but also produce more solution alternatives. Consider the following example:

The parent with the teenaged daughter who has been ignoring the parent's curfew might generate the strategy, "Punish her for coming in late." This strategy can include more specific solutions that are likely to vary in effectiveness, such as "spank her," "make her do extra work around the house," or "take away a privilege." "Take away a privilege" is a somewhat more specific strategy that can still be broken down further into more specific courses of action such as "ground her on a Saturday night" or "deny her the use of the family car for one day." In general, the more specifically one states the solution, the better. However, one should avoid minor, trivial details that are not likely to have a significant impact on the effectiveness or feasibility of the alternatives.

Practice Generating Alternatives

A very entertaining way to teach someone to be creative is to ask the following type of question: "What are all the uses you can think of for an ordinary brick, wire coat hanger, or broom?" Direct individuals to use the three brainstorming principles in answering these questions. In addition, following the *externalization* principle, suggest that they write their ideas down.

These hypothetical problems can be used as exercises to help individuals apply the various GOA skills. It is of greatest importance to direct clients to use these principles in applying them to personally-relevant problems. Use the problem(s) that have been described in various PSSM, "Problem-Solving Worksheet", or PDF forms, especially those that have already been "well defined and formulated."

Additional Aids for Increasing the Quantity and Quality of Solution Ideas

After generating a list of solution alternatives using the principles previously described, one may be able to increase the quantity and quality of solution ideas by using the following procedures:

1. *Combinations.* "Look over your list of solution alternatives and consider how individual solutions can be combined to produce new solution ideas."
2. *Modifications and elaborations.* "Look over your list of solution alternatives and consider how different solutions can be modified or elaborated on to improve the idea or produce a new one."
3. *Role models.* "In real-life problem solving, you might be able to generate more solution ideas for a particular problematic situation by considering how you can act more like a role model or 'hero' who is similar to you in some ways, but different in that he or she handles that type of situation well. For example, 'How can I be more effective in meeting women by acting more like John?' 'How would President _____ handle this problem?' "
4. *Visualization.* "One can facilitate the identification of potentially effective solution ideas by employing the visualization principle. To use this procedure, construct the problematic situation in imagination, and then imagine yourself attempting to cope with the situation and achieve the problem-solving goal. Your imagination may help you discover a new approach. A variation of this procedure, using the forced-relationships method, is to imagine an effective model coping with the same situation."

Seeking Information About Solution Alternatives

For some difficult, serious, or uncommon problems, it may be necessary to seek information or advice about possible solutions from books, experts, professionals, or other sources of relevant, authoritative information. Some cues that this procedure might be necessary or important are: (a) one cannot think of any possible solutions after trying for some time; (b) one's list of alternative solutions is extremely limited; and/or (c) one discovers later while making decisions or attempting to carry out the solution that none of the alternatives are satisfactory. Information or advice about possible solutions should not be sought in a dependent way by acting automatically on the advice received, but in an independent, problem-solving manner by making available more good-quality solution alternatives to choose from. Therefore, it is important to not only get information about possible solutions, but about the *pros* and *cons* of each solution as well.

Emotional Blocks to Being Creative

Feelings of distress, such as anxiety or depression, can often interfere with a person's attention, concentration, and general ability to be creative. If an individual experiences difficulty generating alternatives due to emotional blocks, then the PST counselor should recycle back to various problem-orientation exercises (e.g., reversed advocacy role-play, visualization of successful problem solving) to help him or her to overcome such inhibitions. In addition, relaxation or other stress management exercises may be appropriate to teach at this stage.

Homework

- Generate alternative solutions to personally relevant problems that one is currently experiencing (especially those that have been already well defined) using the various brainstorming principles. Clients should be directed to make lists and bring them into the next session for discussion.

Module 11. Decision Making (DM)

The overarching objective for this third rational problem-solving task is to evaluate (i.e., judge and compare) the available solution alternatives and select the best one(s) for implementation. As per our definition of an *effective solution* (see chapter 2), the best solution plan is the one that is expected to be successful in achieving the problem-solving goal, while *also* maximizing significant benefits and minimizing significant costs. Refer to chapter 3 in this volume and chapter 6 in *Solving Life's Problems*. If you are using this self-help guidebook in conjunction with therapist-led PST, assign the relevant reading and exercises in chapter 6.

Effective decision making entails the following activities:

- Screening out *obviously* ineffective solutions
- Predicting possible consequences
- Evaluating solution outcomes
- Identifying effective solutions and developing a solution plan

Rough Screening of Solution Alternatives

The decision-making task can be made easier if one conducts an initial *rough screening* of the list of possible alternatives in order to eliminate any that are clearly inferior. Remember that the only criteria that should have been used during the process of generating alternatives is one of *relevancy*. Therefore, it is possible that several ineffective ideas were generated "in the spirit of brainstorming." Rather than spending time going through to rate each alternative, it is advisable to conduct such an initial screening. At this point, alternatives can be considered "clearly ineffective" if they have (a) obvious unacceptable risks associated with their implementation, and/or (b) low feasibility. *Unacceptable risks* refer to likely serious negative consequences that significantly reduce the effectiveness of the solution. *Low feasibility* refers to the low likelihood that the solution could actually be implemented by the problem solver due to the lack of ability, lack of resources, or other major obstacles.

Predicting Consequences

Individuals are taught to think of two major categories when predicting consequences: (a) *likelihood* estimates, and (b) *value* estimates. *Likelihood* estimates involve two assessments:

1. The likelihood that a given solution alternative will actually achieve the stated problem-solving goal(s); that is, *will this solution work?*
2. The likelihood that the problem solver will actually be able to implement the solution in an optimal manner; that is, *can I carry it out?*

Value estimates involve predicting the total expected positive consequences (i.e., benefits, gains) *and* negative consequences (i.e., costs, losses) of a particular solution alternative, including long-term, as well as immediate consequences, and social, as well as personal consequences.

Personal consequences that should be considered include the following:

1. Effects on emotional well-being (pleasure versus pain)
2. Time and effort expended
3. Effects on physical well-being
4. Effects on psychological well-being (e.g., depression, anxiety, self-esteem)
5. Effects on economic well-being (e.g., job security)
6. Self-enhancement (e.g., achievements, knowledge)
7. Effects on other personal goals, values, and commitments

Some of the more important *social consequences* that should be considered include:

1. Effects on the personal or social well-being of significant others
2. Effects on the rights of others
3. Effects on significant interpersonal relationships
4. Effects on personal or social performance evaluations (e.g., reputation, status, prestige)

It is clear from these checklists that solutions for real-life problems may have many different consequences. Considering the limited capacity of the conscious mind to handle large amounts of information, it is important to write down the major significant expected consequences (e.g., "I am likely to feel very guilty, my parents will be very hurt, in the long run I could lose my job"). This will help to facilitate the task of evaluating one's solution alternatives.

Evaluating Solution Outcomes

Because the conscious mind does not have the capacity to weigh every expected consequence of each solution alternative when judging and comparing alternatives, the evaluation task is simplified by asking oneself the following four questions:

1. Will this solution solve the problem?
2. Can I really carry it out?
3. What are the overall effects on myself, both short-term and long-term?
4. What are the overall effects on others, both short-term and long-term?

For each alternative idea remaining after the initial screening, individuals should use a simple rating scale in response to these four questions (e.g., −1 = negative; 0 = neutral; +1 = positive). More complex rating systems can be developed for high risk problem solving, where the consequences of a relatively ineffective solution might be serious (e.g., scale of 1–5, where 1 = slightly satisfactory and 5 = very satisfactory). Further, if appropriate, individuals could place more weight or emphasis on a particular outcome criterion by establishing a minimum rating for a given criterion. For example, if it was felt that emotional well-being was particularly important for a given problem, one might decide to eliminate any solution alternative that is not rated as a "+" for this criterion. Individuals can also add new outcome criteria or eliminate criteria, depending on their appraisal of the significance of different outcomes for different problematic situations. For example, in some situations, financial cost might be a particularly significant criterion to consider when judging solution alternatives (e.g., "what to do when your washing machine breaks down"). Instead of considering this criterion as part of the overall personal effects criterion, it can be given special emphasis by considering it separately. The point here is to establish a systematic method of conducting the cost-benefit analysis. However, unless the problem is extremely complex, we advocate using a rather simple scale (i.e., −1 to +1) in order to make the decision-making process more user-friendly.

Keeping in mind the externalization rule, the various solution alternatives and ratings should be written down. To simplify the task of comparing alternatives, they can be summarized in a chart, such as the one in Table 8.9 (see also the "Decision-Making Worksheet" in chapter 6 of *Solving Life's Problems* guidebook). This chart shows a list of possible solution alternatives for the problem: "How can I get my spouse to talk to me about our marital problems more seriously?" We deliberately left out possible ratings to highlight the idea that they would be substantially different based on the person experiencing the problem, as well as the prevailing circumstances of the other individuals involved.

Difficulties in Anticipating and Evaluating Solution Alternatives

It is not always easy to predict and evaluate specific consequences of solutions before they are experienced, especially subjective consequences such as feelings and emotions. Two visualization procedures that might be helpful include behavior rehearsal and imaginal rehearsal. *Behavior rehearsal* or role play (with the PST counselor or other group member if conducting group PST) is particularly useful with regard to solving interpersonal problems (e.g., dealing with the offensive behavior of another person). *Imaginal rehearsal* involves experimenting with different coping

TABLE 8.9   Decision-Making Worksheet

Alternatives	Solve the Problem?	Can I Carry It Out?	Personal Effects	Social Effects
1. Pay him money				
2. Talk to him during dinner				
3. Write him an e-mail				
4. Send him a letter				
5. Leave him a voice message				
6. Forget it				
7. Yell at him				
8. Get a friend to do it				
9. Hire a messenger				

options via visualization. Both of these rehearsal procedures may help a person identify and evaluate the various social and emotional consequences of different solution possibilities. Similar types of questions found in the visualization exercise in module 4 can be used to enhance the individual's ability to better experience the consequences.

Identifying Effective Solutions and Developing a Solution Plan

On the basis of the systematic evaluation of the available solution alternatives, individuals are directed next to ask the following three questions:

1. Is the problem solvable? (i.e., "Is there a satisfactory solution?")
2. Do I need more information before I can select a solution or solution combination for implementation?
3. What solution or solution combination should I choose to implement?

If the problem is appraised as *unsolvable* or the answer to the second question is *positive*, then individuals should return to the problem definition and formulation task to seek more information and reformulate the problem in such a way that makes it solvable (e.g., identifying goals that emphasize acceptance, emotional control, or personal growth). However, if the problem is viewed as *solvable* and the answer to the second question is *negative*, the problem solver is directed to now go to the third question and begin to develop an overall solution plan.

The solution plan should be consistent with the general goal of attempting to resolve the problem satisfactorily while maximizing positive consequences and minimizing negative effects. The solution plan may be *simple* or *complex*. For a simple plan, based on the evaluation ratings, one can choose a single solution or course of action. When there is one solution that is expected to produce a highly satisfactory outcome, such a simple plan may suffice. There are two types of complex plans—a *solution combination* and a *contingency plan*. For a solution combination, one might choose a combination of solution alternatives to be implemented concurrently. This is done when it appears that the combination is likely to have greater utility than any solution alone or when several obstacles are targeted for change either sequentially or simultaneously. As noted previously, many problems in life are complex and involve multiple obstacles to overcome prior to effective problem resolution. Therefore, identifying several specific solution tactics to comprise an overall solution plan at times is highly advisable. Contingency plans involve choosing a combination of solutions to be implemented contingently, that is, implement solution A first; if that does not work, implement solution B; if that does not work, carry out solution C, and so forth.

Another type of contingency plan occurs when one first implements a particular course of action (A) and, then, depending on the outcome of A, the problem solver carries out either B or C. A contingency plan is chosen when there is enough uncertainty about any one solution or solution combination that it seems advisable to have a contingency plan to save time in case the initial solution choice(s) is unsuccessful. Once the solution plan has been prepared, the final step before solution implementation is to fill in the details as to exactly how, when, and where the solution plan will be implemented.

Homework

- Evaluate alternatives that were previously generated for real-life problems using criteria as contained in Table 8.9 (or complete the "Decision-Making Worksheet" from *Solving Life's Problems*).

Module 12. Solution Implementation and Verification (SIV)

The overarching objective for this last rational problem-solving task is to assess the solution outcome and verify the effectiveness of the solution plan after it has been implemented. At this point in the process, the problem has been solved only symbolically, as the effectiveness of the solution plan in real-life has not yet been verified. The only way to accomplish this is to carry out the solution plan and evaluate its outcome objectively. Refer to chapter 3 in this volume and chapter 7 in *Solving Life's Problems*. If you are using this self-help guidebook in conjunction with therapist-led PST, assign the relevant reading and exercises in chapter 7.

SIV involves the following four components:

1. Solution implementation
2. Self-monitoring
3. Self-evaluation
4. Self-reinforcement

Solution Implementation

Solution implementation involves actually carrying out the solution plan. Successfully implementing a solution is likely to be influenced by a number of factors other than problem-solving ability. The problem solver may experience unexpected environmental obstacles (e.g., worsening of the problem, decreased resources) or personal obstacles (e.g., emotional inhibitions, lack of required abilities or performance skills). It is also possible that individuals overestimated the environmental rewards for the particular solution, and as a result, they might be less motivated to complete the solution plan at this stage. If effective solution implementation is not possible because of these obstacles, the problem solver can (a) return to previous phases in the problem-solving process in order to identify an alternative solution that may be implemented more effectively, or (b) focus on overcoming these newly discovered obstacles.

At this point, training in specific coping performance skills and arousal-oriented coping techniques (e.g., relaxation training, meditation) might be appropriate for some individuals who are experiencing obstacles to solution implementation, or who have serious deficits in performance skills or anxiety-management skills. This would also be an appropriate time to use the behavioral-rehearsal and imaginal-rehearsal techniques noted in module 11. However, at this time, instead of focusing on the evaluation of solution outcomes, the procedures would focus on the repeated rehearsal of coping responses for the purpose of skill enhancement and anxiety reduction. In addition, the PST therapist might model the thinking process of carrying out the solution optimally by thinking aloud the various steps to take and the strategies necessary to overcome new obstacles (e.g., "First I need to state my goals and to think about the positive consequences that will occur when I solve this problem. Now I need to take a deep breath and go ahead and carry out the solution. When I begin talking to my boss, I realize that I might get anxious, so I need to practice what I might say to him right before I see him. Then I will remind myself to speak calmly and deliberately so I don't get more nervous . . ." and so forth). Last, in the spirit of externalization, the PST counselor and client can develop a brief user's manual, in written form, that specifies how the solution should be implemented.

If a person is experiencing significant hesitancy in carrying out a solution plan, the following exercise can be used. First, participants are instructed to brainstorm a list of consequences that are likely if a given problem is *not* solved. During this task, patients are reminded to use their brainstorming and decision-making skills in order to generate the likely personal, social, short-term, and long-term consequences of not solving the problem. It is important that the PST counselor aids the person in monitoring this list to ensure that these predicted consequences represent *realistic* effects of not solving the problem, rather than a compilation of unrealistic, negatively biased consequences. The purpose of this list is to highlight and remind individuals of the risks and costs involved in *not* solving the problem, in comparison to the benefits and relief they will experience if they *do* solve the problem. Thus, the next step is for participants to list and review the predicted consequences that will result from solving the problem and comparing both lists in order to conduct a cost-benefit analysis regarding the nest step, that is, whether to try to solve the problem or give up.

Self-Monitoring

Self-monitoring involves both self-observation and recording of the solution performance and its outcome. There are several ways to record or measure one's performance such that an assessment of the solution outcome will be accurate and valid. The type of measure that is most appropriate for a particular problem depends on the type of coping behavior or performance that one is assessing. The following are some common options:

1. *Response Frequency.* One simply counts the number of responses. Examples include the number of cigarettes smoked, the number of times a child gets out of his or her seat or talks out of turn in class, the number of times a teen age daughter violates curfew, or the number of requests for dates.
2. *Response Duration.* One can also record the amount of time it takes to perform a response. For example, the time it takes to complete a report, time spent studying, time spent exercising each day, time spent commuting to work, and time spent sleeping.
3. *Response Latency.* Individuals can also record the time between the occurrence of a particular antecedent event or cue and the onset of a particular response. For example, the number of

minutes late to class, the amount of time beyond curfew, the amount of time late for dinner, or the amount of time a child takes to get a job done following a request.

4. *Response Intensity.* One might be able to rate the degree of intensity of something, such as the degree of anxiety, the intensity or severity of a headache, the degree of depression, the intensity of sexual arousal, or the degree of pleasure or satisfaction associated with a particular activity. This can often be accomplished using a simple rating scale, such as 1 to 5, where 1 = little to no anxiety, and 5 = severe anxiety.

5. *Response Product.* This measure here is not of the behavior itself, but of the *by-products* or *effects* of the behavior. Examples include the number of dates accepted, the number of boxes packed per hour, the number of sales made, the number of chapters studied, the number of arrests made, and the number of problems solved.

Self-Evaluation, Self-Reward, and Troubleshooting

When the solution performance is completed or has been recorded for a sufficient period of time to assess progress, individuals are then directed to evaluate the solution outcome using similar outcome criteria and rating procedures employed in the decision-making task to judge each solution alternative. Essentially, the problem solver should ask the following specific questions:

1. Did this solution solve the problem?
2. What are the overall effects on myself, both short-term and long-term?
3. What are the overall effects on others, both short-term and long-term?

If the match between the actual outcome and the anticipated outcome at the time of decision making is at least satisfactory, then individuals can go to the final step in solution implementation and verification, namely, *self-reinforcement.* In other words, they should reward themselves for a job well done. This can simply be a positive self-statement, such as "Congratulations, you handled that problem very well!" It is also possible to provide oneself with a more tangible reward, such as an enjoyable leisure activity or the purchase of a desirable gift. In addition to self-reinforcement, a powerful reward is likely to be the reinforcement resulting from the positive solution outcome itself, which should also increase one's sense of mastery and competence.

However, if the discrepancy between the actual solution outcome and the anticipated outcome is unsatisfactory, then the problem solver needs to troubleshoot and recycle, that is, to return to the problem-solving process and determine where corrections must be made in order to develop a more effective solution plan (i.e., "Was the solution plan optimally carried out?" "Were enough alternatives generated?" "Were all important consequences identified?" "Was the goal realistic?" etc.). If one cannot succeed after several attempts, it may be important to recognize the futility of further independent problem-solving efforts, and either reformulate the problem as one that must be accepted, or seek help from someone who might be more knowledgeable about that particular type of problem. It is during this process that the PST counselor needs to be very diligent in providing meaningful feedback and encouragement.

Homework

- Carry out the solution plan for real-life problem(s).
- Monitor the consequences and determine the match between the anticipated effects and the actual effects.
- Engage in self-reinforcement.

Module 13. Guided Practice

It is during this stage of PST that attempts are made to enhance expertise and transfer learning both over time and across problem situations via guided practice. We strongly recommend that the therapist extends much time and effort to this stage of training.

At this point, training in the overall model has been completed, whether implemented by going through each of the previous 12 modules or conducted in a truncated manner based on an individualized treatment plan. During guided practice sessions, the majority of time should be spent "putting it all together" and solving real-life problems with direction and guidance from the PST counselor, both in session and as homework assignments. In addition, the therapist should attempt to facilitate the maintenance and generalization of effective problem-solving performance by

1. Continuing to provide positive reinforcement and corrective feedback;
2. Reviewing positive problem-orientation cognitions and strengthening them by recognizing individuals' progress in learning to cope more effectively with everyday problems;

3. Directing patients' attention to the wide range of real-life problems for which the problem-solving approach is applicable, including individual personal problems, interpersonal problems, marriage and family problems, and community problems; and
4. Anticipating obstacles to implementing the problem-solving approach or specific solutions in real-life and preparing strategies for dealing with them, using the problem-solving method.

If performance deficits continue at this point, it may be advisable for the PST counselor to troubleshoot and determine which modules need to be revisited, or if an initial individualized assessment led to incorrect treatment decisions to skip various modules, which ones need to now be carried out.

Module 14. Rapid Problem Solving

Unexpected problems often occur in life that require a quick decision and immediate action, thus, precluding the careful, deliberate problem solving described in this program thus far. However, even if an individual has as little as one minute to solve a problem, several basic problem-solving principles can still help to maximize problem-solving effectiveness, even under these time-limited conditions. This module describes a model for rapid problem solving.

A Rapid Problem-Solving Model

The following are steps to take if confronted with a problem that requires a rapid but effective, problem-solving response:

Step 1. Make the following self-statements:

a. "Take a deep breath and calm down"
b. "There is no immediate catastrophe"
c. "Think of this problem as a challenge"
d. "I can handle it"
e. "Stop-and-think"

Step 2. Ask yourself the following questions:

a. "What's the problem?" (State the discrepancy between *what is* and *what should be*.)
b. "What do I want to accomplish?" (State a goal.)
c. "Why do I want to achieve this goal?" (Broaden the goal, if appropriate.)

Step 3. Think of a solution; now think of several other alternative solutions (at least two or three).

Step 4. Think of the most important criteria for evaluating your solution ideas (at least two or three; e.g., "Will it achieve my goal?" "What effect will it have on others?" "How much time and effort will it take?" Think of any other important criteria.).

    a. Decide quickly on the solution alternative that seems best
    b. Think of one or two quick ways to improve the solution

Step 5. Implement the solution and ask the following question:

    a. Are you satisfied with the outcome?
    b. If not, try out your second choice if you still have time.

If an individual finds it difficult to apply this model in three minutes or less, he or she can reduce the time further by eliminating Step 2c and Step 4b. Without these steps, the model may still increase the effectiveness of problem solving under severe time pressure.

Module 15. Communication Skills and Interpersonal Problem Solving

This module provides for a training outline with specific regard to problem solving for couples with deficits in their ability to resolve interpersonal conflicts successfully. The procedures in this module are based in part on Behavioral Marital Therapy and Integrated Couples Therapy (see Cordova & Mirgain, 2004).

    A. Developing a collaborative problem orientation

        1. Both partners in the relationship should accept responsibility for the conflicts (i.e., disputes or disagreements), as well as for finding the solutions.

        2. Both partners should accept the goal of finding solutions that both partners can accept or be satisfied with (versus proving who is right and who is wrong or trying to find the *right* or *correct* solution).

        3. *Cognitive restructuring* may be needed at this point to facilitate adoption of a collaborate set; for example, correcting cognitive distortions such as absolutistic thinking (turning preferences into rigid, dogmatic *musts* and *shoulds*) and polarized thinking ("I'm right, you're wrong").

    B. Communication training ground rules *(Do's and Don'ts)*

        1. Be open and honest

        2. Express feelings appropriately (i.e., assertively rather than aggressively)

3. Allow your partner equal time to explain his or her point of view (don't monopolize the discussion)
4. Listen and empathize when your partner explains his or her point of view
5. Don't interrupt when your partner is talking (except to ask for clarification)
6. Don't put your partner down (name calling, judging, or character attacks)
7. Don't blame or moralize
8. Don't yell, curse, or use foul language
9. Don't threaten or try to coerce your partner
10. Don't *mind-read* or try to psychoanalyze your partner
11. Don't side-track (*do* focus on one issue at a time)
12. Don't overgeneralize (i.e., by using *always*, or *never*)
13. Don't catastrophize (i.e., *awfulizing*)

C. Problem-solving/conflict resolution training

1. *Problem definition and formulation.* Each person explains his or her view of the problem or conflict (encourage specificity). The other person is encouraged to listen and try to empathize (i.e., put oneself in the other person's shoes and try to imagine how he/she feels). The goal is to find a solution that both partners can accept (*win-win* approach). Cognitive restructuring may be needed at this point to correct cognitive distortions such as absolutistic thinking (rigid, dogmatic *musts* and *shoulds*), catastrophizing, arbitrary inferences, overgeneralizations, and polarized thinking.

2. *Generation of alternative solutions.* Three common types of solutions are:

   a. *Sacrifice or good faith agreement.* One partner unconditionally agrees to meet their partner's expectations or demands. The partner who sacrifices is usually the partner who feels less strong about his or her position. Also, over time, sacrificing works effectively only if sacrificing is volunteered equally by both partners across different conflicts or issues.

   b. *Compromise.* Compromising does not necessarily have to be 50–50 or meeting each other half way. A successful compromise is whatever both partners are willing to accept.

   c. *Exchange.* An exchange is a negotiated quid pro quo, that is, one partner agrees to accept the other partner's demands in exchange for some *reward* from the partner (e.g., sacrificing on another issue, something desirable that the partner gives to or does for the other person).

   3. *Decision Making.* The major decision-making criteria are (a)
      maximum benefits (positive consequences) for both partners,
      and (b) minimum costs (negative consequences) for both part-
      ners. In other words, a good solution is one that maximizes
      satisfaction and minimizes distress for *both* partners.
   4. *Solution implementation and verification*
      a. The solution is spelled out in terms of a behavioral contact
         (verbal or written) that specifies the behavioral changes
         that each partner agrees to make.
      b. Partners implement the solution
      c. Partners monitor the outcome
      d. Partners positively reinforce each other for keeping the
         agreement
      e. Recycling and trouble-shooting, if necessary
D. Promoting Acceptance and Tolerance

When partners are unable to agree upon a solution, the therapist
attempts to promote the notion that *acceptance and tolerance* of the
other person's unwanted behavior can often meet the major criterion for
an effective solution (i.e., mutual satisfaction). Acceptance and tolerance
are facilitated through training in empathic understanding as well as cognitive restructuring aimed at de-catastrophizing and eliminating absolutistic thinking (i.e., the tendency to turn preferences intro rigid, dogmatic
musts and *shoulds*). With regard to the latter, the therapist encourages
partners to adopt the problem orientation belief that it is often more
important to be happy in the relationship than it is to be right (i.e., to get
one's way).

CHAPTER NINE

Case Illustrations

In the previous chapter, it was explained that PST can be applied in a variety of different ways. However, it was also recommended that therapy, in general, should be conducted within an overall PST framework, where other treatment procedures are applied at appropriate points during the training program, as needed. Using this general approach, the goals of therapy not only include the reduction in maladaptive behavior and psychological distress, but also the facilitation of effective problem-solving performance in order to produce more generalized and durable positive changes in adaptive functioning and prevent future psychological problems.

Three clinical cases are presented in this chapter that illustrate the application of PST within a broader, individualized therapy program for clinical disorders involving generalized anxiety, depression, and coping with cancer. The goal of problem-solving-oriented therapy in each case was to reduce negative stress effects and maladaptive behavior by developing a more adaptive, problem-solving coping style and facilitating effective, independent problem-solving performance.

CASE 1: GENERALIZED ANXIETY

Mrs. S. was a 36-year-old housewife and part-time art teacher. At the time she came into therapy she had been married for 8 years, to a bank vice-president. The couple had one child—a 6-year-old boy. It was Mrs. S.'s second marriage. The first having ended in divorce. Mrs. S. contacted the therapist for therapy after she had been arrested for shoplifting at a local drug store. She had stolen only a lipstick, but the store manager had suspected her of shoplifting at the drug store for some time as she frequently bought items and then returned them for refunds. He believed that she had been buying an item, stealing another one of the same type, and then later returning one of them and getting a refund using the receipt from the item she had bought. Mrs. S. denied this accusation, claiming that the theft was her first one, and that she frequently browsed in stores and bought things because she was bored and had nothing else to do. She would later realize that she did not really need many of the things that she had bought, or that she had spent too much money, so she often returned them.

Mrs. S. did not believe that the shoplifting was a problem, except for the fact that she did not understand why she did it. Her major presenting complaints were a high level of general anxiety, depression, and poor self-esteem. She described herself as extremely tense, uptight, impatient, indecisive, and fearful. She reported worrying about "everything" (e.g., chemicals in the food, people who might try to take advantage of her, her health). She even worried about worrying too much—that worrying might eventually make her physically ill.

In addition to anxiety, Mrs. S. reported feeling very unhappy, bored, and dissatisfied with her life. Her self-confidence and self-esteem were very poor. She perceived herself as inadequate, incompetent, and lacking in control over her life and her emotions. She reported that her self-esteem had been deteriorating steadily since she left her full-time job about 6 years before as an art teacher in an elementary school. Mrs. S. had stopped working soon after she became pregnant with her son. She had started working again after he started school, but she could only find a job working 45 minutes each day as an art teacher in a junior high school. In addition to the short working time each week, Mrs. S. was not satisfied with the job as she had much more difficulty managing the behavior of the junior high school students in her class than she had had managing the elementary school students in her previous job.

In addition to gathering information about the dimensions of the emotional and self-esteem problems and their development over time, the pretreatment assessment phase of therapy focused also on the identification of current life problems and stressors, consequences of problem behaviors and emotional responses, assessment of problem solving and other coping skills, and initial structuring for therapy. The latter included an explanation and discussion of the rationale and course of problem-solving therapy, with the major goals being to develop a problem-solving cognitive set and strengthen expectations of benefit. Problem solving and other coping skills were assessed using a self-report measure of problem solving and the Problem-Solving Self-Monitoring (PSSM) method (see chapter 4). In addition to these assessment methods, self-ratings were used to assess anxiety, mood, and self-esteem throughout the course of therapy. These variables were rated on a scale from 0 to 10, with 10 being the negative end of the scale in each case. During the first 3 weeks, the ratings were made daily at a randomly selected time in the morning, afternoon, and evening. Thereafter, the ratings were made during three randomly selected days each week.

Mrs. S. was seen in therapy for 28 sessions. The major specific problems and stresses identified and focused on during therapy fell into five problem areas: (a) her mother's health; (b) her son's well-being (health and school problems); (c) work and other personal achievements; (d) social relationships; and (e) marriage. In addition to the problems in these areas, a major problem that occurred during therapy was related to her husband's expected transfer to a new job in another state within the next 3 months.

About 4 months before entering therapy, Mrs. S. was informed that her mother had cancer. At the time Mrs. S. started therapy, the prognosis of her mother was still uncertain. About 2 months after learning about her mother's cancer, Mrs. S.'s son caught a bad cold that developed into pneumonia. Both of these illnesses created considerable stress for Mrs. S., which reduced her ability to deal effectively with these problems. Shortly after beginning therapy, more anxiety was produced when Mrs. S. was informed by her son's school teacher that he had a reading problem that was interfering seriously with his school performance. This problem was also handled poorly by Mrs. S.

With regard to work and personal achievements, Mrs. S. was not involved in any meaningful work or constructive activity that could give her a sense of mastery or competence. During her brief work period each day as an art teacher, she did not believe that she was managing the class effectively. Mrs. S. was also unhappy because she had no close friends. As she engaged in few activities outside of the home, she rarely had opportunities to meet people. On the few occasions when she did meet someone new, the person failed to show an interest in her as a friend.

At first, Mrs. S. described her husband as a wonderful person for being so patient and understanding about the shoplifting and about her anxiety problems. Later, however, she complained that he was against her going for therapy before the shoplifting incident because he believed "you should not discuss your personal problems with a stranger." Moreover, she complained that her husband never praised her or gave her recognition for anything. Instead, he frequently criticized her and put her down. They spent very little time together because he commuted a long distance to work each day, and as a result, would arrive home sometime between 7:30 P.M. and 11 P.M., eat dinner, and go right to bed. On weekends, he frequently spent hours doing paperwork related to his job. When she complained about their lack of time together, he told her that there was nothing he could do about it and that she was wrong to complain. With regard to the husband's expected job transfer, Mrs. S. was fearful because she did not know anything about the area, and she was concerned that they would not be able to find a satisfactory residence in so short a period of time.

The problem-solving and coping-skills assessment revealed significant deficits in problem-solving coping. The major deficits were in problem orientation and problem definition and formulation, which precluded any further effective problem solving (e.g., generation of alternative solutions, decision making, etc.). Mrs. S. tended to appraise a problem as a "threat to be avoided" instead of a challenge or "problem to be solved" that caused fear and anxiety. She also tended to appraise the threat to her well-being (or a loved one's well-being) as being more serious or significant than it actually was on the basis of minimal information, which exacerbated the anxiety. She blamed herself for the problem, ignoring the important role of other factors, and tended to conclude, inappropriately, that there was nothing she could do to change the problem or reduce its stressfulness. This contributed to a feeling of helplessness and a sense of losing control. For example, when the teacher told Mrs. S. about her son's reading problem, her immediate response was: "I failed him. If I didn't have so many problems, he wouldn't have problems." She then cried and apologized profusely to the teacher for her son's reading problem instead of beginning to gather information about the problem and considering alternatives for dealing rationally and effectively with it. When a woman from the neighborhood whom Mrs. S. met and had lunch with one day seemed to ignore her the next day, Mrs. S. blamed herself, thinking that she had said or done something wrong. She felt rejected and upset and did nothing further to clarify the problem or try to spend more time with the person.

The anxiety generated by Mrs. S.'s negative problem orientation, together with her failure to gather sufficient information to clarify, understand, and reappraise a problem accurately, tended to result in misconceptions and distortions which created "pseudo-problems." These pseudo-problems, reflecting Mrs. S.'s fears and anxieties, were more threatening than the real problems. For example, Mrs. S. believed, incorrectly, that the woman whom she had met in the neighborhood was rejecting her. When her son showed signs of developing a cold, she thought that he had developed pneumonia again. When her husband informed her that he was going to be transferred to a new job within 3 months, she believed, without clarifying the problem, that it would be impossible to find a satisfactory home in so short a period of time.

In addition to Mrs. S.'s deficits in problem orientation and specific problem-solving skills, it was determined during training that she also had deficits in emotion-focused coping skills, which are important for overcoming cognitive and emotional obstacles to effective problem solving (see chapter 6). Moreover, when it was necessary to implement her problem solutions, it was determined that she had deficits in some of the instrumental skills that were required to implement certain problem solutions effectively (i.e., assertiveness skills and communication skills). Toward the latter part of therapy, it also became increasingly clear that it was going to be necessary for the husband to become involved in conjoint communication/problem-solving training, as he sometimes responded very negatively to her assertive problem solutions and other attempts to communicate and resolve the conflicts between them. However, he was very resistant to the idea of therapy.

A major goal of therapy was to help Mrs. S. develop a more effective problem-solving coping style. Instead of viewing a stressful problem primarily as a threat and worrying about it, she gradually learned to approach the problem as a challenge or problem to be solved. This prompted her to gather relevant information and to state the problem in problem-solving terms. Some of the problem statements that were developed and focused on in her therapy were the following:

1. What can I do to minimize my distress about my mother's cancer?
2. What can I do to help my mother adjust to having cancer? (an alternative statement of the problem involving her mother's cancer)
3. My son is showing symptoms of a cold. What can I do to prevent a more serious illness from developing?
4. What can I do to ensure a safe, healthy diet for my family?
5. What can I do to find a satisfying, productive full-time job?
6. What can I do to give myself a greater sense of personal achievement and accomplishment? (a broader statement of problem 5)
7. How can I reduce disruptive behavior in my classroom?
8. What can I do to overcome feelings of boredom when I am home alone?
9. How can I meet more people?
10. How can I communicate with people in a way that will ensure that they will enjoy my company and want to be my friend?
11. How can I get my husband to praise me more often and recognize the good things that I do to please him?
12. What can I do to get my husband to stop criticizing me and putting me down so often?
13. What can my husband and I do to make available more time to spend together?

14. How can my husband and I improve the quality of the time we spend together?
15. How can I persuade my husband to participate with me in marital counseling?

Instead of simply providing solutions to these problems and helping Mrs. S. implement them effectively, the therapist attempted to teach her how to generate alternative solutions on her own, evaluate the solutions, select the best solution or solution combination, implement it, and evaluate the outcome. When Mrs. S. was not able to generate any more solution alternatives using the principles she was taught, the therapist sometimes suggested additional alternatives in order to maximize her effectiveness and build her response repertoire for future, similar problems. When certain solutions required instrumental skills that Mrs. S. did not have (e.g., assertiveness skills), training was provided in these skills using skill-training methods such as coaching, modeling, behavior rehearsal, performance feedback, and positive reinforcement.

In addition to this training in problem-solving and solution-implementation skills, training was also provided in emotion-focused coping skills when cognitive and emotional obstacles to effective problem solving occurred (e.g., exaggerated appraisals of threat, irrational assumptions, intense emotional arousal). Mrs. S. required training in cognitive skills (e.g., cognitive restructuring), as well as behavioral skills (e.g., muscle relaxation). For example, Mrs. S. was taught to test the validity of threatening beliefs and assumptions instead of accepting them automatically. A problem-solving approach was used for this purpose. When the woman in the neighborhood ignored Mrs. S., Mrs. S. assumed that she had said or done something wrong and that, as a result, the woman disliked her and did not want to be her friend. Instead of accepting this threatening assumption, Mrs. S. was taught to generate as many alternative explanations for the woman's behavior as possible (e.g., she was in a bad mood, she was preoccupied and did not see Mrs. S., she has poor eyesight and did not recognize Mrs. S.). She was then asked to generate or seek as many facts as possible for and against each explanation and to decide which one was most likely to be valid.

To deal with excessive emotional arousal, Mrs. S. was trained in progressive muscle relaxation and meditation. In addition, a desensitization procedure was used, which involved verbal problem solving in the session while at the same time attempting to apply relaxation skills (e.g., muscle relaxation, slow and deep breathing).

During the first 4 weeks of therapy, which focused primarily on assessment, Mrs. S.'s average weekly anxiety ratings were consistently high (i.e., 8–10) and her average weekly mood and self-esteem ratings were consistently poor (i.e., 8–10). As she developed more effective problem-solving-oriented coping skills during the next 12 weeks of therapy, her anxiety ratings dropped to the moderate (i.e., 4–7) range, whereas her mood and self-esteem ratings changed to fair (i.e., 4–7) and then to good (i.e., 0–3). At about the 16th week of therapy, Mrs. S.'s anxiety ratings increased to the high range again and her mood and self-esteem ratings deteriorated from good to fair for a few weeks. These changes occurred when Mrs. S.'s husband informed her about the expected job transfer within the next 3 months. Her immediate response was: "We don't know anything about that area. How are we going to find a place to live in three months? What if we don't like it there?" Mrs. S. experienced considerable anxiety because she appraised the problem as a significant threat to the well-being of the entire family and was inclined to believe that it could not be satisfactorily solved before gathering sufficient information to clarify and understand the nature of the problem. When she was encouraged to view the situation as a problem to be solved and to use her problem-solving skills, she was able to clarify that she was concerned mainly about the health and safety of the neighborhood in which they would live and about the quality of the schools. This clarification led to relevant information-gathering strategies during the next few weeks, which resulted eventually in the purchase of a satisfactory home within the 3-month period.

As Mrs. S. made progress in coping with the job-transfer problem, her average weekly anxiety ratings were reduced to low-moderate again and her mood and self-esteem ratings returned to good. The ratings remained at this level for the next several weeks of therapy, after which treatment was terminated because the family moved. At that point, Mrs. S. felt that she could handle all of her current problems on her own except for some of the marital problems (e.g., the lack of positive feedback, the lack of time together). It was recommended that the couple seek marital counseling in their new location. However, in a follow-up telephone conversation 3 months later, Mrs. S. indicated that her husband was still refusing to become involved in marital therapy. As a result, her dissatisfaction with the marriage remained, but she was coping well with her other problems.

CASE 2: DEPRESSION

Mr. C. was a 48-year-old high school guidance counselor who had been separated from his wife for approximately 1 year. He had been married for 26 years and had three children, aged 24, 22, and 20. There were no previous marriages. Mr. C.'s wife had insisted on the separation after a long history of serious marital problems and several previous separations. She was in the process of filing for a divorce at the time that Mr. C. entered therapy.

Mr. C. was a large, handsome man, and slightly balding. He stood about 6'4" and weighed about 220 lbs. His presenting problems included moderate to severe depression, with occasional suicidal ideation, fear and anxiety about the future, poor anger control, and poor self-esteem. Mr. C.'s depression was related primarily to his wife's rejection and its effect on his self-esteem. He reported that he loved his wife and could not accept that his marriage was over. For the past year, he had been trying desperately to win his wife back by attempting to see her and talk to her as often as possible, but he was rejected consistently. His wife told him flatly that she no longer loved him and that there was no chance for a reconciliation. Even his children were urging him to accept the fact that the marriage was over and to start a new life of his own. However, he could not bear the thought of his wife being with another man, and he did not believe that he could ever love another woman. He was afraid that he would be alone and unhappy the rest of his life. Although he occasionally thought of suicide, he reported that these were fleeting thoughts and that he never seriously considered acting on them.

Mr. C. accepted most of the responsibility for his past marital problems. He attributed most of the problems to his poor anger control. Instead of approaching conflicts and disagreements with his wife in a calm and rational manner, he angrily insisted that he was right, refused to compromise in any way, and attempted to coerce her into giving in to his demands by using threats and verbal abuse. Physical violence was frequent, but was limited to throwing objects and hitting walls—no one was ever hurt. When Mr. C.'s aggression did not get him his way, he punished his wife by refusing to communicate with her for days and even weeks at a time. Mr. C. tended to use a similar, although less intense aggressive approach to interpersonal conflicts and disagreements with peers in the work setting and in other social situations. As a result, he alienated many people and had no close friends.

Because of the constant rejection from his wife, his inability to control his anger, the lack of satisfying social relationships, and his inability to do anything about these problems, Mr. C.'s self-esteem was at a very low point when he entered therapy. He felt very inadequate and helpless, perceiving that he had no control over himself, his present life, or his future. However, one personal asset that prevented a complete breakdown in his self-confidence was the fact that he was considered a good guidance counselor and was well liked by the students, if not by his peers.

Mr. C. was seen in therapy for 33 sessions. Assessment methods included a problem-solving inventory, the PSSM method and self-ratings of mood, anxiety state, and self-esteem. Specific current problems and stresses that were focused on in therapy can be grouped into six categories: (1) his wife's relationship with another man; (2) interpersonal conflicts and disagreements in the work setting; (3) his relationships with women; (4) friendships; (5) feelings of loneliness; and (6) feelings of inadequacy. Following the initial assessment and structuring phase, therapy focused on training in problem-solving-oriented coping skills.

The assessment revealed that Mr. C. had deficits in problem orientation and problem-solving skills. For example, he tended to perceive problems primarily as threats to his well-being, and did not approach them as problems to be solved. Instead of taking the time to gather information, clarify the problem, and generate alternative solutions, he responded impulsively and automatically to the perceived threat, often in an angry and aggressive manner. Whenever he did stop to think before acting, he often failed to anticipate important consequences, especially the long-term effects of his actions on his social relationships. After responding ineffectively, he often failed to recognize all the negative consequences, or he disregarded them and failed to correct his behavior.

Mr. C. could not tolerate seeing his wife with her new boyfriend, Dave. As Mr. C. still had hope of winning his wife back, he perceived Dave as a threat to his relationship with her. Because Dave was not well-educated and worked only as a laborer, Mr. C. also perceived the relationship between Dave and his wife as a threat to his self-esteem. Mr. C. responded impulsively to this threat with extreme anger and aggression. On one occasion when he met Dave outside of his home after Mr. C. visited his son, he threatened him with physical violence if Dave ever saw his wife again. A few weeks later, when he saw Dave dancing with his wife at a Parents Without Partners (PWOP) social function, Mr. C. invited him to "go outside and fight." When PWOP officials saw what was happening, they forced Mr. C. to leave the dance.

While learning to clarify and define this problem in therapy, Mr. C. initially stated the problem as follows: "How can I make Dave get out of my wife's life?" However, while exploring the possibility that this problem was not the *real* (primary) problem, he realized that it was secondary to the more important problem: "How can I win my wife back?" A review of past attempts to solve this problem and the failure to come up with any new alternatives that might work helped Mr. C. to realize that he had to accept this problem as insoluble and begin to seek a new relationship. Although it was a difficult step for Mr. C., he reformulated his problem with Dave in the following manner: "How can I control my anger and aggressive behavior toward Dave?" One of his solutions was to keep telling himself that the relationship with his wife was over for good and that Dave and his wife had every right to see each other if they so decided. Mr. C. was taught to use cognition-oriented facilitative coping (rational restructuring) to deal with the threatening assumption that the relationship between Dave and his wife somehow meant that he (Mr. C.) was inadequate. A second solution to this problem was to avoid as many situations as possible where he might see Dave with his wife. A contingency plan related to this solution was that if he did happen to be in the same situation with Dave and his wife, he would act friendly (you can't be friendly and too aggressive at the same time) and then leave the situation as soon as possible.

This solution proved to be almost life-saving on one occasion. Mr. C. met Dave and his wife one day at another PWOP dance. Because of the previous incident when Mr. C. goaded Dave to go outside to fight, Dave brought three tough friends along to wait outside for Mr. C. and physically harm him after he left the dance in order to convince him to leave Dave alone. These men waited in a nearby bar for the dance to end at about midnight. However, Mr. C. implemented his solution and left the dance at about 10:30 P.M. The men who were there to attack him were drinking beer at the bar and never saw him leave. Thus, Mr. C.'s solution enabled him to avoid getting hurt.

With regard to interpersonal conflicts and disagreements in the work setting, Mr. C. also tended to perceive these problems as threats to his self-esteem, and he responded in a similar impulsive, angry, aggressive manner. His problem appraisal in these situations was based on several distorted or irrational beliefs and assumptions. He believed that there were only two sides to every issue or conflict—a *right* side and a *wrong* side. As he always believed that his point of view was the right one, he assumed that the other person's point of view had to be wrong. Furthermore, he believed that if a person held to a wrong viewpoint, and could not recognize the right viewpoint, then that person had to be stupid or incompetent, and therefore, did not deserve to be treated with respect. Thus, it became clear that Mr. C. felt very threatened when someone challenged his views or disagreed with his demands, because he did not want to be perceived as wrong and incompetent.

In order to reduce anger, avoid impulsive and aggressive responding, and make time available for rational problem-solving thinking, Mr. C. was taught to use cognitive restructuring techniques to correct these irrational assumptions. For example, he was taught that two people could hold different viewpoints without either one being wrong (i.e., different evaluative criteria). He was also taught to understand that a person could make a mistake and be wrong in a particular instance without being stupid or incompetent.

Once he was able to inhibit his impulsive, aggressive responses and devote time to problem definition and formulation and the generation of alternative solutions, Mr. C. began to generate more appropriate assertive strategies for dealing with interpersonal disputes and disagreements. In addition, once he realized that he did not have to win every argument or dispute, he was able to consider alternative strategies for resolving conflicts, such as compromising, negotiating a quid pro quo agreement (i.e., one person agrees to something in exchange for something else), and sacrificing (i.e., one person *gives in* or defers to the other person's demands). As some conflict situations required quick thinking and quick action (e.g., an unexpected confrontation), Mr. C. was also taught a rapid problem-solving method. Specifically, he was taught how to respond initially to an unexpected confrontation so as to give himself at least a few minutes to think before acting (e.g., "I can't talk to you about this right now. Where are you going to be? I'll get back to you in a few minutes." "I don't have an answer for you right now. Let me think about it a few minutes and I'll get back to you." "I'm not sure how I feel about this right now. Let me think about it awhile and I'll get back to you").

With regard to his relationships with women, Mr. C. initially had little hope of finding another woman whom he could love and who would love him. As noted previously, he also maintained the hope that he would win his wife back. As a result, he was devoting very little time and effort to exploring ways of meeting women at the time he entered therapy. After Mr. C. accepted the need and desirability of developing new relationships, problem-solving training focused on such problems as: "Where can I go to meet women?" "How can I let women know that I am available?" "How should I approach a woman whom I don't know and start a conversation?" "How can I make myself as attractive as possible to women?" "How and when should I make sexual advances?" "What kind of woman would satisfy me the most?" Mr. C. soon became adept at generating a variety of solutions to these problems and implementing them. For example, he decided that he preferred to meet women at PWOP functions, church-related activities, and work-related activities (e.g., seminars, conferences, workshops). He preferred to avoid singles bars and personal ads in the newspaper. He bought new clothes to make himself look more attractive, and he asked friends and relatives to let people know that he was single and available. During the generation-of-alternatives training, the therapist suggested additional alternatives when Mr. C.'s response repertoire was depleted and only a few good alternatives were generated. However, this aid was not often necessary. In order to maximize solution implementation effectiveness, some training in instrumental skills was required (e.g., communication and conversational skills). However, in most cases, once Mr. C. considered all the alternatives carefully and decided on the best solution, he was usually able to implement it effectively. He was soon meeting women and dating frequently.

Mr. C. was unhappy about the fact that he had no close friends, although he had several acquaintances with whom he was on friendly terms. In addition to solving his anger-control problems, problem-solving training also focused on other positive strategies for developing closer relationships with particular individuals. Some of the solution strategies generated by Mr. C. included friendly greetings, being a good listener, expressing empathy, giving reassurance and support, expressing positive feelings, giving positive feedback, offering help, and inviting the person to participate in activities together more often. Very little training was required in the specific instrumental skills needed to implement these strategies. Most of these skills were already present in Mr. C.'s response repertoire and were already being applied in his counseling activities. Problem solving helped him to generalize these skills to his everyday social relationships.

Early in therapy, Mr. C. often felt lonely because he spent much of his time in his apartment alone. He also felt inadequate because he was not experiencing much positive reinforcement in his life. These feelings were problematic because they aggravated his depression, which in turn, threatened to interfere with effective problem solving. Therefore, although it was recognized that these negative feelings would probably be reduced once the current antecedent problems causing them were solved, it was also believed that by focusing on these feelings directly as problems to be solved, Mr. C. might be able to get some immediate relief from depression, which might facilitate further problem-solving therapy related to the antecedent problems. These emotional problems were stated as follows—"What can I do to feel better when I feel lonely?" "What can I do to feel better about myself?" With regard to the first problem, Mr. C. found that several of his relatives and acquaintances were quite willing to talk to him and offer support and understanding when he felt lonely and depressed. However, as he did not want to make too many demands on relatives and friends, he considered a variety of other strategies as well, and found that a particularly effective one was to take a long drive in the country.

For the problem of feeling inadequate, Mr. C. generated alternatives, which included reminding himself of the students he helped as a guidance counselor, putting in extra time counseling, taking a continuing education course and attending workshops to improve his counseling skills, helping a friend, developing some new hobbies, and taking steps to pursue a life goal of getting into school administration. These strategies, once implemented, proved to be helpful in reducing feelings of loneliness and inadequacy early in therapy.

As therapy continued and improvement was observed in problem-solving-oriented coping, progress was reflected in Mr. C.'s self-ratings of mood, self-esteem, and anxiety. During the first 7 weeks of therapy, average weekly self-ratings showed high anxiety and poor mood and self-esteem. In the eighth week, anxiety ratings reduced to moderate. Two weeks later, mood and self-esteem ratings improved to fair. By the 25th session, anxiety was low-moderate and mood and self-esteem were good. When these ratings stabilized over a period of several weeks, and Mr. C. felt that he could cope with his current problems on his own, therapy was faded and then terminated. A few weeks before therapy ended, Mr. C. was divorced from his wife. He handled this event well. A follow-up telephone conversation 6 months after termination revealed that Mr. C. was continuing to do well. He was no longer depressed. Anxiety was moderate to low. Self-esteem was very good and was being reinforced by frequent positive feedback from women. Although he was dating frequently, he was not yet in love. However, he felt confident that he would fall in love and be married again some day.

CASE 3: COPING WITH CANCER

Lisa H. was a 35-year-old office manager of a large software company. She had been divorced for a little more than 2 years at the time of her initial visit. She had one daughter, Karen, who was 9 years old. Her divorce resulted as a function of an affair that her ex-husband had with a coworker. Lisa and her ex-husband, John, had been high school sweethearts and married soon after graduation. She had worked to put him through college as an accounting major, while also earning an associates degree on a part-time basis at a 2-year junior college. Part of the reason John told Lisa that he wanted a divorce was sexual and interpersonal incompatibility. He felt that "they had changed and had different goals in life." Although the divorce was devastating, Lisa resolved to cope with it as best she could, with the goal of minimizing the impact on her daughter. To some degree, she was glad that the divorce proceedings themselves were not prolonged or destructive, that her ex-husband moved to another state, and that he was reliable about providing child support. On the other hand, one of the major fall-outs was the change in her social life, where many of her previous friends were couples and were no longer interested in socializing with her. Additionally, although she felt she still could trust men, she was very unwilling to put Karen through another painful divorce.

Lisa was referred for therapy by her oncologist. She had recently been diagnosed with early stage breast cancer and was soon to undergo surgery, followed by chemotherapy. Although the prognosis was fairly positive because of early detection, the physician identified significant psychosocial concerns that prompted a referral. During the initial interview, Lisa presented as anxious, sad, and very concerned about her daughter's future. Although she was somewhat comforted about knowing that she would be receiving excellent medical care, and that her prognosis was positive, she was very scared about the consequences of the actual cancer treatment. Having read multiple articles about breast cancer in popular magazines, she was well aware of the major negative side effects that would be likely, including hair loss, nausea, fatigue, pain, and estrogen changes. Moreover, stating that as a function of being brought up as an only child, she felt uncomfortable talking about sexual issues, such as her breasts and the effects that breast surgery would have on her future sexual relationships. Although she was not interested in getting married again quickly, she hoped one day to have a better relationship and provide Karen with a live-in dad.

Although she was experiencing significant psychological distress, Lisa's primary interest in coming to therapy was to get help in talking to her daughter about the cancer. She was scared that having undergone a divorce, Karen might become especially frightened of losing her mommy also. Since the divorce, they had become closer, spending more time together, and relying less on other family members and friends. Now, Lisa was concerned that the cancer treatment would change everything, making her less accessible to Karen and her needs. Her work environment was positive, where her supervisors and coworkers respected and treated her well, but she did not have anyone in particular with whom she felt close. Lisa was financially stable, but had little reserves. She was also concerned about surgical scars and how it would make her feel sexually.

Based on the interviews and her responses to a variety of self-report inventories and questionnaires, it was determined that she was experiencing moderate levels of depression and anxiety, with no suicidal ideation. She was particularly concerned about her daughter's future and how to tell Karen about the cancer. She also described strong feelings of isolation and loneliness, but she was too scared to do anything about them. She reported that her self-esteem since the divorce had improved considerably, in part due to reading and taking the advice offered by various self-help books, as well as the increase in her computer skills as a result of taking a series of evening classes at a local community college. However, she was aware that she was beginning to depend too much on her relationship with her daughter for social activities, and she realized that she had to begin making friends in the near future.

Specific assessment of her problem-solving ability and attitudes was accomplished through completion of the SPSI-R and *Coping Attempts*

Worksheets (see chapter 8). Subsequent discussions of her responses to these materials revealed that she had a strong tendency to avoid problems that were emotional in nature (e.g., anxiety, fear), but she had the opposite tendency to impulsively try to solve problems if they were work-related. Moreover, she often felt a lack of confidence when it came to dealing with interpersonal problems, regardless of where they occurred. Interestingly, many of her responses to the Rational Problem-Solving Skills scale were couched in dichotomous terms—that is, she felt she was able to effectively define problems, generate alternatives, make decisions, and effectively carry them out, but only if they pertained to work-related issues. When problems involved relationships and emotions, she felt that all her "good common sense just gets up and flies out the window."

Based on these initial findings and clinical impressions, it was felt that a significant part of treatment would be to help Lisa transfer her effective skills to other areas of her life, and to focus on helping to facilitate her coping with the cancer diagnosis and the cancer treatment. To that end, *formal* training in the problem-solving model was modified. Specifically, the entire problem-solving process was described, emphasizing the importance of the role that one's problem orientation plays. Because she was somewhat familiar with many of the concepts underlying the rational problem-solving skills, training in these areas were shortened. However, with regard to various orientation variables, significant effort had to be extended to help her adopt a more positive problem-solving set. In addition, continued discussions uncovered Lisa's feelings of guilt surrounding the negative impact on her daughter regarding the divorce. She felt that if she had only been a better wife, she could have been a better mother, in that John would not have sought another relationship, he would not have had the affair, and consequently, the divorce would not have taken place. As a result of the cancer diagnosis, Lisa's guilt escalated—she began to feel that she would "pass cancer onto Karen." As such, significant effort was made to help Lisa overcome the feelings of guilt.

At times, the guilt made her overprotective of Karen, and resulted in spoiling her (e.g., giving into requests for extra desserts and later bedtime curfews). Although Lisa knew better, she felt emotionally unable to combat the guilt. The *Reversed Advocate Role-Play* exercise (see chapter 8) was found to be particularly helpful in reducing Lisa's guilt and assigning responsibility for the divorce and cancer more realistically. In addition, Lisa found the use of the *STOP and THINK* technique particularly helpful in making herself engage in cognitive restructuring strategies when she started to feel guilty (see chapter 8). Moreover, she pasted pictures of stop signs on her refrigerator to help in this process.

Continued discussions and work on her guilt further revealed that it tended to serve as a means of avoiding having to deal with the anxiety of telling Karen that she had cancer. Lisa continued to want to protect Karen from also feeling scared, but she was finally convinced that Karen would be able to discern that something was going on and would be likely to put her own interpretation on the situation, potentially making it worse. To help increase Lisa's motivation to want to tell Karen about the cancer, she was encouraged to brainstorm a list of reasons why it would be important to do so. After several attempts, the following list was developed:

1. Karen may put the worst interpretation on the situation, as she was aware that her mother was seeing a doctor.
2. Karen might get upset if she found out from someone else; she might think that her mother was keeping something from her because she wasn't trustworthy.
3. If Karen picked up that "something was going on," but did not know what it was, any problems resulting from the divorce could get exacerbated.
4. Lisa felt that honesty between her and her daughter was the most important part of their relationship.
5. Lisa would want Karen to be able to feel comfortable talking to her about anything.
6. No matter how bad talking about the cancer was, Karen would be able to understand.

Lisa was instructed to write these reasons down and take them with her to work in order to prompt her to think about them, rather than avoid the decision. After a week, Lisa felt convinced that telling Karen about the cancer was an important task. Again, using the brainstorming techniques, Lisa generated a list of various ways to talk to her daughter. Using the decision-making tools, she finally decided that they would take an extended vacation, during which time she would talk to Karen. She had previously prepared a series of questions that she thought Karen might ask, along with appropriate answers. She also anticipated that Karen's reaction might make her feel upset, thus making it more difficult to discuss the overall issue. To deal with that possibility, Lisa decided to try to break up the discussion into small segments, in order for Karen to be able to react to the news without feeling overwhelmed. One additional major obstacle was Lisa's underlying belief that if she did not conduct this discussion perfectly, then this was evidence that she was a bad mother. This prompted the use of the reversed advocate role-play exercise again, in addition to having Lisa carry a list of positive self-statements that were geared to facilitate a more positive orientation.

Because of all the prior planning, when Lisa actually did talk to Karen, it went better than she anticipated. Karen did ask many questions, but Karen had concrete and reassuring answers. In fact, as mentioned earlier, Lisa's cancer was characterized by a good prognosis, so Lisa ultimately felt that she could be honest and uplifting at the same time. At one point during the weekend, Karen brought up the question of whether her father might be coming back to help Lisa with her fight against the cancer. This made Lisa both upset and somewhat angry, as memories of her helping John financially get through college came to mind, in sharp contrast to those memories of being told about "the other woman." In the past, this increase in distress would have led Lisa to want to avoid thinking and talking about the stressful situation and engage in some work-related activity. Instead, because of the training to *STOP and THINK,* the actual increase in negative affect led her to engage first in some deep breathing, and then to explain to Karen that her father would not be involved in her medical care. What used to lead to emotional suppression, now led to meaningful discussions.

Over the next few weeks, Karen would often ask her mother questions about the cancer and occasionally cried. Previously, Lisa would try to get Karen to stop crying by "kidding around and making her laugh." Then she would attempt to distract her by talking about something else or engaging in a different activity. Because of the training she underwent in problem orientation, she was able to change this behavior. Now, she viewed Karen's crying as a signal that a problem exists, and then told herself to *STOP and THINK.* She realized that it would do more harm to attempt to ignore such problems, and therefore, used this signal to try to cope with the problem more appropriately. Therefore, Lisa asked Karen what she was feeling, why she was crying, and attempted to try to help her to better cope with these feelings, rather than trying to dismiss them. During therapy, it was important to reinforce such changes and to point out that her changes would have a positive impact on Karen. Moreover, it facilitated a more honest and closer relationship between them, which was very important to Lisa.

During the period of time where Lisa was recovering from the breast surgery and undergoing chemotherapy, she missed several sessions due to fatigue and nausea. Those sessions that she was able to make were centered around body-image concerns, coping with various side effects of the cancer treatment, and mild feelings of depression. Each of these were addressed using the problem-solving model, in addition to providing referrals for various local support groups and programs (e.g., American Cancer Society). Having other women to talk to about concerns that even remotely dealt with sexual issues provided Lisa with an opportunity to share problems and ask questions in a low stress environment.

Consequently, she ultimately felt that she could view sex in the right perspective and not feel that it was a taboo subject. In addition, discussions that occurred during the support groups were often brought into the problem-solving therapy, where she attempted to apply various parts of the model to help her make better decisions. In particular, the problem-definition-and-formulation exercises helped her to better define her immediate and long-term goals regarding the future.

To that end, Lisa decided that she wanted to build up a social network of adults who would be friends with her as a single person, and not necessarily as part of a couple. At a later point in time, she would be more receptive to dates or a more long-term relationship with a man, but not at the present. She used the problem-solving model to generate various ideas about how to increase opportunities to meet people and make friends. A natural outlet was the support groups she had been attending, as well as the parent-teacher groups at Karen's school. Lisa also began to volunteer at her local church regarding a homeless kitchen. In engaging in these activities, she realized that part of her previous hesitancy was due to the concern that she wasn't interesting enough. Going back to the list of positive self-statements, she was able to overcome this concern rather quickly. At the time of termination, after 18 sessions, her cancer was in remission, she was making new friends, and her relationship with her daughter continued to be very close. A 6-month follow-up found her similarly doing well.

SUMMARY AND DISCUSSION

Three clinical cases are presented to illustrate the application of PST as part of a broader, individualized therapy program for clinical disorders involving generalized anxiety (Mrs. S.); depression (Mr. C.); and coping with cancer (Lisa H.). All three cases were characterized by a negative coping style, which included the perception of uncontrollability and ineffective problem-solving performance. In two of these cases, this negative coping style was associated with negative stress effects such as anxiety, depression, and low self-esteem. In the third case (Lisa), the threatening nature of the problem was very real—that is, cancer. However, she also tended to avoid emotion-laden situations that were not life-threatening (e.g., telling her daughter about the cancer). Problem-solving-oriented therapy seemed to be successful in developing a more adaptive problem-solving coping style, increasing effective problem-solving performance, and reducing negative stress effects, although the amount of improvement was limited in the case of Mrs. S.

In addition to the common emphasis in these cases on goal-oriented coping (discovering and implementing problem solutions), the three clients required different amounts of training in coping emotion-focused. All patients required some training in cognitive restructuring to correct negative problem-orientation cognitions (e.g., exaggerated, threatening problem appraisals) and distortions in problem definition and formulation (e.g., perfectionistic behavioral standards). Mrs. S. also required training in relaxation and desensitization skills because of her emotional oversensitivity to stressful problematic situations, which could not be reduced sufficiently through cognitive restructuring and problem solving alone. Although Mr. C. showed strong emotional reactivity as well, relaxation training was not conducted because cognitive restructuring and problem solving were successful in reducing emotional arousal.

The case of Mrs. S. illustrates how the generalization of problem-solving training effects may be limited when the client's social environment fails to set the occasion for, and reinforce, independent problem-solving behavior. In these cases, it is necessary to involve significant others from the client's social environment in the therapy in an attempt to create a more supportive environment, which encourages and reinforces problem-solving behavior. In the case of Mrs. S., the husband punished assertive problem solutions and refused to participate in conjoint problem solving to resolve interpersonal conflicts.

CHAPTER TEN

Outcome Studies

This chapter provides an overview of PST treatment outcome investigations. Because the past several years have witnessed an increase in the number of clinical trials evaluating the efficacy of PST across a variety of populations and patient problems, we necessarily need to be somewhat limited in this review due to space considerations. As such, we will only focus on those PST studies that have been published during the past 2 decades (i.e., 1985–2005), where PST is either a singular intervention being assessed or at least one significant component of a larger treatment package, and that target adults as the primary recipients of PST. For studies published prior to 1985, the reader is directed to the two previous editions of this volume (D'Zurilla, 1986; D'Zurilla & Nezu, 1999), as well as A. M. Nezu, D'Zurilla, Zwick, and Nezu (2004). For investigations focusing on PST for children and adolescents, please refer to Frauenknecht and Black (2004). As will be apparent in this chapter, researchers have applied PST to a wide variety of patient populations and program goals. Target populations have ranged from hospitalized psychiatric patients to average individuals and groups who want to maximize their overall personal-social competence. In different studies, PST has been used as a clinical intervention, part of an overall treatment package, a maintenance strategy, or as a prevention program. The studies described in this chapter are grouped according to the following categories: psychiatric and schizophrenic patients, depression, suicide, social phobia, generalized anxiety disorder, posttraumatic stress disorder, distressed couples, parent-child problems, parent and family caregivers, primary care patients, persons with mental retardation, stress management, ineffective coping, substance abuse, offenders, HIV/AIDS prevention, obesity/weight control, and medical patients.

PSYCHIATRIC AND SCHIZOPHRENIC PATIENTS

As noted in chapter 7, several investigators have identified PST to be a particularly important clinical intervention with regard to patients with major mental illness, such as schizophrenia (Falloon, 2000). For example, Hansen and colleagues (1985) trained seven chronic aftercare psychiatric patients in five problem-solving component skills: problem identification, goal definition, solution evaluation, evaluation of alternatives, and selection of a best solution. The effects of training were assessed using measures of problem-solving ability and verbal problem-solving performance, which focused on actual problematic situations the patients were likely to encounter in the community. The results showed that training significantly increased both problem-solving ability and problem-solving effectiveness, with improvement generalizing from problematic situations used in training to unfamiliar, untrained situations. Before training, the patient sample showed a significant deficit in problem-solving effectiveness compared to a criterion sample of 20 normal control subjects living in the community. Following training, the patients' problem-solving effectiveness was equal to that of the criterion sample.

Wallace and Liberman (1985) randomly assigned 28 male patients with schizophrenia to either intensive social skills training or holistic health therapy. The social skills training was directive and structured and aimed at interpersonal problem solving deemed important for effective functioning in social arenas within the hospital setting. In addition to training in various rational problem-solving skills (e.g., generating alternatives, decision making), patients in this condition were also taught to better deliver an appropriate social response using verbal and nonverbal behaviors. Patients in the holistic health therapy received a program that emphasized coping with stressors that might have precipitated previous psychotic episodes. Coping skills included yoga, meditation, walking, and group discussions about the relationship between stress and well-being.

A comprehensive assessment battery was conducted at pretreatment, posttreatment (i.e., after 9 weeks of the in-patient treatment), and for 24 months in the community. Results indicated that patients in the social skills group evidenced significantly greater acquisition, generalization, and durability of social skills. Moreover, their overall social adjustment in the community was rated as better by significant others, and they experienced fewer relapses and rehospitalizations as compared to their control counterparts.

Bradshaw (1993) compared a coping skills training program with PST for a group of 14 patients diagnosed with schizophrenia at a day treatment program. Each group met weekly for 1.5 hours during a 24-week period. The coping skills group focused on managing physiological arousal, cognitive restructuring, and learning social skills. Goal attainment scaling was used as a dependent variable and consisted of participants' goals set at pretreatment. The participant's case manager assigned a goal attainment score for each of the four goals at pretreatment, posttreatment, and at a 6-month follow-up. The scores were based on interviews with the patient and a family member, as well as information gleaned from intake evaluations and progress notes. It was found that individuals in the coping skills group were significantly better able to attain their goals than PST individuals at posttreatment. However, this difference disappeared at the 6-month follow-up assessment point.

Marder et al. (1996) compared a social skills training package that included a significant PST component to supportive group therapy for 80 male outpatients diagnosed with schizophrenia. After these patients were stabilized with low doses of medication, they were randomly assigned to either condition. Both treatments were provided twice weekly for 6 months and then weekly for the next 18 months. Results indicated the superiority of the social skills protocol on certain measures of social adjustment over the control. In addition, it was noted that this advantage was greatest when it was combined with active drug supplementation.

Training in problem solving was also a significant component of a larger cognitive-behavioral therapy (CBT) protocol to treat chronic schizophrenia in a study conducted by Tarrier et al. (1998). Additional components within the intensive intervention included teaching patients specific methods of coping with their symptoms, as well as training them in strategies to reduce the risk of relapse. This CBT protocol was conducted during 20 sessions over the course of 10 weeks and was compared to a control group that received supportive counseling. Both active treatments also included a routine care component and were also compared to a routine care alone control condition. The adjunct treatments were conducted either in outpatient settings or in the patient's home.

Results indicated that compared to patients receiving the supportive group therapy, CBT patients experienced significant improvements regarding both the number and severity of positive symptoms of schizophrenia. Moreover, significantly more patients treated with CBT showed an improvement of 50% or greater in their symptoms. The group of patients receiving only the routine care alone also experienced more exacerbations and days spent in the hospital.

Liberman, Eckman, and Marder (2001) conducted a study to determine whether PST actually had an impact on the problem-solving skills of persons with schizophrenia. Seventy-five adult outpatients diagnosed with schizophrenia were randomly assigned to one of two groups—4 months of weekly PST group sessions, or 4 months of supportive group therapy. The impact of training was measured by the Assessment of Interpersonal

Problem Solving Skills (AIPSS), a psychometrically sound interview and role-play instrument. The AIPSS consists of 13 videotaped vignettes, 10 of which represent interpersonal problems. Subjects are requested to take the role of the protagonist and to respond to a series of questions that parallel various problem-solving steps, for example, "Was there a problem in that scene?" (problem recognition) and "Please tell me what you would do or say if you were in that situation" (generating alternatives).

Results indicated that although both sets of patients did improve at posttreatment regarding their ability to identify problems, PST participants demonstrated significant improvements in all other problem-solving dimensions addressed by the AIPSS (i.e., generating alternatives, decision making, role-play skills, overall role-play performance). Because the actual training in problem solving included scenarios that were different from those included in the AIPSS, the authors concluded that 4 months of PST did yield generalizable outcomes that could be of help to patients in many realms of functioning.

In an effort to enhance the generalization of important social skills into the community, Glynn et al. (2002) compared a clinic-based skills training approach with a similar program supplemented by manual-based generalization sessions in the community. Training in social problem solving was one of three major skills sets included in both treatment conditions, the other two involving medication management and effective living skills. Results indicated that providing generalization training in the community led to significant posttreatment improvements in instrumental role functioning, social relations, and overall adjustment. Moreover, these rates of improvement in social functioning were coupled with low rates of psychiatric exacerbation.

DEPRESSION

A. M. Nezu and his colleagues (A. M. Nezu, 1987; A. M. Nezu et al., 1989) developed a model of major depressive disorder that underscores the significant role that problem-solving deficits play in the etiopathogenesis of depression. In support of this formulation, research by many differing investigators have identified a significant relationship between ineffective problem-solving skills and depressive symptomatology (see A. M. Nezu, Wilkins, & Nezu, 2004 for a review of this literature). In addition, research has documented the mediating nature of problem solving, whereby problem solving is viewed as an intervening variable that significantly accounts for the causal relationship between stress and depression (A. M. Nezu, 2004). Given this, PST has also been evaluated extensively as a treatment for depression.

In an outcome study focusing on adult unipolar depression, A. M. Nezu (1986d) randomly assigned clinically depressed individuals in an outpatient setting to one of three conditions: (1) PST; (2) problem-focused therapy (PFT); or (3) wait-list control (WLC). Both therapy conditions were conducted in a group setting over eight weekly sessions lasting from 1.5 to 2 hours. PFT involved discussions of the subjects' current life problems with a problem-solving goal, but systematic training in problem-solving skills was not provided.

Assessment was conducted at pretreatment, posttreatment, and at a 6-month follow-up. Both traditional statistical analyses and an evaluation of the clinical significance of the results identified substantial reductions in depression in the PST group that were maintained over the 6-month follow-up period, as measured by two different self-report measures of depression (i.e., Beck Depression Inventory [BDI] and the depression scale of the Minnesota Multiphasic Personality Inventory). Moreover, the improvement in depression in the PST condition was significantly greater than in the PFT and WLC conditions. The superiority of PST over PFT was also maintained at the 6-month follow-up evaluation. Further results revealed that PST participants increased significantly more than the other two groups in problem-solving effectiveness, as well as changing significantly in locus-of-control orientation from external to internal. These improvements were also maintained at the 6-month follow-up. Overall, these results provide support for the basic assumption that PST produces its effects by increasing problem-solving ability and strengthening personal control expectations.

The purpose of a subsequent study by A. M. Nezu and Perri (1989) was twofold: (a) to provide for a partial replication of the A. M. Nezu (1986d) investigation, and (b) to assess the relative contribution of the problem-orientation component in treating depressed individuals. A dismantling research strategy was used to address these goals by randomly assigning individuals who had been reliably diagnosed, according to Research Diagnostic Criteria, as experiencing major depressive disorder to one of three conditions: (a) PST, (b) abbreviated PST (APST), and (c) a wait-list control. In addition to the BDI, the Hamilton Rating Scale for Depression (HRSD), a measure completed by two independent clinician raters, was used to assess depression. Both treatment conditions included 10, 2-hour therapy sessions conducted in groups by pairs of therapists counterbalanced by condition. Members of the PST condition received training in both the problem orientation and rational problem-solving skills components of the model. APST participants were provided with a similar package, with the exception of training in problem orientation. Individuals in the WLC condition were requested to wait until the program was able to accommodate them at a later date. In this manner, by conducting such a component analysis, the degree to which training in problem orientation actually contributes to a positive treatment outcome could be determined.

Pre-post analyses indicated that individuals in the PST condition were significantly less depressed at posttreatment, according to both the BDI and HRSD, as compared to the APST and WLC participants. Further, APST subjects reported significantly lower posttreatment depression scores than WLC participants. Decreases in depressive symptoms were also significantly correlated with increases in problem-solving ability. Further, these results were clinically significant using a metric whereby a *recovered* individual was defined as a treated subject (i.e., PST and APST participants) who had a posttreatment score two standard deviations beyond the mean of the dysfunctional population (i.e., untreated subjects or WLC participants). Specifically, following this approach, over 85% of PST subjects, 50% of APST participants, and only 9% of WLC subjects experienced clinically meaningful decreases in depressive symptoms as measured by the BDI. According to the HRSD, these percentages were found to be 79%, 50%, and 9%, respectively.

A 6-month follow-up assessment revealed no significant differences between posttreatment and follow-up scores for either treatment condition. In other words, the therapeutic benefits obtained by participants in both treatment conditions were maintained 6 months after completing treatment. In general, these overall results provide further support for the efficacy of PST for major depression, and they underscore the importance of including training in the problem-orientation component.

Continuing this line of research, Arean et al. (1993) applied the A. M. Nezu et al. (1989) intervention model of depression specific to an older population. Seventy-five individuals over the age of 55 years were randomly assigned to either PST, Reminiscence Therapy (RT), or a wait-list control (WLC) group. Both PST and RT conditions were conducted within a group format with one of three therapists who were trained in both treatment approaches. Each group met over 12 weekly sessions with each session lasting approximately 1.5 hours. Participants in the PST condition were trained in the PST model as contained in the A. M. Nezu et al. (1989) treatment manual. RT involved reviewing one's life history in order to gain perspective and satisfaction with major positive and negative life events, and it was based on a psychodynamic formulation that had previously received empirical support for its efficacy for geriatric depression.

Overall results indicated that participants in both therapy conditions were significantly less depressed on three differing measures of depression at posttreatment as compared to WLC individuals. Moreover, the effects found at posttreatment for PST and RT conditions were maintained

3 months after the completion of treatment. However, individuals in the PST condition reported significantly lower depression at posttreatment than RT participants on two of the three depression measures (i.e., HRSD and the Geriatric Depression Scale). Moreover, at posttreatment, a significantly greater proportion of individuals in the PST condition (88%), compared with participants in the RT (40%) and WLC (10%) groups, no longer met the diagnostic criteria for major depression.

Also focusing on a geriatric depressed population, Lopez and Mermelstein (1995) evaluated a cognitive-behavioral program that was designed to improve geriatric rehabilitation outcome. PST was considered a major component of their approach, although additional coping skills training strategies were used (e.g., increasing pleasant events, relaxation training). Because this treatment program took place in a hospital setting, ethical issues prevented these authors from conducting a well-controlled investigation (e.g., treatment versus no-treatment control). However, focusing on the 21 patients with elevated depression scores who completed this program, they reported that their cognitive-behavioral intervention led to significant decreases in depression scores by the time of discharge.

Alexopoulos, Raue, and Arean (2003) compared PST with supportive therapy (ST) with regard to a group of elderly individuals who were reliably diagnosed with major depression, but who also exhibited impairment in executive functioning (e.g., initiation, perseveration, response inhibition). Treatment occurred over a 12-week period. The mean age of the recruited sample was 74 years. Results indicated that PST was more effective than ST in engendering remission of depression, fewer posttreatment depressive symptoms, and less overall disability. In addition, using the Social Problem Solving Inventory (D'Zurilla & Nezu, 1990) to measure problem solving, further analyses indicated that a substantial reason that accounted for the reductions in depression and disability involved patients' improvement in two skill areas—generating alternatives and decision making.

Teri, Logsdon, Uomoto, and McCurry (1997) focused on individuals who were depressed and also diagnosed with Alzheimer's disease. Specifically, 72 patient-caregiver dyads were randomly assigned to one of four conditions and assessed at pretreatment, posttreatment, and at a 6-month follow-up. Two active behavioral treatments were investigated, one emphasizing increasing patient pleasant events and one emphasizing caregiver problem solving, and both were compared to an equal-duration "standard care" condition, as well as to a wait-list control. Participants in both active treatments showed significant improvement in depression and diagnostic status as compared to patients in the two control groups. These therapeutic gains were maintained at the 6-month follow-up assessment.

In addition, caregivers in each behavioral condition also showed significant improvement in their own depressive symptoms, whereas caregivers in the two other conditions did not.

Because depression is often treated or managed more often in the primary care sector rather than by mental health specialists, increased focus on this population has occurred during the past decade (Eisenberg, 1992). For example, in the United Kingdom, Mynors-Wallis, Gath, Lloyd-Thomas, and Tomlinson (1995) compared PST with an antidepressant medication regimen for the treatment of depression in a primary care population. Ninety-one adults with major depression were randomly assigned to PST, amitriptyline, or a drug placebo. In all three treatment conditions, participants were offered six or seven sessions lasting from 30 to 60 minutes over 3 months. Therapists included a psychiatrist and two general practitioners who were trained in PST and drug administration. For both "medication" conditions, both patients and therapists were unaware as to the accurate nature of the capsules.

In addition to the HRSD, two other outcome measures were employed—the BDI and a self-report measure of social functioning and adjustment. Results indicated that at 6 and 12 weeks posttreatment, the PST group was significantly less depressed on both measures of depression and more socially adjusted than the placebo group. No significant differences were found between the PST and amitriptyline conditions, suggesting the comparability in efficacy between the psychosocial intervention and drug treatment.

In a subsequent study also focusing on the treatment of major depression in primary care, Mynors-Wallis, Gath, Day, and Baker (2000) compared the following four treatment conditions: PST as provided by research general practitioners; PST as given by research practice nurses; antidepressant medication (either fluvoxamine or paroxetine) provided by research general practitioners; and a combined PST and medication package. Results indicated that patients in all four conditions showed clear improvement over the course of 12 weeks. The combined treatment of PST and antidepressant medication was found to be no more effective than either treatment alone. In addition, there was no difference in outcome irrespective of who delivered PST (i.e., physicians versus nurses).

Contrary to theoretical predictions, however, a subsequent analysis found that the PST implemented in this study did not lead to a greater resolution in the patients' perception of their problem severity in comparison with the drug treatment, nor did it engender a greater sense of mastery or self-control (Mynors-Wallis, 2002). The measure used to assess problem solving involved the Personal Questionnaire Rapid Scaling Technique. Patients were asked to specify three individual problems and then to respond to a series of paired adjectives asking "How much of a problem is . . . ?" In essence, based on a 10-point scale, patients provided ratings of the severity of their problems. In addition, the measure of self-control and sense of mastery was based on two questions that incorporated a 9-point Likert scale—"(1) I feel I have my life under control; and (2) I feel overwhelmed by events" (p. 1316). Close scrutiny of this evaluation approach suggests that these measures are of unknown psychometric properties, leading one to question the validity of Mynors-Wallis's conclusions. Moreover, he did not directly address changes in problem-solving ability, a more important mechanism of action to address. Last, the analytic approach used found no differences at posttreatment among the four conditions regarding these two measures, suggesting that these measures were less an evaluation of responsible independent mechanisms of action, but rather state dependent measures of depressed mood.

In addition to major depression, PST has also been the focus of study as a potentially effective treatment of dysthymia and minor depression in primary care. For example, the Treatment Effectiveness Project (Barrett et al., 1999) represents the first large-scale evaluation in the United States of PST for primary care (PST-PC). PST-PC is described as a collaborative treatment approach where a patient's symptoms are first identified and linked to various problems in living. Such problems are then defined and clarified, and attempts are made next to solve them in a structured manner (Hegel, Barrett, & Oxman, 2000). This project involved a multisite randomized clinical trial, whereby PST-PC was compared to paroxetine and placebo. Williams et al. (2000) described the results of this evaluation with specific regard to a group of 415 older primary care adults (i.e., older than 60 years). PST-PC was provided across six treatment sessions over 11 weeks. For both the paroxetine and placebo participants, the six visits, also over 11 weeks, included general support and symptom and adverse effects monitoring.

Results indicated that patients receiving the active medication showed greater symptom resolution than placebo patients. Whereas no differences at posttreatment were found between PST-PC and placebo patients, their symptoms improved more rapidly than placebo patients during the latter treatment weeks. With regard to patients diagnosed with minor depression, both the paroxetine and PST-PC conditions led to improved overall mental health functioning as compared to placebo participants, but only with regard to those individuals in the lowest tertile of baseline functioning. These authors concluded that both paroxetine and PST-PC showed moderate benefits for this population, but the benefits of the psychosocial treatment were fewer and had slower onset. In addition, it appeared that the PST-PC effects were more subject to site differences than those of the drug treatment.

Barrett et al. (2001) reported the results of the same trial, but with regard to its focus on 241 adults aged 18 to 59 years. This investigation was conducted in two of the four sites involved in the previous trial. Results indicated that all three treatment conditions led to a significant decline in depressive symptoms over the 11-week period, where no differences between interventions or by diagnosis were identified. However, the remission rates for dysthymia regarding the paroxetine and PST-PC conditions were significantly higher as compared to the placebo condition. The remission rates for patients with minor depression were similar across conditions. This suggests a differential effect as a function of diagnosis specific to remission rates, but not overall changes in depressive symptomatology. As such, the authors conclude that general clinical management ("watchful waiting") may be an appropriate treatment option.

PST, as adapted for implementation in community settings, was one of two interventions that were evaluated for treating various depressive disorders in a European-based, multisite project, entitled the Outcomes of Depression International Network (Dowrick et al., 2000). The second psychosocial treatment was a group psychoeducation program focused on the prevention of depression developed by Munoz et al. (1995). The 452 participants were initially identified through a community survey. Nine sites in Finland, Ireland, Norway, Spain, and the United Kingdom were involved. PST was provided across six individual sessions, whereas the educational programs were group administered across eight sessions. Both treatments were compared to a control condition. Results indicated that overall, the PST program was considered more acceptable than the course on prevention of depression. Outcomes at 6 months were positive for both treatment approaches, whereby compared to controls, treated individuals were less likely to remain as a case of depression and more likely to report improved mental and social functioning. However, participants in the PST condition were less likely to report depressive symptoms as compared to the other two conditions.

On a smaller scale, Lynch, Tamburrino, and Nagel (1997) compared PST (as outlined by A. M. Nezu et al., 1989) to a control condition with regard to 29 individuals diagnosed with minor depression emanating from various family physician practices. Six 20-minute PST sessions were provided and conducted over the telephone. Results indicated that at posttreatment, treated subjects were less depressed, and reported more improved social health, mental health, and self-esteem as compared to control participants. Contrary to these results, this same team found that a subsequent attempt to compare PST to a stress management and treatment-as-usual (TAU) control revealed no differences among the three conditions with regard to another sample of mildly depressed patients in primary care settings (Lynch, Tamburrino, Nagel, & Smith, 2004). Unfortunately, according to the authors, a high dropout rate across conditions created significant limitations in interpreting these results. However, similar to the logic of Barrett et al. (2001) as noted previously, because patients in the TAU condition also improved, these authors concluded that watchful waiting may be a reasonable approach to treating this particular population.

PST has also been included as the form of psychotherapy that is an inherent part of a collaborative care program that is combined with antidepressant medication for the treatment of late-life depression as experienced by primary care patients (Unutzer et al., 2001). The program, entitled IMPACT, involves meeting with a depression clinical specialist, who is supervised by both a psychiatrist and primary care physician, in order to support the treatment of depression of an elderly primary care patient for 12 months. A stepped-care protocol involves initially providing drug treatment or PST-PC depending on the choice of the patient. Treatments are switched (i.e., from medication to PST-PC or visa versa) or modified (e.g., change in antidepressant medication) if symptoms do not remit. If a patient is resistant to treatment, electroconvulsive therapy, inpatient treatment, or other services may be recommended. Although the randomized controlled trial designed to evaluate the efficacy of IMPACT was not able to assess the independent effects of PST-PC by itself due to the complex nature of the stepped care program, Unutzer et al. (2002) did find that overall, the IMPACT protocol, as compared to usual care control patients, led to significant reductions in baseline depressive symptoms, as well as less functional impairment and more improved quality of life.

SUICIDE AND SUICIDAL IDEATION

PST has also been systematically studied as a treatment for suicidal adults and adolescents. For example, Patsiokas and Clum (1985) compared PST to both a cognitive restructuring and nondirective control group regarding the treatment of psychiatric inpatients admitted for suicide attempts. Participants recorded instances of suicidal thoughts on a daily basis and participated in 10, 1-hour individual therapy sessions. Results indicated that changes in hopelessness and suicidal intention occurred for all three conditions. However, at posttreatment, only the PST condition was significantly different from the nondirective group regarding measures of hopelessness. In addition, only patients receiving PST demonstrated improved problem-solving ability as measured by the Means-End Problem-Solving procedure (MEPS).

Lerner and Clum (1990) compared PST to supportive therapy for 18 adults who were experiencing clinically significant suicidal ideations. Each treatment group consisted of 10 sessions lasting 1.5 hours per session during a 2-month period. Participants in the supportive group were taught active listening skills and shared their experiences regarding suicide. Assessments were conducted pretreatment, posttreatment, and at a 3-month follow-up and consisted of the MEPS, PSI, BDI, Hopelessness Scale (HS), and the UCLA Loneliness Scale. Results indicated that individuals in the PST condition rated the quality of treatment and therapists significantly higher as compared to the supportive therapy group. At posttreatment, PST individuals were found to be significantly less depressed than individuals in the supportive therapy group. At the 3-month follow-up, participants in the PST condition continued to be less depressed and were additionally less lonely and less hopeless than participants in the supportive therapy group. The authors concluded that both PST and supportive therapy approaches were effective in reducing suicidal ideation, but that PST was more effective for reducing depression and hopelessness, both being key risk factors for suicidal behavior.

Another study evaluated the efficacy of PST for patients at high risk of repeated suicide attempts (Salkovskis, Atha, & Storer, 1990). Twenty individuals ranging in age from 16 to 65 years who met at least two of the following criteria were included in the study: (a) made at least two previous suicide attempts, (b) took antidepressants as part of an overdose, and/or (c) scored at least 4 on a 6-point scale designed to predict repeated suicidal behavior. This information was obtained during a structured interview completed by a psychiatrist. Participants were randomly assigned to either PST or a control group, as defined by standard hospital treatment. A community psychiatric nurse, who had experience working with suicide attempters, provided PST to the participants in the experimental group. Treatment was begun during a 24-hour crisis intervention admission in a hospital for eight of the participants in the PST condition. Four other PST participants received treatment in their homes. Five treatment sessions, lasting 1 hour, were conducted at the time of the index suicide attempt, 1-week post-attempt, 2-weeks post-attempt, and 1-month post-attempt.

Posttreatment assessments were conducted at the participant's home 1-week, 1-month, 3-months, 6-months, and 1-year post-index suicide attempt. A structured interview that measured thoughts, plans, and attitudes related to future suicide attempts was performed at each posttreatment assessment. The participants also completed three self-report measures, the BDI, the HS, and the Profile of Mood States. In addition, at the first posttreatment assessment, a problem list was constructed in which all of the participant's current or impending problems were ranked in order of importance. It was found that PST participants were more hopeful, less fatigued, and less depressed, as measured by both of the self-report depression scales, than individuals in the control group. Furthermore, at 6-months post-attempt, significantly more individuals in the control group repeated a suicide attempt than individuals in the PST condition.

McLeavey, Daly, Ludgate, and Murray (1994) evaluated the effectiveness of PST with 39 adolescents and adults who had intentionally self-poisoned themselves. Individuals were randomly assigned to either a PST or control group. Treatment consisted of five individual 1-hour sessions conducted by professionals with extensive experience with self-poisoning individuals. The control condition was based on principles of crisis intervention. Results indicated that individuals who received PST had significantly more improved problem-solving abilities, more positive attitudes about problems, and higher self-esteem than individuals in the control condition at posttreatment. However, there were no significant differences regarding self-reported levels of hopelessness. At 6-months posttreatment, individuals who received PST had significantly better attitudes and self-concept about problems. There were no significant differences in the level of hopelessness at 6-months posttreatment.

SOCIAL PHOBIA

DiGiuseppe, Simon, McGowan, and Gardner (1990) compared PST to rational-emotive therapy, cognitive therapy, self-instructional training, and assertion training for the treatment of social anxiety. Seventy-nine adults were randomly assigned to the four treatment conditions or a wait-list control group. Treatment for all therapy conditions was conducted in a group format that met weekly for 10 weeks for 1.5-hour sessions with one of three therapists who were trained in each of the therapies. Each treatment consisted of an educational component, a skill acquisition and initial rehearsal component, skill consolidation, and a continued rehearsal component. Results indicated that participants in all of the therapy groups reported significantly less social avoidance and distress, less fear of negative evaluations, and diminished behavioral manifestations of anxiety at posttreatment, as compared to pretreatment. In addition, participants in all of the therapy groups, except the assertiveness training condition, reported significantly less generalized anxiety and depression at posttreatment. There were no significant differences regarding level of hostility or pulse rate among the treatment groups on any of the measures at posttreatment. Participants in the WLC condition reported no significant differences between pretreatment and posttreatment levels of social anxiety, general anxiety, depression, and behavioral measures. It was concluded that the four cognitive-behavioral treatment programs were equally effective for the treatment of social anxiety.

GENERALIZED ANXIETY DISORDER

PST has more recently been included as a major component of an overall cognitive-behavioral therapy package for the treatment of generalized anxiety disorder (GAD). Ladouceur, Dugas, Freeston, Gagnon, and Thibodeau (2000), for example, compared a GAD intervention that targeted intolerance of uncertainty, erroneous beliefs about worry, poor problem orientation, and cognitive avoidance to a delayed treatment control. Training in problem orientation was focused on dealing with worries that are amenable to problem solving by having patients remain focused on the problem and not pay undue attention to related minor details. Worries about situations not amenable to problem solving were treated with cognitive exposure in order to decrease the threatening nature of the worry itself. Results indicated that the CBT treatment package lead to both statistically and clinically significant changes at posttreatment and that these gains were maintained at 6- and 12-month follow-ups. Moreover, 20 of 26 treated patients no longer met diagnostic criteria following treatment.

Dugas et al. (2003) treated GAD by targeting intolerance of uncertainty via the reevaluation of positive beliefs about worry, cognitive exposure, and PST. Treatment consisted of 14 weekly, 2-hour group sessions and was compared to a wait-list control. PST in this study included training in both orientation and skills dimensions. Results indicated that the cognitive-behavioral intervention demonstrated significantly greater improvement on all dependent measures (i.e., self-report and clinician ratings of GAD symptoms, intolerance of uncertainty, anxiety, depression, and social adjustment) as compared to the control. Moreover, treated participants made further gains over the course of a 2-year follow-up period.

In an attempt to determine the efficacy of each of the two major treatment components of their GAD intervention, Provencher, Dugas, and Ladouceur (2004) more recently conducted a case replication series of 18 primary GAD patients who received 12 sessions of their cognitive-behavioral treatment. The therapy was individualized according to the main worries of a given patient. Specifically, PST was provided for worries concerning current problems, and cognitive exposure was applied to worries concerning hypothetical situations. Results indicated that both intervention strategies led to statistically significant improvements on all outcome measures and that over 73% of the patients met stringent criteria for clinical significance. Moreover, treatment gains were maintained at a 6-month follow-up. These authors concluded that each strategy was efficacious for GAD.

POSTTRAUMATIC STRESS DISORDER (PTSD)

McDonagh et al. (2005) recently conducted a clinical trial to evaluate a CBT approach for the treatment of chronic PTSD in adult female survivors of childhood sexual abuse. The CBT package included prolonged exposure, in vivo exposure, and cognitive restructuring, and was compared to both a "present-centered therapy" (PCT) approach, which included psychoeducation, journal writing, and problem-solving training, and a wait-list control. Results indicated that both the CBT and PCT interventions were more effective than the control across several measures of posttraumatic and related symptomatology. Specifically, both treatments engendered marked improvements in PTSD symptom severity, state anxiety, and trauma-related cognitive schemas, all of which displayed little change for control participants. The CBT intervention was found to be superior to the PCT in achieving remission from the PTSD diagnosis at follow-up, but this difference was not found either for completers or "intent-to-treat" analyses at posttreatment. In fact, the two active treatments did not differ significantly at any assessment point on any other outcome measure, including PTSD severity. Moreover, the CBT condition had a significantly greater dropout rate than the PCT group.

DISTRESSED COUPLES

Cognitive-behavioral approaches to treating distressed couples and marital therapy have generally involved both behavior-exchange procedures and training in communication/problem-solving skills (e.g., Jacobson & Margolin, 1979). Early studies, in general, underscored the promise of this overall approach in helping couples in distress (e.g., Jacobson, 1978). In an attempt to determine the relative contributions of each of these two major components, Jacobson (1984) compared a treatment package that included both sets of strategies with each component presented alone: behavior exchange (BE) and communication/problem-solving training (CPT). Participants included 33 married couples who were randomly assigned to one of four conditions: (a) BE, (b) CPT, (c) BE + CPT, or (d) wait-list control. Treatment involved 12 to 16 sessions. Dependent measures included global marital satisfaction, problem checklists, and spouse reports of behavior at home. Results at posttest indicated that the three active treatments were equally effective in improving marital satisfaction and reducing presenting problems. At the 6-month follow-up, however, 44% of the BE couples reversed their progress, whereas virtually all couples receiving CPT—either alone or in conjunction with BE—generally maintained their treatment gains or continued to improve.

In a later report, Jacobson and Follette (1985) presented data from an additional 24 couples. In terms of marital satisfaction, differences between groups began to emerge at the 6-month follow-up. BE couples deteriorated in marital satisfaction again at very high rates, whereas deterioration was rare among CPT and BE + CPT couples. Moreover, some of the couples in both these conditions continued to improve from posttest to follow-up, whereas none of the BE couples improved. Collectively, these studies underscored the clinical importance of training in communications and problem solving.

Johnson and Greenberg (1985) compared PST to an emotionally focused therapy (EFT) and a wait-list control. In the EFT approach, couples are helped to recognize negative interaction patterns and encouraged to express more primary emotions, such as fear of abandonment and need for attachment, that may have been suppressed. Both treatments were administered in eight sessions. Whereas both treatments significantly improved the quality of the dyadic relationships, the effects of EFT were superior to the problem-solving intervention regarding marital adjustment, intimacy, and target complaint level. At follow-up, marital adjustment scores for the EFT participants were still significantly higher than those in the PST condition.

Kaiser, Hahlweg, Fehm-Wolfsdorf, and Groth (1998) conducted a study to investigate the efficacy of a cognitive-behavioral program for married couples that was preventive in nature. Participants responded to newspaper announcements indicating that the program was intended not as marital therapy but to assist couples before problems actually developed. The program included communication and problem-solving training, couples' discussions to clarify relationship expectations, and exercises to enhance their sexual relationship. Results indicated that, compared to a wait-list control, treated couples emitted more positive verbal and nonverbal communication behaviors on a role-play task, displayed less negative communication behaviors, and reported significantly less relationship problem areas. At a 1-year follow-up, intervention couples reported fewer problem areas in comparison to baseline levels.

PARENT-CHILD PROBLEMS

PST has also been used to help parents of children with behavioral or psychological problems. Pfiffner, Jouriles, Brown, Etscheidt, and Kelly (1990) assessed the effects of PST as an adjunctive treatment addressing non-child-related problems for 11 single mothers of noncompliant or aggressive children. The mothers were randomly assigned to either a parent training or parent training + PST condition. Mothers in both conditions had eight weekly 90-minute individual sessions. Individuals in the parent-training condition were taught basic operant child management skills (e.g., increasing adaptive behavior through positive attention and rewards; decreasing inappropriate behaviors by ignoring and negative consequences; reducing inappropriate behavior by changing antecedents).

Assessments were conducted pretreatment, posttreatment, and at a 4-month follow-up. The mothers completed the Achenbach Child Behavior Checklist, which assesses child behavior problems, competencies, and appropriate behavior. An observational measure of deviant child behavior was obtained during a 5-minute cleanup period. Results indicated that mothers in both treatment conditions reported decreases in externalizing behavior problems at posttreatment and follow-up. In addition, there were significant reductions in observations of deviant child behavior for individuals in the parent training + PST condition, but not for families in the parent-training only condition. Furthermore, mothers in the parent training + PST condition reported significantly fewer child behavior problems at follow-up relative to mothers in the other group.

Spaccarelli, Cotler, and Penman (1992) evaluated the efficacy of PST as an adjunct to parenting-skills training in a group program for parents who self-referred based on concerns regarding child behavior problems. Fifty-three parents were randomly assigned to either parent training plus PST, parent training plus extra discussion, or a wait-list control condition. Both treatment conditions received the same 10-hour program of parent training. The PST adjunct component involved an additional six hours of training in problem solving. The extra discussion component served as a legitimate attention placebo in that it involved 6 hours of therapist-led discussions of how parents could apply the skills they learned to actual problem behaviors they were encountering.

At posttreatment, participants in both treatment conditions demonstrated significant improvements in parenting behaviors. However, recipients of the additional training in problem solving, as compared to their control counterparts, reported significantly larger reductions in the intensity of their child behavior problems. In addition, only the PST training participants were associated with significant improvements in parent attitudes concerning their child's adjustment, as well as their own functioning as parents. Treatment gains were maintained for both conditions at a 4–6 month follow-up, but no differences between them were identified. This last set of results, however, is difficult to interpret due to high levels of attrition regarding follow-up assessment attendance.

PARENT AND FAMILY CAREGIVERS

Due to the significant distress and levels of burden often experienced by family caregivers of persons with medical problems, PST has also been evaluated as a potentially effective alternative for this population (C. M. Nezu, Palmatier, & Nezu, 2005). For example, Gendron, Poitras, Dastoor, and Pérodeau (1996) conducted an investigation comparing a CBT group intervention to a support group for informal caregivers of patients with dementia. The CBT groups focused on assertion, problem-solving, and cognitive restructuring, whereas the support group emphasized information giving and social exchanges between participants. Both programs lasted for 8 weeks. Results indicated that the only positive benefit accrued from the CBT program, relative to the support group, involved the increased ability to be assertive with one's extended family network.

Focusing on family caregivers of physically or cognitively impaired older adults, Gallagher-Thompson et al. (2000) compared PST to a program geared to increase pleasant events (Life Satisfaction Class) and a wait-list control with regard to reducing depression and feelings of burden. Both active treatments were conducted in a classroom format and met weekly for 10 weeks for 2 hours each time. Results indicated that both treatments engendered significant improvement as compared to the wait-list control. Few differences were identified between the two classes with the exception of the superiority of the Life Satisfaction class over PST with specific regard to depression status (i.e., change in diagnostic status).

Zarit, Anthony, and Boutselis (1987) reported that two intervention groups that included social problem-solving training components demonstrated improvements in caregiver burden and psychiatric symptoms, but these results were not significantly greater than the outcomes for caregivers in a wait-list group. However, a reanalysis of this study revealed that both intervention groups were more effective than the wait-list group in reducing caregiver distress in each of the areas studied (Whitlatch, Zarit, & von Eye, 1991).

Roberts et al. (1999) reported that caregivers of individuals with dementia who were trained in problem-solving skills did not significantly improve on measures of distress, psychosocial adjustment to the patient's illness, or caregiver burden during the 6-month and 1-year follow-up periods. However, the majority of caregivers (i.e., 92%) rated the counseling program as very helpful. In addition, a smaller subset of caregivers that revealed greater deficits in many logical analysis problem-solving skills at baseline measurement, but who went through the problem-solving counseling, did report less psychological distress and greater psychosocial adjustment at the 1-year follow-up period. These mixed results may suggest that PST can be especially useful for individuals who reveal greater problem-solving deficits and high distress levels at baseline.

Grant, Elliott, Weaver, Bartolucci, and Giger (2002) compared PST, a sham intervention, and a control with regard to 74 caregivers of individuals who suffered a stroke. PST in this study consisted of an initial 3-hour home visit between a trained nurse and the family caregiver within 1 week after discharge. This was followed by weekly (the first month) and biweekly (the second and third months) telephone contacts over a period of 12 weeks. Family caregivers assigned to the sham intervention received the same number of weekly and biweekly telephone contacts. Participants were simply asked to identify professional and skilled health services the stroke survivor received since the last contact.

Results indicated that compared with the sham and control conditions, family caregivers receiving PST training had better problem-solving skills, greater caregiver preparedness, less depression, and significant improvements in measures of vitality, social functioning, mental health, and role limitations related to emotional problems. However, no differences were found among the groups regarding caregiver burden. Satisfaction with health care services was found to decrease over time for control participants, while remaining comparable in the two treatment groups.

Wade, Wolfe, Brown, and Pestian (2005) focused on families of children who suffered moderate to severe traumatic brain injury and recently reported preliminary efficacy results regarding a Web-based family problem-solving intervention geared to improve parent and child adaptation. In this open trial, eight parents and six children participated in the intervention. Families were provided with computers, Web cameras, and high speed Internet access. Therapists conducted weekly videoconferences with the families after they completed self-guided Web exercises regarding problem solving, communication, and antecedent behavior management strategies. Pre-post results revealed significant improvements in injury-related burden, parental psychiatric symptoms, depression, and parenting stress. In addition, although no significant improvement was found among the children regarding self-reported depression, there was a significant decrease in antisocial behaviors in the injured child.

PRIMARY CARE PATIENTS

In addition to applying PST to treat both major and minor depression among primary care patients, such approaches have also been applied to treat other psychological and physical problems experienced by persons initially seen in primary care settings. For example, Catalan, Gath, Bond, Day, and Hall (1991) conducted a randomized clinical trial in a general practice setting that included 47 patients with recent onset emotional disorders of poor prognosis as determined by a standardized psychiatric interview (e.g., Present State Examination). These patients were randomly assigned to either a 4-session PST protocol conducted by a psychiatrist, or a control group wherein the general practitioner was allowed to provide any type of treatment of choice, whether psychological, social, pharmacological, a combination of these, or nothing at all. Although both conditions led to significant improvements in psychiatric symptomatology, the improvement was significantly better in the PST group than in the control group, both at the end of treatment and at a 16-week follow-up period.

Wilkinson and Mynors-Wallis (1994) conducted a noncontrolled study that combined PST with reattribution techniques in the treatment of 11 patients presenting in a primary care setting with unexplained physical symptoms. Results from this pilot investigation indicated that PST for this population was both feasible to deliver and acceptable to patients. Moreover, patients were found to experience a significant reduction in their overall psychiatric morbidity.

In a subsequent investigation, Mynors-Wallis, Davies, Gray, Barbour, and Gath (1997) assessed whether community nurses could serve as PST therapists in treating emotional disorders in primary care. Seventy patients with an emotional disorder were randomly assigned to one of two treatment conditions: (a) PST with a trained nurse, and (b) treatment as usual from a general practitioner. Interview and self-report assessments of psychiatric symptomatology, general health, social adjustment, and quality of life were conducted at pretreatment, 8-weeks, and 26-weeks posttreatment. Results revealed no significant differences in general clinical outcome between the two conditions, but patients receiving PST had fewer disability days and fewer days off from work. It should be noted that, although this study was not intended to specifically compare PST with a psychopharmacological intervention, in essence, because many of the patients in the standard care group received medications (e.g., antidepressants), given the lack of differences between both groups, it can be concluded that PST was as effective in some cases as drug therapy for this population.

PERSONS WITH MENTAL RETARDATION

As a means of improving the social competence of 33 moderately and mildly retarded adults, Castles and Glass (1986) compared the relative effectiveness of PST, social skills training (SST), and a combined PST + SST approach. The three treatment groups met twice weekly for 15, 1-hour sessions. Results indicated that, compared to a control group, SST subjects improved in social skills, PST participants improved in problem solving, and subjects receiving problem-solving training in the two conditions also improved on a measure of personal-social responsibility. However, generalization effects were found to be limited.

The effects of group anger management training with 54 mildly retarded adults were evaluated by Benson, Rice, and Miranti (1986). Four self-control-based training protocols were compared: relaxation training, self-instruction, PST, and a combined program. Results analyzing various self-report measures, videotaped role-plays, and supervisor ratings indicated that all four programs yielded significant decreases in aggressive responding with no between-group differences.

Tymchuk, Andron, and Rahbar (1988), using a multiple baseline design, provided nine mothers with mental retardation with training in decision-making skills using vignettes describing child-raising situations. Results indicated that the identification and use of specific decision-making aids in both trained and untrained situations were significantly improved as a result of the group training protocol.

Assessing the social validation and generalization of problem-solving skills training with mildly mentally retarded adults, Foxx, Kyle, Faw, and Bittle (1989) compared three experimental subjects with three control participants. Experimental subjects received baseline, training, probes, and pre-post training generalization evaluations, whereas control subjects received only the pre-post training assessments. Results indicated that (a) specific training led to increases in the participants' verbal problem-solving skills when given cues, and (b) this improvement persisted when the cues were eliminated, indicating that generalization occurred.

C. M. Nezu and colleagues (1991) compared PST with assertiveness training for 28 adults diagnosed with mental retardation, as well as having a second diagnosis of an anxiety, schizophrenic, adjustment, impulse-control, or personality disorder. Subjects were randomly assigned to either problem solving/assertiveness (PS-A), assertiveness/problem solving (A-PS), or a WLC condition. Participants in the PS-A condition received five weekly 1-hour sessions of PST followed by five weekly 1-hour sessions of assertiveness training. Members in the A-PS condition received assertiveness training first, followed by PST. Assertiveness training focused on substituting aggressive behavior with assertive behavior, which included voice intensity and quality, latency and duration of response, eye contact, body language, and listening ability. PST was based on the format of A. M. Nezu and colleagues' (1989) treatment manual adapted for a developmentally disabled population.

Assessments were conducted pretreatment, mid-phase, posttreatment, and at a 3-month follow-up. Participants completed a self-report inventory of current psychological symptoms, a behavioral task designed to measure problem-solving ability, a measure that assessed behavioral responding to situations that serve as a stimulus for underassertive or aggressive behavior, and a measure of subjective distress. In addition, each participant's caregiver assessed overall adaptive functioning at pre- and posttreatment. Results indicated that at mid-phase, individuals in both treatment conditions reported significantly less psychological distress symptoms, as well as higher levels of assertive behavior. These changes were found to be equivalent between conditions. Further, also at mid-phase, it was found that individuals in the PS-A condition had significantly improved their problem-solving abilities, whereas participants in A-PS condition did not.

Analyses focused on mid-phase to posttreatment changes revealed that participants in both of the treatment conditions did not have additional changes in levels of distress, psychological symptoms, or assertive behavior. However, individuals in the A-PS condition were found to have significantly improved their problem-solving abilities since mid-phase. Further, no changes in psychiatric symptoms, assertiveness, and problem-solving ability were found to occur for individuals in the WLC at either mid-phase or posttreatment. It was also found that individuals in both treatment conditions had improved their overall level of adaptive functioning at posttreatment, as rated by their caregivers, with no differences emerging between the two groups. WLC subjects did not show changes during this time. Results from the 3-month follow-up indicated that treatment gains were maintained for both experimental conditions across all measures. Thus, the results indicate that PST can be adapted for a population that is cognitively limited and does not require the learner to possess superior, or even average, intellectual abilities.

Cunningham, Davis, Bremner, Dunn, and Rzasa (1993) compared a coping modeling/problem-solving training program to a mastery modeling program for 50 staff members from group homes for developmentally handicapped adolescents and young adults. Each staff member identified a resident for whom he or she had primary responsibility and whose guardian consented to the study. The staff-resident pairs were randomly assigned to one of the two training programs or a wait-list control group. Each training program lasted for 12 weeks. In the coping modeling/PST condition, the participants identified staff errors depicted in videotaped demonstrations, discussed consequences and alternatives, and formulated rationales supporting the solutions. Participants in the mastery modeling program learned new strategies didactically through videotaped demonstrations of models correctly executing the new skills.

Participants in the two training programs spent an equal amount of time in each 2-hour session reviewing homework, observing the same video-tapes, role-playing, and formulating homework projects. Compared to the coping modeling/PST participants, the mastery model participants were late to more sessions, had a greater decline in group attendance, completed less homework, used more noncompliant verbalizations in-session, had lower personal accomplishment on the job, and were less satisfied with their training program.

Loumidis and Hill (1997) evaluated the effects of PST on maladaptive behavior and specific problem-solving skills in 29 adults with intellectual disabilities. Thirteen of these adults resided in a hospital for people with intellectual disabilities and 16 of them lived in the community. The study also included an untrained control group that were matched with the trained subjects on age, intellectual ability, and degree of maladaptive behavior. Problem-solving skills were assessed using a structured interview format in which subjects were asked to respond to hypothetical problems. The hospital group received 23 training sessions lasting 40 minutes, whereas the community group received 15, 1-hour sessions. The results showed that the trained community group, but not the trained hospital group, improved significantly more than the control group on degree of maladaptive behavior as rated by independent judges and several problem-solving skills, including measures of means-ends thinking, evaluative checking and decision making, and effectiveness of solutions. Although the two trained groups were matched on intellectual ability and degree of maladaptive behavior, the hospital group was significantly older and had lower adaptive functioning than both the trained community group and the control group.

STRESS MANAGEMENT

D'Zurilla and Maschka (1988) conducted a preliminary study in which the PST approach to stress management was compared to a social support intervention. Participants included 27 high-stressed, middle-aged community residents who were randomly assigned to either PST or Supportive Communication Training (SCT). Each intervention was conducted in group formats and involved 14 weekly sessions lasting approximately 1.5 hours each. SCT was based on two forms of support: socio-emotional aid (e.g., empathetic understanding, warmth) and informational aid (e.g., advice, factual information). In this approach, the therapist provided both forms of support, as well as training participants in the mutual exchange of support. At posttreatment, the PST group showed a significantly greater reduction than the SCT group on a measure of psychological stress, as well as significantly greater increases in problem-solving ability, self-esteem, and life satisfaction. These effects were maintained at a 6-month follow-up assessment. In addition, new significant differences emerged in favor of the PST group on measures of personal problems and psychological symptomatology. Moreover, increases in problem-solving ability in the PST group were found to be significantly related to improvement on several outcome measures, which supports the theory underlying PST.

INEFFECTIVE COPING/COPING ENHANCEMENT

PST has also been evaluated as a means to enhance overall general coping. Heppner, Baumgardner, Larson, and Petty (1988), for example, conducted a study that evaluated the utility of an 8-week PST program. Specifically, 40 undergraduate college students were randomly assigned to either a PST or delayed treatment control. Results indicated that the PST program was effective at enhancing students' appraisal of their overall problem-solving abilities. Moreover, these changes were maintained at a 1-year follow-up assessment. Training appeared to be most effective for individuals who initially were characterized as having limited problem solving.

Wege and Möller (1995) evaluated the effectiveness of a PST program with a group of 27 South African undergraduate students. Initially, a group of 13 individuals were identified as ineffective problem solvers according to their scores on a problem-solving task that measured the quality of choices made by subjects in specific problem situations. They then underwent eight sessions of group PST of 50 minutes each. Simultaneously, a group of 16 subjects were identified as effective problem solvers and constituted the "no treatment control." Results indicated that PST led to improved general self-efficacy expectancies, greater confidence in problem-solving ability, a more internal locus of control orientation, and improved problem-solving skills. These improvements were further maintained at a 2-month follow-up.

SUBSTANCE ABUSE

Carey, Carey, and Meisler (1990) compared PST to a control group for individuals diagnosed with an alcohol-related disorder, polysubstance-related or cannabis-related disorder, who had also received an additional diagnosis of a mood disorder, schizophrenia, anxiety, adjustment, or delusional disorder. The 18 participants were individuals from a day treatment program for mentally ill chemical abusers who were randomly assigned to treatment condition. The control group received the standard day treatment protocol. Individuals in the treatment group received PST, which met for 1-hour sessions twice per week for 6 weeks, in addition to the standard protocol. Contrary to the hypothesis, no significant differences were found between the two groups on any of the measures at either posttreatment or follow-up regarding self-reported stress and problem-solving ability.

Platt, Husband, Hermalin, Carter, and Metzger (1993) applied PST to individuals with opioid-related disorders. The PST approach specifically focused on job training designed to help methadone patients resolve their vocational problems. Similar to the D'Zurilla and Nezu (1982) approach, the PST intervention used here was based on a model developed by Platt and colleagues and entailed problem recognition, generation of alternatives, assessment of likely consequences, using a stepwise process to reach goals, understanding causal sequences and relationships, and taking other people's perspectives in a problem situation. Participants were randomly assigned to either the PST or control group. Individuals in the control group received the standard methadone treatment provided at their clinic. PST subjects received the standard services in addition to 10 weekly PST group sessions. Results indicated that PST participants had a significant increase in rate of employment at posttreatment and at a 6-month follow-up. Moreover, at follow-up, the PST group had a significantly higher employment rate as compared to the control group. Unfortunately, at a 12-month follow-up, participants in the problem-solving group showed a significant decline in employment rate.

OFFENDERS

Training in social problem-solving skills has been a component of several different programs geared to decrease recidivism rates among a variety of offender populations for the past several decades, both in Europe and in the United States (McMurran & McGuire, 2005). This is based in part on the empirical literature that has identified links between social problem solving and aggression (Keltikangas-Järvinen, 2005), as well as with personality disorders (Dreer, Jackson, & Elliott, 2005; McMurran, Egan, & Duggan, 2005). In addition, studies have found specific problem-solving deficits among groups of offenders (Antonowicz & Ross, 2005) as noted in chapter 7.

One such program is the *Reasoning and Rehabilitation* (R&R) program developed by Ross, Fabiano, and Ross (1986). It is estimated that R&R has been delivered to more than 50,000 offenders in 17 different countries and most states in the United States (Antonowicz, 2005). R&R is a multifaceted program, including training in social problem solving, designed to teach offenders social cognitive skills and values that are essential for prosocial competence. Although the program has evolved throughout the years, a current manual exists comprised of 35 group administered sessions, each 2 hours in length (Ross & Ross, 1995).

The first empirical evaluation of the R&R program in reducing recidivism was conducted with a high-risk population of adult male probationers in Canada (Ross, Fabiano, & Ewles, 1988). Participants were randomly assigned to one of three conditions: regular probation, regular probation plus life skills training, and regular probation plus R&R training. Results indicated that only 18% of the R&R recipients were convicted of an offense during a 9-month follow-up period from program entry, as compared to 48% for the life skills group and 70% for the regular probation only control. Moreover, none of the R&R subjects were incarcerated upon conviction whereas such rates for the life skills group was 11% and 30% for the control group.

Since this evaluation, there have been numerous attempts to assess the efficacy of the R&R program. Antonowicz (2005) has identified 22 such evaluations that have taken place in both institutional and community settings. Although the majority of these studies point to positive results for the R&R program, as a group, they vary in their methodological rigor. Moreover, it is difficult to determine the actual contribution that PST actually makes regarding offender improvement in comparison to the other therapy components.

Think First is another offender treatment program that relies heavily on PST as a major intervention component. The major aspects of Think First include problem-solving training, self-management training, social interaction training, and values education. The overall goal of Think First is to help individuals acquire, develop, and apply a series of social problem-solving and allied skills that will enable them to manage difficulties in their lives, as well as help them avoid future reoffenses (McGuire, 2005). Currently, two programs exist—one implemented in probation and other community corrections settings and one applied in prisons and mental health settings for incarcerated offenders. The first program entails four pregroup sessions, three conducted on an individual basis and one as an introductory group meeting. This is followed by 22, 2-hour group sessions and six individual postgroup sessions. The prison version involves 30, 2-hour group meetings.

Unfortunately, because of the inherent difficulties in conducting such research with this population (e.g., a community's intolerance of having offenders in "no treatment control" conditions), there are no randomized controlled trials of the Think First program as implemented in either community (i.e., probation) or institutional (i.e., prison) settings. As McGuire (2005) notes, it is more likely that probation programs using this approach use quasiexperimental designs. For example, McGuire and Hatcher (2001) provide pre-post data for 225 offenders who completed the program in probation settings. Significant improvements were identified regarding problems, criminal attitudes, impulsivity, self-esteem, and empathy. Whereas other similar program evaluation studies regarding both the short-term and follow-up are generally positive and encouraging, the program's efficacy has yet to be demonstrated within the context of a methodologically well-controlled study.

Stop & Think is a program that has adopted the D'Zurilla and Nezu (1999) treatment model specifically for personality disordered offender inpatients (McMurran & Duggan, 2005; McMurran, Fyffe, McCarthy, Duggan, & Latham, 2001). This program is based on the notion that personality disorder is partially a function of interpersonal problem-solving deficits (e.g., McMurran, Egan, Blair, & Richardson, 2001). An overarching problem-solving strategy is taught by having patients ask the following six questions when confronted with a problem: (1) Bad feelings? (2) What's my problem? (3) What do I want? (4) What are my options? (5) What is my plan? and (6) How am I doing? Stop & Think is currently being evaluated, but initial pilot data, based on nine male patients, indicate statistically significant improvement in patients' overall problem-solving ability, as measured by the SPSI-R (McMurran et al., 2005).

Based on both clinical experience and research findings that point to problem-solving deficits among various populations of sexual offenders (C. M. Nezu et al., 2005; C. M. Nezu, D'Zurilla, & Nezu, 2005; C. M. Nezu, Fiore, & Nezu, in press; C. M. Nezu, Greenberg, & Nezu, in press), *Project CBT* (for cognitive-behavior therapy) was developed in Philadelphia, Pennsylvania, by C. M. Nezu, Nezu, and colleagues (2003). This research project represents a randomized controlled trial of PST for sex offenders who are on parole for having committed a sexual offense. Participants are initially randomly assigned to one of two conditions: (1) Group PST conducted over 20, 1.5-hour group sessions, or (2) a wait-list control. The pool of subjects are those sex offenders released from prison and on parole and required to engage in some form of follow-up counseling. Because of the natural limited resources available in the greater Philadelphia area for sex-offender treatment, it is typical for individuals to be on some type of waiting list for services, thus eliminating community concerns about sex offenders not being in treatment. At the end of the 20 sessions, those receiving group PST are then further randomly assigned to one of two additional conditions—no further treatment contact (patients are told to apply problem solving to their daily lives during this time) or 10 additional booster sessions with a buddy (i.e., another program participant) and therapist in order to practice problem solving in a structured and more individualized format. Assessment occurs at baseline, 20 weeks, 30 weeks, and 3 months posttreatment. Results regarding the efficacy of PST, as well as the added value of booster sessions, await final data collection and analysis.

HIV/AIDS PREVENTION

Kelly et al. (1994) focused on a group of 197 women designated high-risk for HIV (e.g., multiple sex partners, diagnosed sexually transmitted disease, unprotected sex with high-risk male partner) seen in an urban primary health care clinic. They were randomly assigned to one of two treatment groups: (a) a cognitive-behavioral HIV/AIDS intervention that included skills training in condom use, sexual assertiveness training, problem solving, self-management, and peer support; and (b) a comparison group that involved health education on topics such as nutrition and healthy meal preparation. Results indicated that at a 3-month follow-up, women undergoing the HIV/AIDS intervention were found to significantly improve with regard to sexual communication and negotiation skills. In addition, unprotected sexual intercourse declined significantly and condom use increased from 26% to 56% of all intercourse interactions. Women in the comparison group showed no change.

OBESITY AND WEIGHT-CONTROL PROBLEMS

Black (1987) evaluated the efficacy of a weight-control program that consisted of a minimal intervention, followed by a PST program for weight control. Participants included seven moderately obese women. The minimal intervention consisted of verbal instructions regarding nutrition, physical activity, gradual weight loss, and self-monitoring of weight and calories consumed and expended. The duration of this intervention varied for different subjects, ranging from 6 weeks to 12 weeks. The PST program involved 20, 2-hour sessions over a 10-week period. Major findings of this investigation were: (a) weight loss increased dramatically during the PST program compared to the minimal-intervention program; (b) weight loss was variable during minimal intervention, but very homogeneous during PST; (c) weight loss continued after treatment, with six subjects losing weight by the 3-month follow-up and three subjects continuing to lose weight by the 12-month follow-up; (d) clinically significant weight losses occurred for five subjects; and (e) greater weight loss was associated with better problem-solving ability and less frequent problems.

In a further study, Black and Threlfall (1986) evaluated the efficacy of a stepped approach to weight control. In this approach, treatment began with a minimal intervention with more intensive procedures added for particular subjects as needed. In this investigation, such a procedure involved a home-study bibliotherapy program based on the same problem-solving procedure used in the previous study. This investigation focused on 26 moderately obese subjects and their partners who helped with the home-study PST program. The minimal-intervention program was introduced first; if subjects were not losing weight, the PST program was added. It was necessary to add the PST program for 22 of the 26 subjects. The duration of the program was 1 year, after which there was a 3-month follow-up evaluation.

Results showed that the subjects substantially decreased in weight and percentage overweight by the end of the 1-year program and maintained the improvement at follow-up. Six subjects reached ideal weight by the 3-month follow-up and nine subjects were in the acceptable range for body-mass index. Overall, subjects lost an average of 22.1 pounds by the 3-month follow-up. An important additional finding was that subjects who complied well with the requirements of the PST program lost significantly more weight than those who complied poorly.

PST served as the framework within which social support was incorporated into a maintenance package in a series of investigations by Perri and his colleagues (e.g., Perri & Nezu, 1992) geared to prevent weight loss relapse. For example, Perri and colleagues (1987) tested two differing maintenance programs: (a) a peer-support group that used a problem-solving approach within the context of a self-help group; and (b) a protocol where therapists directed patients' use of problem-solving strategies to cope with difficulties with weight-loss maintenance. Results indicated that the therapist-led program was superior to the peer-support group and a control condition. The importance of including therapist-led problem-solving groups as part of a maintenance program was further supported in a subsequent investigation by Perri and colleagues (1988). Collectively, these studies led Perri and his colleagues to develop a continuous-care/problem-solving model of obesity management whereby obesity is conceptualized as a chronic disorder necessitating long-term and continuous care that focuses on the solving of weight-related problems (Perri, Nezu, & Viegener, 1992).

Beyond applying PST as the major treatment modality to decrease psychological distress and improve functioning, it has also been used as an adjunct to foster the effectiveness of other behavioral intervention strategies. For example, Perri and colleagues (2001) hypothesized that

PST would be an effective means by which to foster improved adherence to a behavioral weight loss intervention by helping subjects to overcome various barriers to adherence such as scheduling difficulties, completing homework assignments, or the interference of psychological distress. More specifically, after completing 20 weekly group sessions of standard behavioral treatment for obesity, 80 women were randomly assigned to one of three conditions: (a) no further contact (BT only); (b) relapse prevention training; and (c) PST. At the end of 17 months, no differences in overall weight loss were observed between relapse prevention and BT-only or between relapse prevention and PST. However, PST participants had significantly greater long-term weight reductions than BT-only participants, and a significantly larger percentage of PST participants achieved clinically significant losses of 10% or more in body weight than did BT-only members (approximately 35% versus 6%). As such, these findings suggest that PST can be an effective adjunctive treatment to enhance adherence to other treatment modalities (see also A. M. Nezu & Nezu, in press, b).

MEDICAL PATIENTS

PST has been used with medical patients with different kinds of medical conditions to help them cope more effectively with the symptoms and problems associated with their illnesses and its treatment (e.g., chemotherapy for cancer patients). The goals of therapy are to facilitate recovery from the illness, reduce emotional distress, and increase quality of life.

Back Pain

Recent research has identified a strong association between problem-orientation variables and levels of functional disability among persons experiencing low back pain (LBP). For example, van den Hout, Vlaeyen, Heuts, Stillen, and Willen (2001) found that a negative orientation toward problems was associated with higher levels of functional disability in persons with LBP. In addition, Shaw, Feuerstein, Haufler, Berkowitz, and Lopez (2001), using the SPSI-R, found low scores on the positive orientation scale and high scores on impulsivity/carelessness and avoidant style scales to be correlated with functional loss in LBP patients. Based on such findings, van den Hout, Vlaeyen, Heuts, Zijlema, and Wijen (2003) evaluated whether PST (based on the A. M. Nezu, 1986c, protocol for depression) provided a significant supplemental value to a behavioral graded activity protocol in treating patients with nonspecific low back pain with regard to work-related disability. Their results indicated that in the second half-year after the intervention, patients receiving both graded activity and problem solving (GAPS) had significantly fewer days of sick leave than their counterparts who received graded activity plus group education (GAGE). Further, work status was more favorable for the GAPS participants in that more employees had a 100% return-to-work and fewer patients received disability pensions 1-year posttreatment. These results point to the potential efficacy of PST as a secondary prevention strategy.

Hypertension

García-Vera, Labrador, and Sanz (1997) combined PST with education and relaxation training for the treatment of essential hypertension. Overall, compared to participants comprising a wait-list control condition, treated patients were found at posttreatment to have significantly lowered blood pressure. These positive results were further found to be maintained at a 4-month follow-up assessment. Whereas studies evaluating the efficacy of a treatment package cannot provide data specific to any of the included intervention components, a subsequent analysis of their outcome data (García-Vera, Sanz, & Labrador, 1998) revealed that reductions in both systolic and diastolic blood pressure were significantly correlated with improvements in problem solving as measured by the SPSI-R. Moreover, problem solving was found to mediate the antihypertensive effects of their overall stress management protocol, suggesting that PST was at the very least an important and active treatment ingredient.

Head-Injured Adults

Foxx, Martella, and Marchand-Martella (1989) tested a PST-based protocol with six closed head-injured adults, ranging in age from 24 to 31 years. Training focused on four general areas: (a) community awareness and transportation; (b) medication, alcohol, and drugs; (c) asserting one's rights; and (d) emergencies, injuries, and safety. Three patients were in an experimental condition that included baseline, problem-solving training, probes, and pre-posttraining generalization evaluations. The second three participants served as controls and only underwent the pre-posttraining assessments. The 6-month posttraining results indicated that the experimental participants' problem-solving skills had generalized to similar and dissimilar types of situations, whereas the control group showed little change. Moreover, these 6-month scores were comparable to those of three normal controls.

Arthritis

DeVellis, Blalock, Hahn, DeVellis, and Hockbaum (1987) conducted a study to evaluate the efficacy of PST versus a control group concerning arthritis-related problems (e.g., adherence to exercise, rest, wearing splints). Results indicated that, compared to the control group, PST helped patients solve their compliance problems and their lifestyle problems more successfully, although support for the second finding was only statistically marginal.

Recurrent Headaches

PST was combined with applied relaxation in order to treat recurrent headaches and implemented via the internet and e-mail in a study by Ström, Pettersson, and Andersson (2000). Specifically, 102 headache sufferers were randomly assigned to either the treatment condition or to a wait-list control. The intervention was delivered over the course of 6 weeks with a new segment sent to participants on a weekly basis in order to encourage consistent participation. Pre-post analyses indicated that the PST plus relaxation intervention led to a statistically significant reduction in headaches and that among 50% of these, the reduction was clinically significant. One of the more important outcomes of this study was the notion that a low-cost method of treatment delivery (i.e., Internet and e-mail) could be clinically effective. Unfortunately, due to a high attrition rate (56%) across both conditions, the generalizability of these results is limited.

Cancer

Research has indicated that large numbers of cancer patients experience substantial difficulty in coping and adjusting to this illness (A. M. Nezu, Nezu, Felgoise, & Zwick, 2003). Given the prevalence of psychological distress experienced by adult cancer patients, researchers have looked to the potential efficacy of various psychosocial interventions as one means of addressing this public health concern, including PST (A. M. Nezu et al., 1999).

Several of these outcome investigations included PST as part of an overall multicomponent CBT package. For example, Telch and Telch (1986) included training in problem solving as part of a group administered CBT protocol that also involved instruction in the following: relaxation and stress management skills, assertive communication, cognitive restructuring, management of emotions, and planning pleasant events. This intervention was compared to a supportive group therapy protocol, as well as to a no-treatment control condition. Results indicated that patients receiving the CBT protocol fared significantly better than participants in the other two conditions. In fact, patients in the supportive group therapy condition evidenced little improvement, whereas untreated cancer patients actually experienced significant deterioration in their overall psychological adjustment.

Another multicomponent treatment package that included PST focused on patients who were newly diagnosed with malignant melanoma (Fawzy et al., 1990). Cancer patients were randomly assigned to one of two conditions—a 6-week structured group intervention that included PST, stress management training, group support, and health education, and a no-treatment control. At the end of 6 weeks, patients receiving the structured intervention began showing reductions in psychological distress as compared to control participants. However, 6 months posttreatment, the group differences were very pronounced. Moreover, 5 years following the intervention, treated patients continued to show significantly lower levels of anxiety, depression, and total mood disturbance (Fawzy, Fawzy, & Canada, 2001).

In addition, at the end of the original 6-week program, patients receiving the treatment evidenced significant increases in the percentage of large granular lymphocytes, suggesting a positive treatment effect on immune functioning. Further, 6 months posttreatment, this increase in granular lymphocytes continued, and increases in natural killer cells were also evident. Last, although not originally structured to determine the effects of treatment on actual health outcomes, Fawzy and colleagues (1993) did find at 6 years posttreatment that treated patients experienced longer overall survival as compared to control participants, and there was also a trend for a longer period to recurrence for the treated patients. This same intervention was later adapted for a Japanese population and found to be effective for Japanese women with breast cancer (Hokasa, 1996).

Mishel and colleagues (2002) paired training in problem solving with a cognitive reframing strategy as a means of helping 134 Caucasian and 105 African American men with localized prostate carcinoma to manage their levels of uncertainty and symptom control. Participants were randomly assigned to one of three experimental conditions—the combined psychosocial treatment provided only to the patient himself, treatment provided to the patient and a selected family member, and the control (medical treatment as usual). Both forms of treatment were provided by trained nurses through weekly phone calls for 8 weeks. In general, regardless of ethnicity, participants who received either form of the intervention improved significantly as measured at the 4-month post-baseline assessment. It is during this period of time that cancer treatment side effects are most prevalent. As such, it is particularly noteworthy that the combined PST and cognitive reframing treatment led to significant improvement in control of incontinence at 4-months post-baseline.

Other investigations focused on PST as a singular intervention and not as part of a larger treatment package. For example, Allen and colleagues (2002) assessed the efficacy of PST, as compared to a no-treatment control, with regard to a population of 164 women diagnosed with breast cancer and for whom a first course of chemotherapy had been recently initiated. PST consisted of two in-person and four telephone sessions with an oncology nurse who provided problem-solving skills training to the women over a 12-week period. This treatment program was designed to empower women with breast carcinoma to cope more effectively with a range of difficulties when diagnosed in mid-life. Participants in both conditions were assessed for physical and psychosocial adjustment.

At a 4-month evaluation, participants in general tended to have significantly less unmet needs and better mental health as compared to baseline. At the 8-month assessment, differences between the treated and control conditions emerged, pointing to the efficacy of the training. In general, PST led to improved mood and more effective coping with problems associated with daily living tasks. Further, the intervention was effective for the majority of women in resolving a range of problems related to cancer and its treatment, including physical side effects, marital and sexual difficulties, and psychological problems. However, an unexpected finding emerged with regard to women who had baseline scores characteristic of poor problem solving. In essence, such individuals, relative to the control participants, were less likely to resolve such cancer-related problems. Qualitative analyses suggested that such individuals became especially overwhelmed by expectations to *go it alone* after only one in-person treatment session. As such, these authors concluded that an important outcome of this study was the advisability of prescribing treatment based on one's level of need or risk. In other words, for individuals who are initially identified as poor problem solvers, a more intensive program (e.g., more face-to-face sessions) may be necessary as compared to those who at baseline are average or good problem solvers.

A. M. Nezu and colleagues (2003) recently reported the results of Project Genesis (A. M. Nezu, Nezu, Friedman, Houts, & Faddis, 1997), a 5-year study evaluating the efficacy of PST for 132 adult cancer patients. This intervention was based on a treatment manual (A. M. Nezu, Nezu, Friedman, Faddis, & Houts, 1998) that was adapted from previous research conducted with patients experiencing major depression (e.g., A. M. Nezu et al., 1989). In this clinical trial, adult cancer patients who were experiencing significant distress (e.g., depression) were randomly assigned to one of three conditions: (a) 10, 1.5-hour sessions of individual PST; (b) 10, 1.5-hour sessions of PST provided simultaneously to both the cancer patient and his or her designated significant other (e.g., spouse, family member); and (c) a treatment as usual control. The condition that involved a significant other was included to assess the enhanced effects of formalizing a social support system where the role of the significant other was conceptualized as a problem-solving coach.

Results at posttreatment across several self-report, clinician-ratings, and ratings by the significant other provide strong evidence in support of the efficacy of PST for decreasing emotional distress and improving the overall quality of life of patients with cancer. Specifically, patients in both treatment conditions were found to evidence significant improvement as compared to individuals in the control condition. At posttreatment, no differences were found between these two conditions. However, at a 6-month follow-up assessment, on approximately half of the variables assessed, patients who received PST along with a significant other continued to improve significantly beyond those individuals receiving PST by themselves, highlighting the advantage of formally including a collaborative person in treatment.

A study by Given and colleagues (2004) focused on 237 adult cancer patients recently diagnosed with a solid tumor and who were undergoing a first course of chemotherapy. Participants were randomly assigned to either a symptom management intervention, or conventional care. The cognitive-behavioral intervention was based on the PST model of D'Zurilla and Nezu (1999) in order to generate a listing of possible strategies to provide to patients and their caregivers in order to more effectively cope with a variety of cancer-related problems (e.g., alopecia, depression, fatigue, pain, insomnia). Based on discussions between a nurse and patient-caregiver dyad, various interventions were selected for implementation. Treatment occurred within 10 contacts (in person and telephone) over the course of 20 weeks.

Results indicated that treated patients who had higher baseline symptom severity levels reported lower depression at 10, but not at 20 weeks. Unexpectedly, patients in the experimental condition characterized by higher baseline depression were found to be more depressed at 10 weeks than control patients. Further, the intervention was found to be more effective in lowering depression at 10 weeks as a function of its impact on other symptoms rather than on depression directly. However, at 20 weeks, a significant main effect for treatment on depression was identified. As such, these authors concluded that the intervention influenced depression differentially over time. Specifically, it appeared to lower depression through enhanced ability to manage symptoms unrelated to depression and only later did it impact depression directly.

In a subsequent assessment of the impact of this intervention on the limitations imposed on patients by symptoms of cancer and its medical treatment, Doorenbos and colleagues (2005) recently reported that on average, after 10 weeks, patients receiving the problem-solving–based intervention reduced such symptom limitations by a statistically significant 13 points more than the control group. Moreover, this positive treatment effect was maintained over the course of the remainder of the treatment. Parenthetically, these authors concluded that this intervention was particularly helpful to younger individuals in managing cancer-related symptom limitations.

Family members who are responsible for the day-to-day care of cancer patients can also experience high levels of distress and frequent problems. As such, training in problem-solving skills may be a particularly useful approach in helping family caregivers in general cope more effectively in this role (C. M. Nezu, Nezu, & Houts, 1993). For example, Toseland, Blanchard, and McCallion (1995) reported a study that evaluated the efficacy of an intervention for spouses of cancer patients that included support, problem-solving, and coping skills. In this study, 40 male and 40 female spouses of cancer patients were randomly assigned to this intervention or a usual treatment condition. Results indicated that little change occurred over time for caregivers in either the treatment or control condition. However, this lack of effects were probably due to the low level of distress and problems that existed across this sample at pretreatment. Thus, when focusing on a subsample of distressed caregivers, significant effects were in fact evident. For example, distressed caregivers undergoing the PST-based intervention were found to significantly improve in their physical, role, and social functioning, as well as their ability to cope with pressing problems. The actual cancer patients related to this subsample of distressed caregivers receiving the intervention were also found to be significantly less depressed at posttreatment. Moreover, in a subsequent article that provided results of a 6-month post-baseline follow-up, Blanchard, Toseland, and McCallion (1996) reported that, overall, patients whose spouses received the PST intervention became significantly less depressed than did control patients.

Houts, Nezu, Nezu, and Bucher (1996) described a problem-solving-based program geared to improve the caregiving skills of family caregivers of cancer patients. The "Prepared Family Caregiver Course" adapted the D'Zurilla and Nezu (1982) PST model as a means of providing the following types of information to family caregivers of cancer patients: (a) understanding the problem; (b) when to get professional help; (c) what can be done to deal with, as well as prevent, a problem; (d) identifying obstacles when they arise and planning to overcome them; and (e) carrying out and adjusting the plan. Manuals have been developed (e.g., Houts, Nezu, Nezu, Bucher, & Lipton, 1994; Houts et al., 1997) that contain guided problem-solving plans across a variety of physical (e.g., fatigue, hair loss, appetite difficulties) and psychosocial (e.g., depression, anxiety) problems that cancer patients commonly experience. These manuals use the acronym COPE to highlight various problem-solving operations, where C = creativity, O = optimism, P = planning, and E = expert information. Although no controlled studies have yet been conducted with this protocol, Bucher, Houts, Nezu, and Nezu (1999) offered positive program evaluation data concerning participant satisfaction and acceptability of the treatment approach.

Schwartz and colleagues (1997) assessed the impact of a brief PST intervention regarding cancer-specific and general distress among 341 women with a first-degree relative who had recently been diagnosed with breast cancer. This investigation included two conditions: PST and a general health counseling (GHC) protocol. Both interventions were conducted during a single 2-hour individual session with a health educator. Initial analyses indicated that both approaches led to decreases in both cancer-specific and general distress, but no between-group differences emerged. However, when PST participants were divided into those who practiced the skills and those who did not, significant differences emerged. Specifically, PST-practicers had significantly greater decreases in cancer-specific distress compared to both nonpracticers and GHC participants. In addition, controlling for baseline education and distress differences between the groups did not reduce the magnitude of these results.

Adding to this same sample to eventually include 510 women who had a first-degree relative with breast cancer, Audrain and colleagues (1999) asked a different question—does a brief PST intervention increase the likelihood of adherence to breast self-examination? Whereas initial results found no differences between conditions, a cancer-specific distress by treatment interaction was identified. Specifically, among women who participated in the PST condition, those with high levels of distress were two times more likely to improve in adherence than women low in cancer-specific distress. No such effect was identified among control participants. The authors suggest that women with a family history of breast cancer who have high levels of distress may be most likely to benefit from this coping skills approach when attempting to promote adherence to breast cancer screening.

Sahler and colleagues (2002) focused on the well-being of mothers of newly diagnosed pediatric cancer patients. Ninety-two such mothers were randomly assigned to one of two conditions—PST and a control (standard psychosocial care). The problem-solving intervention consisted of eight 1-hour individual sessions and was adapted for this population based on the work of D'Zurilla and Nezu (1999). At posttreatment, results indicated that mothers in the PST condition has significantly enhanced problem-solving skills and significantly decreased negative affectivity as compared to their control counterparts. Moreover, analyses revealed that changes in self-reports of problem-solving behaviors accounted for 40% of the difference in mood scores between the two conditions. In addition, the intervention appeared to have the greatest impact on improving constructive problem solving, whereas improvement in mood was most influenced by decreases in dysfunctional problem solving.

In an extension of their previous investigation, Sahler and colleagues (2005) further assessed the efficacy of PST among a sample of 430 English- and Spanish-speaking mothers of pediatric cancer patients. Again, the 8-week PST condition was compared to a usual care control. Replicating their previous study, results from this study indicating that mothers receiving the PST protocol reported significantly enhanced problem-solving skills and significantly decreased negative affectivity. Whereas treatment effects appeared to be greatest at posttreatment, several differences were maintained at the 3-month follow-up. Interestingly, the efficacy of PST for Spanish-speaking mothers exceeded that for English-speaking mothers. Moreover, results suggest that young, single mothers befitted the most from the problem-solving intervention.

Diabetes

Problem solving has been identified as a central component of chronic illness self-management (Bodenheimer, Lorig, Holman, & Grumbach, 2002) and is considered a key component of many successful diabetes management programs (Glasgow, Toobert, Barrera, & Stryker, 2004). For example, Anderson and colleagues (1995) conducted a randomized control trial that evaluated an intervention geared to empower patients regarding their diabetes management. The intervention included goal setting, problem-solving training, and stress management training implemented over six weekly sessions and was compared to a wait-list control. At the end of 6 weeks, the control group completed the six-session empowerment program. Results indicated that the intervention group showed gains over the control group on four of eight self-efficacy subscales and two of five diabetes-attitude subscales. In addition, the intervention group showed a significant reduction in glycated hemoglobin levels. Within groups, analysis of data from all program participants showed sustained improvements in all of the self-efficacy areas and two of the five diabetes attitude subscales and a modest improvement in blood glucose levels.

Glasgow and colleagues (1992) developed a one-session, self-management training program for persons over 60 years having type 2 diabetes that especially targeted problem-solving skills and self-efficacy. The study randomized 102 adults to immediate or delayed treatment. Results from the first wave at posttreatment indicated that treated patients showed significantly greater reductions in caloric intake and percent of calories from fat than control patients. The self-management program also engendered greater weight reductions and increases in the frequency of glucose testing. These positive treatment effects were found to be maintained at a 6-month follow-up.

Glasgow and colleagues (2004) developed the Diabetes Problem-Solving Inventory (DPSI) in order to assess how patients coped with challenges to diabetes self-care. Glasgow also conducted mediation analyses to determine whether problem solving was related to improved outcomes regarding a multiple lifestyle behavior change program (called the Mediterranean Lifestyle Program; MLP) developed for post-menopausal women with type 2 diabetes at risk for coronary heart disease. The MLP program (Toobert, Glasgow, Barrera, & Bagdade, 2002) addressed changes in diet, physical activity, stress management, and social support. This study randomly assigned 116 patients to a usual care control condition and 163 patients to the MLP program. Of interest to this discussion, the mediation analyses indicated that (a) DPSI scores improved significantly more in the MLP group than in controls, and (b) this increase in problem solving was a partial mediator of positive outcome (e.g., changes in self-efficacy, decreases in caloric intake).

The Pathways Study (Katon et al., 2004) applied the IMPACT program, as described earlier in the section on depression, to reduce depression levels among diabetic patients who were also depressed. Patients were randomly assigned to the Pathways case management protocol or to usual care. Results indicated that whereas depression outcomes were improved (e.g., less depression severity over time for treated subjects as compared to controls), this improved depression care alone did not result in improved diabetes outcomes (i.e., improved glycemic control).

SUMMARY AND CONCLUSIONS

Since the publication of the first and second editions of this volume, there has been a significant increase in the number and overall quality of outcome studies that have applied PST to a wide variety of patient populations and specific health and mental health problems. These range from hospitalized psychiatric patients to normal individuals and groups interested in maximizing their general problem-solving effectiveness. One application that has particularly seen a growth in the number of investigations involves health psychology or behavioral medicine. As can be seen by this review, PST has been applied extensively for a variety of medical patients and their families, including individuals diagnosed with cancer, diabetes, back pain, arthritis, hypertension, headaches, and obesity. In addition, beyond the traditional mode of therapy implementation (i.e., face-to-face individual and group sessions), PST has also been successfully applied via Internet and telephone protocols.

Although not all the studies cited in this overview provide uniform support for the efficacy of PST, the preponderance of the data strongly underscore its effectiveness as a clinical intervention across ages, patient samples, problems, treatment settings, and manner of implementation. It has been found to be as effective as pharmacotherapy when treating depression (i.e., Mynors-Wallis et al., 1995), equal to or better than other forms of psychosocial interventions for a variety of problems (e.g., Arean et al., 1993; Alexopoulos et al., 2003; Lerner & Clum, 1990; A. M. Nezu, 1986c), and more effective than placebos (vast majority of cited studies).

However, whereas the results of the investigations in general provide strong evidence for the efficacy of PST, it is important to highlight various methodological limitations that were identified in order to encourage researchers to conduct more well-controlled studies in the future as a means of better understanding the nature and scope of the efficacy of PST.

One problem in many of the studies described is that PST is often included as part of a larger treatment package that includes other intervention strategies. Whereas the goal of many such projects may not have been to understand the unique contribution of PST to treatment outcome, it is difficult to isolate the specific effects of PST in these studies. What is necessary after an overall treatment package is found to be effective is the use of dismantling research strategies (see A. M. Nezu & Perri, 1989) or mediational component analyses to determine which intervention strategies actually contribute to positive treatment outcome (e.g., García-Vera et al., 1998; Glasgow et al., 2004).

A second problem concerns the lack, at times, of adequate control conditions that are necessary when conducting randomized controlled trials in order to minimize a variety of threats to internal validity (A. M. Nezu & Nezu, in press, a). One concern involves the need for a wait-list or delayed treatment control condition in order to account for the effects of certain extraneous variables on behavior change. This is especially important with regard to various disorders that may be prone to vary over time (e.g., depression, anxiety). Related is the lack of control conditions that allows one to rule out alternative hypotheses concerning the effects of nonspecific factors associated with treatment, such as expectations, motivation, or contact with a therapist. Perhaps the most appropriate types of control conditions are not simply attention-placebos, but rather standard care approaches or alternate forms of treatment (e.g., PST versus social skills training).

A third methodological problem identified during this review is the failure of some investigations to include any measures of social problem solving among the various measures administered. Without such measures, it is not possible to determine whether the training program actually achieved its major immediate objective of improving problem-solving ability or performance, rather than the outcome being produced by nonspecific factors (e.g., expectations). Moreover, what becomes important is to conduct process-oriented analyses to determine whether improvements in problem-solving ability were associated with changes in the outcome of interest (e.g., reduction in depression, anxiety, agoraphobic behavior). For example, within a study that evaluates PST for major depression, if participants receiving PST do not improve in their problem-solving skills, even if this group is characterized by significant reductions in depressive symptoms, the general thesis that PST is responsible for the clinical improvement cannot be supported (see design in A. M. Nezu, 1986c). In essence, PST is firmly predicated on the assumption that the *major* mechanism of action of this clinical intervention is improved problem-solving ability. However, in the absence of such an evaluation, even if one includes adequate control conditions, resulting differences between groups continues to beg the question whether improved problem solving was the responsible factor. As such, it is imperative for future studies to include a measure of problem solving.

Another problem is that some studies used a problem-solving outcome measure only, without including any measures of adjustment, psychopathology, or maladaptive behavior. The failure to include these measures reduces the clinical relevance of the findings.

Many of these studies also did not include a detailed description of the problem-solving training actually conducted in a given study. Several authors indicated that they followed the general model described in this book (e.g., D'Zurilla & Goldfried, 1971; D'Zurilla & Nezu, 1982, 1999; A. M. Nezu et al., 1989). Other authors simply stated that PST was implemented without providing specific details or indicating that a manual was followed. The importance of following a treatment manual cannot be overemphasized. As the A. M. Nezu and Perri (1989) investigation points out, for example, the effects of PST *without* training in the problem-orientation component was not as effective as training in the entire model that we espouse. However, scrutiny of some of the studies reviewed, especially those not in support of PST, led to the finding that they did not include adequate training in this important problem-solving component (see discussion regarding PST for minor depression in primary care).

Another problem, one which parenthetically characterizes the majority of the psychotherapy literature in general, concerns the lack of quality control or treatment integrity checks across PST therapists and across PST patients (see A. M. Nezu & Nezu, in press, c). Psychosocial-based interventions are significantly different compared to psychopharmacologic procedures with regard to the assurance one has that an intervention is actually veridically administered. In other words, a drug protocol is relatively easy to monitor (e.g., count the number of pills administered within a structured protocol). With psychotherapy outcome studies, few investigators have sought to determine whether what is thought to be administered (e.g., PST) is actually implemented correctly. Having a detailed treatment manual certainly facilitates therapist adherence, but without including a specific assessment of treatment implementation (e.g., ratings of therapist adherence based on tapes of sessions), it remains unclear if any given therapist actually conducted treatment in the manner that the researcher intended.

Related to this problem is the issue of therapist *competency* (A. M. Nezu & Nezu, 2005). Even if a given therapist correctly implements a given intervention protocol, there will be variability in the competence or skillfulness in which this is done across differing therapists (or even across a sample of patients seen by the same therapist). Without such an assessment, once again the ability of a given study to comprehensively answer the question of whether a treatment worked is limited.

In addition, some studies failed to include any follow-up evaluations. Without a follow-up, the question of the durability or generalizability of treatment effects cannot be answered. Also important is the need to include a comprehensive assessment protocol when measuring outcome. In the A. M. Nezu and colleagues (2003) study involving adult cancer patients described earlier, including a significant other in PST appeared to appreciably enhance the outcome for the patient at a later point in time (i.e., 6-month follow-up assessment). However, such differences only held true for some of the outcome measures and not all. This set of findings strongly underscores the need to include a comprehensive assessment protocol (e.g., multitrait, multimethod approach) in order to actually capture adequately the entire picture.

In addition to the limitations resulting from these methodological problems, definite conclusions are not possible for a few target populations because only a limited number of outcome studies have been reported thus far (e.g., arthritis, head-injured patients). Such studies must be replicated before conclusions about the efficacy of PST for these particular target populations can be made with confidence.

Despite these limitations, during the past decade, many additional well-controlled studies have been conducted, generally pointing to the overall efficacy of PST as a clinical intervention strategy for a variety of different mental health, substance abuse, and health problems. The evidence indicates that PST contributes not only to immediate treatment effects, but to the maintenance of treatment effects as well. Moreover, the results of several studies indicates that this form of psychosocial intervention may have an impact on health, as well as mental health, outcomes as well.

CHAPTER ELEVEN

Conclusions and Future Directions

PST has been described as a positive clinical intervention that reduces and prevents stress and psychopathology by increasing positive problem-solving attitudes and skills and promoting broad positive changes in coping performance and psychological well-being across a wide range of problematic situations. Empirical support for the theory and practice of PST comes from two areas of research: (a) studies on the relationship between social problem solving and adjustment (see chapters 6 and 7); and (b) studies on the efficacy of PST with a variety of different clinical and vulnerable populations (see chapter 10). Despite the impressive body of research in these two areas, there are still a number of issues that need to be examined in future research in order to firmly establish the empirical foundation for the theory, efficacy, and scope of PST.

SOCIAL PROBLEM SOLVING AND ADJUSTMENT

In this section we present our major recommendations for future research on the relationship between social problem solving and adjustment.

Social Problem Solving and Positive Functioning

Most of the research on social problem solving and adjustment has focused on *maladaptive* functioning (e.g., psychological distress, behavior deviations). According to the theory of PST, problem solving is expected to reduce and prevent psychopathology by increasing *positive* functioning. Hence, in order to establish the validity of this theory, more research is needed that examines the relationship between social problem solving and different measures of behavioral competence and positive psychological well-being (e.g., adaptive coping, interpersonal competence, job productivity, positive affect, hope, optimism, self-esteem, life satisfaction, and feelings of mastery and control). Moreover, in order to establish social problem solving as an important variable in *positive psychology* (Seligman, 1999; Seligman & Csikszentmihalyi, 2000), more research is needed on the role of social problem solving in predicting and enhancing *optimal* or superior functioning that maximizes the quality of life for oneself and society. Such research would focus on measures of exceptional performance, achievement, creativity, and invention in various areas of life and work, such as business and industry, medicine, public service, sports, and marriage and family.

Rational Problem Solving and Negative Affective Conditions

In general, the dimension of rational problem solving (i.e., effective problem-solving skills) has been found to be more strongly and consistently related to behavioral measures of adjustment than to psychological measures. In particular, inconsistent results have been reported on the relationship between rational problem solving and negative affective conditions, such as depression and anxiety. With only a few exceptions, studies using self-report inventories, such as the SPSI-R, have reported nonsignificant correlations between the rational problem-solving scale and negative affective conditions, whereas the MEPS and other performance-based measures have more consistently found significant relationships between deficits in some problem-solving skills (e.g., generation of alternative solutions, decision making) and negative affective conditions. In order to shed some light on this issue and resolve the inconsistencies, future studies are needed that include both types of problem-solving measures in the same study.

Reciprocal Causation Hypothesis

A major assumption of social problem-solving theory is that problem-solving deficits cause or contribute to psychopathology. However, because most of the research on the relationship between social problem solving and psychopathology is cross-sectional, an alternative interpretation is that psychopathology has a negative impact on social problem-solving ability and performance (Mitchell & Madigan, 1984; Schotte et al., 1990). In addition, a third hypothesis, which we strongly endorse, is that the relationship between social problem solving and psychopathology is reciprocal. According to this hypothesis, ineffective problem solving leads to maladaptive functioning (e.g., depression, anxiety), which in turn, inhibits or disrupts subsequent problem solving, resulting in a negative cycle over time of decreasing problem-solving effectiveness and increasing maladjustment or psychological disturbance. Moreover, the reciprocal causal model might also be extended to the relationship between social problem solving and positive adjustment, where effective problem solving enhances positive functioning (e.g., positive affectivity, a sense of mastery and control), which in turn, facilitates subsequent problem solving. Over time, the resulting positive cycle of increasing problem-solving effectiveness and positive functioning might eventually lead to optimal or superior functioning and well-being. The reciprocal causation hypothesis has important implications for theories of psychopathology as well as for treatment. It also has implications for theories of positive psychology and for interventions that are designed to achieve optimal psychological and behavioral functioning. To examine this hypothesis, longitudinal studies are needed that use multiple assessments of problem solving and adjustment variables over time.

Basic Cognitive Abilities

In chapter 2, social problem solving was described as a set of abilities that can be grouped into three levels: (a) the metacognitive level (i.e., problem orientation); (b) the performance level (i.e., problem-solving styles); and (c) the basic cognitive level (i.e., intellectual and information-processing abilities). The present social problem-solving model does not specifically address the abilities at the basic level. It is assumed that most populations, clinical as well as normal, already possess adequate abilities at the basic level to allow them to benefit from training experiences that focus on the metacognitive and performance levels. Hence, most current problem-solving training programs focus only on these two levels. However, there are a number of populations, including persons with mental retardation, brain-injured individuals, individuals with schizophrenia, and young children, that have significant deficits or underdeveloped abilities at the basic cognitive level. Additional research is needed with these populations to identify (a) the basic cognitive deficits that are impacting problem-solving performance, and (b) training methods that are effective in correcting them (for a further discussion of this issue as it pertains to schizophrenics, see Morris, Bellack, & Tenhula, 2004; for a discussion pertaining to young children, see Frauenknecht & Black, 2004). However, as described in chapter 10, research has demonstrated that by significantly altering the method by which PST is conducted, it is an efficacious intervention for persons with mental retardation (e.g., C. M. Nezu et al., 1991).

Ethnic and Racial Differences

Very little research has been done on cultural and racial differences in social problem-solving ability and their relationship to adjustment. In two studies, Asian Americans were found to score higher than White Americans on negative problem orientation (Chang, 1998) and impulsivity/carelessness style (Chang, 1998, 2001). However, the elevated scores on these dysfunctional problem-solving dimensions in Asian Americans has *not* been found to be associated with greater maladjustment. Thus, it appears that the impact of specific problem-solving deficits on adjustment may vary across different ethnic or racial groups. Clearly, more research is needed on the relationship between social problem solving and adjustment in diverse populations.

PROBLEM-SOLVING TRAINING/THERAPY

In this section, we present our major recommendations for future research on the efficacy and process of PST (see also recommendations at the end of chapter 10 regarding how to improve outcome methodology).

Adolescents and Their Parents

Studies have found a link between problem-solving deficits and serious psychological and behavioral problems in adolescents, including depression and suicidal ideation (Sadowski & Kelley, 1993; Sadowski et al., 1994), aggression and delinquency (Freedman et al., 1978; Jaffee & D'Zurilla, 2003; Lochman, Wayland, & White, 1993), substance use (tobacco, alcohol, marijuana), and high-risk automobile driving (Jaffee & D'Zurilla, 2003, 2006). Based on these findings, we recommend more research on PST programs for adolescents as well as their parents. The programs for parents should not only focus on problem solving for dealing more effectively with their adolescents' problem behaviors, but they should also teach parents how to be more effective in teaching constructive problem-solving attitudes and skills to their pre- and early-adolescent children.

Individuals With Cardiovascular Disease

In recent years, problem-solving therapy has been successfully applied as a method for helping patients and their caregivers cope with serious medical conditions and their treatments (see chapter 10). According to Ewart (1990), cancer and cardiovascular diseases have replaced infectious diseases as the leading causes of death in developed nations. Whereas successful PST programs have been developed for cancer patients and their caregivers (e.g., A. M. Nezu et al., 2003), there are no studies on PST for cardiac patients. Like cancer, cardiovascular diseases and recovery from heart attacks and strokes require many difficult behavioral and lifestyle changes and adjustments, such as job adjustments, diet changes, taking daily medications, making time for exercise, and reducing stress in one's life. PST might be particularly useful and effective for helping cardiac patients cope more effectively with these difficult behavioral and lifestyle changes and, thus, improve their physical and psychological well-being (A. M. Nezu, Nezu, & Jain, 2005). A. M. Nezu and his colleagues are currently in the process of developing and evaluating PST protocols for such purposes.

Preventive Behavioral Health

A number of behavioral and lifestyle changes have also been recommended by medical professionals to *prevent* serious medical conditions such as cancer and cardiovascular diseases. These changes include reducing and managing stress more effectively, changing eating habits, losing weight, stopping smoking, controlling alcohol intake, and increasing physical exercise. Despite the frequent communication of these recommendations to the general public through primary care physicians, television commercials, newspapers, and magazines, many high-risk individuals are unable to make these changes because of various lifestyle obstacles and conflicts. Hence, we recommend research on PST as a preventive intervention to help people overcome these obstacles to a healthy lifestyle. As noted in chapter 10, efforts regarding the self-management of diabetes has already begun.

Stress Reduction and Prevention in the Workplace

Except for senior citizens, most American adults spend at least half of their waking hours in the workplace. Hence, daily conflicts and problems at work are a major source of stress for most adults, resulting in such adverse outcomes as absenteeism, low productivity, occupational burnout, lost work days due to illness, high turnover rates, psychological disturbance, and health problems. Social problem solving is likely to be an effective strategy for reducing and preventing stress and its negative effects in the workplace (see D'Zurilla, 1990). However, there is a lack of research on the evaluation of problem-solving training workshops for managers, supervisors, and other employees. If they are proven to be effective, such workshops could have important psychological, health, and economic benefits for individual employees, business owners and executives, and society in general.

Mediators and Moderators of PST Outcomes

According to social problem-solving theory, the major mediator of positive PST outcomes is social problem-solving ability; that is, problem-solving training improves problem-solving ability and performance which, in turn, produces more positive therapy outcomes. In support of this assumption, several outcome studies have found a significant relationship between improvements in social problem-solving ability and positive changes in negative psychological conditions, including psychological stress (D'Zurilla & Maschka, 1988), depression (A. M. Nezu, 1987; A. M. Nezu & Perri, 1989), and cancer-related distress (A. M. Nezu et al., 2003). However, more research is needed to identify *what* specific problem-solving dimensions are the most important mediators of PST outcomes for *what* particular patients with *what* particular adjustment problems. Based on the body of research on social problem solving and adjustment, it appears that positive and negative problem orientation and avoidance style might be important mediators in therapy programs for negative psychological conditions, whereas rational problem solving (i.e., problem-solving skills) and impulsivity/carelessness style might be important in programs focusing on behavioral outcomes. In addition to social problem-solving ability, other variables that might mediate PST outcomes include positive affectivity, optimism, hope, self-efficacy, self-esteem, and a sense of mastery or control. Whereas mediators are variables that are affected by problem-solving training, which in turn, influence or account for therapy outcomes, moderators are variables that interact with treatment to influence the magnitude of outcomes, for better or worse. Such variables might include age, gender, ethnicity, intelligence, educational level, and various personality traits. Research designed to identify moderator variables is particularly important for determining what individuals might benefit most or least from problem-solving therapy.

New Methods for Implementing PST

The traditional mode of implementing PST in published outcome studies is face-to-face individual or group sessions lasting from 1 to 1.5 hours. However, a few studies have successfully implemented telephone and computer-based interventions (see chapter 10). Other possible alternative training methods include self-help manuals and videotapes or DVDs. In order to capitalize on advances in new communication technologies that might make PST more accessible, efficient, and cost-effective, more research is recommended on the efficacy of these alternative modes of intervention. Because some of these alternative methods are likely to be implemented or monitored by subprofessionals (e.g., behavioral technicians, nurses), the evaluation of training methods for these individuals should also be the subject of future research.

CONCLUDING COMMENT

Since the publication of the second edition of this volume (D'Zurilla & Nezu, 1999), research on social problem solving and PST has been increasing at a rapid pace. In general, the results have provided strong support for the theory and practice of PST. The findings indicate that good problem-solving ability, assessed by several different measures, is related to positive psychological and behavioral functioning, whereas problem-solving deficits are associated with a variety of different forms of maladaptive functioning, including psychological distress, behavior deviations, and health problems. In addition, the evidence supports the view that PST is a useful and effective intervention for a variety of different clinical populations, including individuals with different kinds of psychological disorders, behavior disorders, and medical illnesses. Moreover, there is evidence that PST is also an effective preventive intervention with various vulnerable populations, such as individuals under high levels of life stress and individuals at risk for HIV. However, while the research to date has generally been supportive or promising, the recommendations in this chapter indicate that much more work needs to be done to establish the true potential of social problem-solving theory, research, and therapy.

References

Alexapoulos, G. S., Raue, P., & Arean, P. A. (2003). Problem-solving therapy versus supportive therapy in geriatric major depression with executive dysfunction. *American Journal of Geriatric Psychiatry, 11*, 46–52.

Allen, S. M., Shah, A. C., Nezu, A. M., Nezu, C. M., Ciambrone, D., Hogan, J., et al. (2002). A problem-solving approach to stress reduction among younger women with breast carcinoma: A randomized controlled trial. *Cancer, 94*, 3089–3100.

Anderson, R. M., Funnell, M. M., Butler, P. M., Arnold, M. S., Fitzgerald, J. T., & Feste, C. C. (1995). Patient empowerment: Results of a randomized controlled trial. *Diabetes Care, 18*, 943–949.

Antonowicz, D. H. (2005). The reasoning and rehabilitation program: Outcome evaluations with offenders. In M. McMurran & J. McGuire (Eds.), *Social problem solving and offending: Evidence, evaluation and evolution* (pp. 163–182). Chichester, UK: Wiley.

Antonowicz, D. H., & Ross, R. R. (2005). Social problem-solving deficits in offenders. In M. McMurran & J. McGuire (Eds.), *Social problem solving offending: Evidence, evaluation and evolution* (pp. 91–102). Chichester, UK: Wiley.

Appel, P. W., & Kaestner, E. (1979). Interpersonal and emotional problem solving among narcotic drug abusers. *Journal of Consulting and Clinical Psychology, 47*, 1125–1127.

Arean, P. A., Perri, M. G., Nezu, A. M., Schein, R. L., Christopher, F., & Joseph, T. X. (1993). Comparative effectiveness of social problem-solving therapy and reminiscence therapy as treatments for depression in older adults. *Journal of Consulting and Clinical Psychology, 61*, 1003–1010.

Audrain, J., Rimer, B., Cella, D., Stefanek, M., Garber, J., Pennanen, M., et al. (1999). The impact of a brief coping skills intervention on adherence to breast self-examination among first-degree relatives of newly diagnosed breast cancer patients. *Psycho-Oncology, 8*, 220–229.

Auerbach, S. M., & Gramling, S. E. (1998). *Stress management: Psychological foundations.* Upper Saddle River, NJ: Prentice-Hall.

Azar, S. T., Robinson, D. R., Hekimian, E., & Twentyman, C. T. (1984). Unrealistic expectations and problem-solving ability in maltreating and comparison mothers. *Journal of Consulting and Clinical Psychology, 52*, 687–691.

Baddeley, A. D. (1972). Selective attention and performance in dangerous environments. *British Journal of Psychology, 63*, 537–546.

Bandura, A. (1997). *Self-efficacy: The exercise of control.* New York: W. H. Freeman.

Barlow, D. H., Hayes, S. C., & Nelson, R. O. (1984). *The scientist practitioner: Research and accountability in clinical and educational settings.* New York: Pergamon.

Barrett, J. E., Williams, J. W., Oxman, T. E., Frank, E., Katon, W., Sullivan, M., et al. (2001). Treatment of dysthymia and minor depression in primary care: A randomized trial in patients aged 18 to 59 years. *Journal of Family Practice, 50,* 405–412.

Barrett, J. E., Williams, J. W., Oxman, T. E., Katon, W., Frank, E., Hegel, M. T., et al. (1999). The Treatment Effectiveness project. A comparison of the effectiveness of paroxetine, problem-solving therapy, and placebo in the treatment of minor depression and dysthymia in primary care patients: Background and research plan. *General Hospital Psychiatry, 21,* 260–273.

Basquil, M., Nezu, C. M., Nezu, A. M., & Klein, T. L. (2004). Aggression-related hostility bias and social problem-solving deficits in adult males with mental retardation. *American Journal on Mental Retardation, 109,* 255–263.

Bayless, O. L. (1967). An alternative pattern for problem-solving discussion. *Journal of Communication, 17,* 188–197.

Beach, L. R., & Mitchell, T. R. (1978). A contingency model for the selection of decision strategies. *Academy of Management Review, 3,* 439–449.

Beck, A. T. (1976). *Cognitive therapy and the emotional disorders.* New York: International Universities Press.

Beck, A. T., Rush, A. J., Shaw, B. F., & Emery, G. (1979). *Cognitive therapy of depression.* New York: Guilford.

Bellack, A. S. (1979). A critical appraisal of strategies for assessing social skills. *Behavioral Assessment, 1,* 157–176.

Bellack, A. S., Sayers, M., Mueser, K. T., & Bennett, M. (1994). Evaluation of social problem solving in schizophrenia. *Journal of Abnormal Psychology, 103,* 371–378.

Belzer, K. D., D'Zurilla, T. J., & Maydeu-Olivares, A. (1998a). *Correlations between the Social Problem-Solving Inventory-Revised and measures of worry and state and trait anxiety.* Unpublished data, State University of New York at Stony Brook.

Belzer, K. D., D'Zurilla, T. J., & Maydeu-Olivares, A. (1998b). *The relationships between problem-solving self-efficacy, worry, and trait anxiety.* Paper presented at the Association for Advancement of Behavior Therapy Convention, Washington, DC.

Belzer, K. D., D'Zurilla, T. J., & Maydeu-Olivares, A. (2002). Social problem solving and trait anxiety as predictors of worry in a college student population. *Personality and Individual Differences, 33,* 573–585.

Benson, B. A., Rice, C. J., & Miranti, S. V. (1986). Effects of anger management training with mentally retarded adults in group treatment. *Journal of Consulting and Clinical Psychology, 54,* 728–729.

Bernstein, D. A., & Borkovec, T. D. (1973). *Progressive relaxation training: A manual for the helping professions.* Champaign, IL: Research Press.

Biggam, F. H., & Power, K. G. (1998). A comparison of the problem-solving abilities and psychological distress of suicidal, bullied, and protected prisoners. *Criminal Justice and Behavior, 25,* 177–197.

Biggam, F. H., & Power, K. G. (1999). Suicidality and the state-trait debate on problem-solving deficits: A re-examination with incarcerated young offenders. *Archives of Suicide Research, 5,* 27–42.

Black, D. R. (1987). A minimal intervention program and a problem-solving program for weight control. *Cognitive Therapy and Research, 11,* 107–120.

Black, D. R., & Threlfall, W. E. (1986). A stepped approach to weight control: A minimal intervention and a bibliotherapy problem-solving program. *Behavior Therapy, 17,* 144–157.

Blanchard, C. G., Toseland, R. W., & McCallion, P. (1996). The effects of a problem-solving intervention with spouses of cancer patients. *Journal of Psychosocial Oncology, 14,* 1–21.

Blankstein, K. R., Flett, G. L., & Johnston, M. E. (1992). Depression, problem-solving ability, and problem-solving appraisals. *Journal of Clinical Psychology, 48,* 749–759.

Bodenhausen, G. V., Macrae, C. N., & Hugenberg, K. (2003) Social cognition. In T. Millon & M. J. Lerner (Eds.), *Personality and social psychology.* New York: Wiley.

Bodenheimer, T. S., Lorig, K., Holman, H., & Grumbach, K. (2002). Patient self-management of chronic disease in primary care. *Journal of the American Medical Association, 288,* 2469–2475.

Bloom, B. L. (1985). *Stressful life event theory and research: Implications for primary prevention.* D.H.H.S. Publication No. (AMD) 85–1385. Rockville, MD: National Institute of Mental Health.

Bloom, B. S., & Broder, L. J. (1950). *Problem-solving processes of college students.* Chicago: University of Chicago Press.

Bond, D. S., Lyle, R. M., Tappe, M. K., Seehafer, R. S., & D'Zurilla, T. J. (2002). Moderate aerobic exercise, Tai chi, and social problem-solving ability in relation to psychological stress. *International Journal of Stress Management, 9.* 329–343.

Bonner, R. L., & Rich, A. (1988). Negative life stress, social problem-solving self-appraisal, and hopelessness: Implications for suicide research. *Cognitive Therapy and Research, 12,* 549–556.

Borsoi, D., & Toneatto, T. (2003). Problem-solving skills in male and female problem gamblers. *eGambling: The Electronic Journal of Gambling Issues, 8,* 1–13. Retrieved February 27, 2006, from http://www.camh.net

Bowen, L., Wallace, C., Glynn, S., Nuechterlein, K., Lutzker, J. R., & Kuehnel, T. G. (1994). Schizophrenic individuals' cognitive functioning and performance in interpersonal interactions and skills training procedures. *Journal of Psychiatric Research, 28,* 289–301.

Bradshaw, W. H. (1993). Coping-skills training versus a problem-solving approach with schizophrenic patients. *Hospital and Community Psychiatry, 44,* 1102–1104.

Braver, T. S., Barch, D. M., & Cohen, J. D. (1999). Cognition and control in schizophrenia: A computational model of dopamine and prefrontal function. *Biological Psychiatry, 46,* 312–328.

Brilhart, J. K., & Jochem, L. M. (1964). Effects of different patterns on outcome of problem-solving discussion. *Journal of Applied Psychology, 48,* 175–179.

Brodbeck, C., & Michelson, I. (1987). Problem-solving skills and attributional styles of agoraphobics. *Cognitive Therapy and Research, 11,* 593–610.

Bucher, J. A, Houts, P. S., Nezu, C. M., & Nezu, A. M. (1999). Improving problem-solving skills of family caregivers through group education. *Journal of Psychosocial Oncology, 16,* 73–84.

Burks, N., & Martin, B. (1985). Everyday problems and life change events: Ongoing vs. acute sources of stress. *Journal of Human Stress, 11,* 27–35.

Burns, L. R., & D'Zurilla, T. J. (1994). *Correlations between the Social problem-Solving Inventory Revised and measures of extraversion, social adjustment, and interpersonal competence.* Unpublished data, State University of New York at Stony Brook.

Burns, L. R., & D'Zurilla, T. J. (1999). Individual differences in perceived information processing styles in stress and coping situations: Development and validation of the Perceived Modes of Processing Inventory. *Cognitive Therapy and Research 23,* 345–371.

Butler, L., & Meichenbaum, D. (1981). The assessment of interpersonal problem-solving skills. In P. C. Kendall & S. D. Hollon (Eds.), *Assessment strategies for cognitive-behavioral interventions.* New York: Academic Press.

Camp, C. J., Doherty, K., Moody-Thomas, S., & Denney, N. W. (1989). Practical problem solving types and scoring methods. In J. D. Sinnott (Ed.), *Everyday problem solving: Theory and applications* (pp. 211–228). New York: Praeger.

Cantor, N., & Kihlstrom, J. F. (1987). *Personality and social intelligence.* Englewood Cliffs, NJ: Prentice Hall.

Carey, M. P., Carey, K. B., & Meisler, A. W. (1990). Training mentally ill chemical abusers in social problem solving. *Behavior Therapy, 21*, 511–518.

Carver, C. S., & Scheier, M. F. (1982). Control theory: A useful conceptual framework for personality-social, clinical, and health psychology. *Psychological Bulletin, 92*, 111–135.

Castles, E. E., & Glass, C. R. (1986). Training in social and interpersonal problem-solving skills for mildly and moderately mentally retarded adults. *American Journal of Mental Deficiency, 91*, 35–42.

Catalan, J., Gath, D. H., Bond, A., Day, A., & Hall, L. (1991). Evaluation of a brief psychological treatment for emotional disorders in primary care. *Psychological Medicine, 21*, 1013–1018.

Chang, E. C. (1998). Cultural differences, perfectionism, and suicidal risk in a college population: Does social problem solving still matter? *Cognitive Therapy and Research, 22*, 237–254.

Chang, E. C. (2001). A look at the coping strategies and styles of Asian Americans: Similar and different? In C. R. Snyder (Ed.), *Coping with stress: Effective people and processes* (pp. 222–239). New York: Oxford University Press.

Chang, E. C. (2002a). Examining the link between perfectionism and psychological maladjustment: Social problem solving as a buffer. *Cognitive Therapy and Research, 26*, 581–595.

Chang, E. C. (2002b). Predicting suicide ideation in an adolescent population: Examining the role of social problem solving as a moderator and a mediator. *Personality and Individual Differences, 32*, 1279–1291.

Chang, E. C. (2003). A critical appraisal and extension of hope theory in middle-aged men and women: Is it important to distinguish agency and pathways components? *Journal of Social and Clinical Psychology, 22*, 121–143.

Chang, E. C., Downey, C. A., & Salata, J. L. (2004). Social problem solving and positive psychological functioning: Looking at the positive side of problem solving. In E. C. Chang, T. J. D'Zurilla, & L. J. Sanna (Eds.), *Social problem solving: Theory, research, and training* (pp. 99–116). Washington, DC: American Psychological Association.

Chang, E. C., & D'Zurilla, T. J. (1996a). Irrational beliefs as predictors of anxiety and depression in a college population. *Personality and Individual Differences, 20*, 215–219.

Chang, E. C., & D'Zurilla, T. J. (1996b). Relations between problem orientation and optimism, pessimism, and trait affectivity: A construct validation study. *Behaviour Research and Therapy, 34*, 185–195.

Chang, E. C., Sanna, L. J., & Edwards, M. C. (2003). *Relations between problem-solving styles and psychological outcomes: Is stress a mediating variable for young and middle-aged adults?* Unpublished manuscript, Department of Psychology, University of Michigan.

Cheng, S. K. (2001). Life stress, problem solving, perfectionism, and depressive symptoms in Chinese. *Cognitive Therapy and Research, 25*, 303–310.

Clum, G. A., Canfield, D., Van Arsdel, M., Yang, B., Febbraro, G. A. R., & Wright, J. (1997). An expanded model for suicide behavior in adolescence: Evidence for it specificity relative to depression. *Journal of Psychopathology and Behavioral Assessment, 19*, 207–223.

Clum, G. A., & Febbraro, G.A.R. (1994). Stress, social support, and problem-solving appraisal/skills: Prediction of suicide severity within a college sample. *Journal of Psychopathology and Behavioral Assessment, 16,* 69–83.

Clum, G. A., Yang, B., & Febbraro, G. A. R. (1996). An investigation of the validity of the SPSI and SPSI-R in differentiating suicidal from depressed, non-suicidal college students. *Journal of Psychopathology and Behavioral Assessment, 18,* 119–132.

Cone, J. D., & Hawkins, R. P. (Eds.). (1977). *Behavioral assessment: New directions in clinical psychology.* New York: Brunner/Mazel.

Cordova, J. V., & Mirgain, S. A. (2004). Problem-solving training for couples. In E. C. Chang, T. J. D'Zurilla, & L. J. Sanna (Eds.), *Social problem solving: Theory, research, and training* (pp. 193–208). Washington, DC: American Psychological Association.

Cormier, W. H., Otani, A., & Cormier, S. (1986). The effects of problem-solving training on two problem-solving tasks. *Cognitive Therapy and Research, 10,* 95–108.

Cornelius, S. W., & Caspi, A. (1987). Everyday problem solving in adulthood and old age. *Psychology and Aging, 2,* 144–153.

Cunningham, C. E., Davis, J. R., Bremner, R., Dunn, K. W., & Rzasa, T. (1993). Coping modeling problem solving versus mastery modeling: Effects on adherence, in-session process, and skill acquisition in a residential parent-training program. *Journal of Consulting and Clinical Psychology, 61,* 871–877.

Davey, G. C. L. (1994). Worrying, social problem-solving abilities, and problem-solving confidence. *Behaviour Research and Therapy, 32,* 327–330.

Davey, G. C. L., Hampton, J., Farrell, J., & Davidson, S. (1992). Some characteristics of worrying: Evidence for worrying and anxiety as separate constructs. *Personality and Individual Differences, 13,* 133–147.

Davey, G. C. L., Jubb, M., & Cameron, C. (1996). Catastrophic worrying as a function of changes in problem-solving confidence. *Cognitive Therapy and Research, 20,* 333–344.

Davey, G. C. L., & Levy, S. (1999). Internal statements associated with catastrophic worrying. *Personality and Individual Differences, 26,* 21–32.

Davis, G. A. (1966). Current status of research and theory in human problem solving. *Psychological Bulletin, 66,* 36–54.

Davis, G. A. (1973). *Psychology of problem solving: Theory and practice.* New York: Basic Books.

Davison, G. C., Robins, C., & Johnson, M. K. (1983). Articulated thoughts during simulated situations: A paradigm for studying cognition in emotion and behavior. *Cognitive Therapy and Research, 2,* 17–40.

DeLongis, A., Coyne, J. C., Dakof, G., Folkman, S., & Lazarus, R. S. (1982). Relationship of daily hassles, uplifts, and major life events to health status. *Health Psychology, 1,* 119–136.

Denney, N. W., & Pearce, K. A. (1989). A developmental study of practical problem solving in adults. *Psychology and Aging, 4,* 438–442.

DeVellis, B. M., Blalock, S. J., Hahn, P. M., DeVellis, R. F., & Hockbaum, L. (1987). Evaluation of a problem-solving intervention for patients with arthritis. *Patient Education and Counseling, 11,* 29–42.

DiGiuseppe, R., Simon, K. S., McGowan, L., & Gardner, F. (1990). A comparative outcome study of four cognitive therapies in the treatment of social anxiety. *Journal of Rational-Emotive & Cognitive-Behavior Therapy, 8,* 129–146.

Dixon, W. A. (2000). Problem-solving appraisal and depression: Evidence for a recovery model. *Journal of Counseling and Development, 78,* 87–91.

Dixon, W. A., Heppner, P. P., & Anderson, W. P. (1991). Problem-solving appraisal, stress, hopelessness, and suicide ideation in a college population. *Journal of Counseling Psychology, 38,* 1–56.

Dixon, W. A., Heppner, P. P., Burnett, J. W., Anderson, W. P., & Wood, P. K. (1993). Distinguishing among antecedents, concomitants, and consequences of problem-solving appraisal and depressive symptoms. *Journal of Counseling Psychology, 40,* 357–364.

Dixon, W. A., Heppner, P. P., & Rudd, M. D. (1994). Problem-solving appraisal, hopelessness, and suicide ideation: Evidence for a mediational model. *Journal of Counseling Psychology, 41,* 91–98.

Dobson, D. J., & Dobson, K. S. (1981). Problem-solving strategies in depressed and nondepressed college students. *Cognitive Therapy and Research, 5,* 237–249.

Donahoe, C. P., Carter, M. J., Bloem, W. D., Hirsch, G. L., Laasi, N., & Wallace, C. J. (1990). Assessment of interpersonal problem-solving skills. *Psychiatry, 53,* 329–339.

Donnelly, J. P., & Scott, M. F. (1999). Evaluation of an offending behaviour programme with a mentally disordered population. *British Journal of Forensic Practice, 1,* 25–32.

Doorenbos, A., Givens, B., Given, C., Verbitsky, N., Cimprich, B., & McCorkle, R. (2005). Reducing symptom limitations: A cognitive behavioral intervention randomized trial. *Psycho-oncology, 14,* 574–584.

Dowrick, C., Dunn, G., Ayuso-Mateos, J. L., Dalgard, O. S., Page, H., Lehtinen, V., et al. (2000). Problem solving treatment and group psychoeducation for depression: Multicentre randomised controlled trial. *British Journal of Medicine, 321,* 1–6.

Dreer, L. E., Elliott, T. R., Fletcher, D. C., & Swanson, M. (2005). Social problem-solving abilities and psychological adjustment of persons in low vision rehabilitation. *Rehabilitation Psychology, 50,* 232–238.

Dreer, L. E., Jackson, W. T., & Elliott, T. R. (2005). Social problem solving, personality disorder, and substance abuse. In M. McMurran & J. McGuire (Eds.), *Social problem solving and offending: Evidence, evaluation and evolution* (pp. 67–90). Chichester, UK: Wiley.

Dugas, M. J., Freeston, M. H., & Ladouceur, R. (1997). Intolerance of uncertainty in worry. *Cognitive Therapy and Research, 21,* 593–606.

Dugas, M. J., Ladouceur, R., Léger, E., Freeston, M. H., Langlois, F., Provencher, M. D., et al. (2003). Group cognitive-behavioral therapy for generalized anxiety disorder: Treatment outcome and long-term follow-up. *Journal of Consulting and Clinical Psychology, 71,* 821–825.

Dugas, M. J., Letarte, H., Rhéaume, J., Freeston, M. H., & Ladouceur, R. (1995). Worry and problem solving: Evidence of a specific relationship. *Cognitive Therapy and Research, 19,* 109–142.

Durlak, J. A. (1983). Social problem solving as a primary prevention strategy. In R. D. Felner, L. A. Jason, J. N. Moritsugu, & S. S. Farber (Eds.), *Preventive psychology: Theory, research, and practice.* New York: Pergamon.

D'Zurilla, T. J. (1986). *Problem-solving therapy: A social competence approach to clinical intervention.* New York: Springer Publishing.

D'Zurilla, T. J. (1990). Problem-solving training for effective stress management and prevention. *Journal of Cognitive Psychotherapy: An International Quarterly, 4,* 327–355.

D'Zurilla, T. J., & Chang, E. C. (1995). The relations between social problem solving and coping. *Cognitive Therapy and Research, 19,* 547–562.

D'Zurilla, T. J., Chang, E. C., Nottingham IV, E. J., & Faccini, L. (1998). Social problem-solving deficits and hopelessness, depression, and suicidal risk in college students and psychiatric inpatients. *Journal of Clinical Psychology, 54,* 1–17.

D'Zurilla, T. J., Chang, E. C., & Sanna, L. J. (2003). Self-esteem and social problem solving as predictors of aggression in college students. *Journal of Social and Clinical Psychology, 22,* 424–440.

D'Zurilla, T. J., & Goldfried, M. R. (1971). Problem solving and behavior modification. *Journal of Abnormal Psychology, 78,* 107–126.

D'Zurilla, T. J., & Maschka, G. (1988, November). *Outcome of a problem-solving approach to stress management: I. Comparison with social support.* Paper presented at the Association for Advancement of Behavior Therapy Convention, New York.

D'Zurilla, T. J., & Maydeu-Olivares, A. (1995). Conceptual and methodological issues in social problem-solving assessment. *Behavior Therapy, 26,* 409–432.

D'Zurilla, T. J., & Nezu, A. (1980). A study of the generation-of-alternatives process in social problem solving. *Cognitive Therapy and Research, 4,* 67–72.

D'Zurilla, T. J., & Nezu, A. (1982). Social problem solving in adults. In P. C. Kendall (Ed.), *Advances in cognitive-behavioral research and therapy* (Vol. 1, pp. 202–274). New York: Academic Press.

D'Zurilla, T. J., & Nezu, A. M. (1990). Development and preliminary evaluation of the Social Problem-Solving Inventory (SPSI). Psychological Assessment. *A Journal of Consulting and Clinical Psychology, 2,* 156–163.

D'Zurilla, T. J., & Nezu, A. M. (1999). *Problem-solving therapy: A social competence approach to clinical intervention* (2nd ed.). New York: Springer Publishing.

D'Zurilla, T. J., Nezu, A. M., & Maydeu-Olivares, A. (2002). *Manual for the Social Problem-Solving Inventory-Revised.* North Tonawanda, NY: Multi-Health Systems.

D'Zurilla, T. J., Nezu, A. M., & Maydeu-Olivares, A. (2004). Social problem solving: Theory and assessment. In E. C. Chang, T. J. D'Zurilla, & L. J. Sanna (Eds.), *Social problem solving: Theory, research, and training.* Washington, DC: American Psychological Association.

D'Zurilla, T. J., & Sheedy, C. F. (1991). Relation between social problem solving ability and subsequent level of psychological stress in college students. *Journal of Personality and Social Psychology, 61,* 841–846.

D'Zurilla, T. J., & Sheedy, C. F. (1992). The relation between social problem-solving ability and subsequent level of academic competence in college students. *Cognitive Therapy and Research, 16,* 589–599.

Easterbrook, J. A. (1959). The effect of emotion on cue utilization and the organization of behavior. *Psychological Review, 66,* 183–201.

Edwards, W. (1961). Behavioral decision theory. *Annual Review of Psychology, 12,* 473–498.

Eisenberg, L. (1992). Treating depression and anxiety in primary care: Closing the gap between knowledge and practice. *New England Journal of Medicine, 326,* 1080–1084.

Elliott, T. R. (1992). Problem-solving appraisal, oral contraceptive use, and menstrual pain. *Journal of Applied Social Psychology, 22,* 286–297.

Elliott, T. R. (1998). Social problem solving abilities and adjustment to recent-onset physical disability. *Rehabilitation Psychology, 44,* 315–322.

Elliott, T. R., Godshall, F., Herrick, S., Witty, T., & Spruell, M. (1991). Problem solving appraisal and psychological adjustment following spinal cord injury. *Cognitive Therapy and research, 15,* 387–398.

Elliott, T. R., Godshall, F., Shrout, J. R., & Witty, T. E. (1990). Problem solving appraisal, self-reported study habits, and performance of academically at risk college students. *Journal of Counseling Psychology, 37,* 203–207.

Elliott, T. R., Herrick, S., MacNair, R., & Harkins, S. (1994). Personality correlates of self-appraised problem-solving ability: Problem orientation and trait affectivity. *Journal of Personality Assessment, 63,* 489–505.

Elliott, T. R., Johnson, M. O., & Jackson. R. (1997). Social problem solving and health behaviors of undergraduate students. *Journal of College Student Development, 38,* 24–31.

Elliott, T. R., & Marmarosh, C. (1994). Problem solving appraisal, health complaints, and health related expectancies. *Journal of Counseling and Development, 72,* 531–537.

Elliott, T. R., Sherwin, E., Harkins, S., & Marmarosh, C. (1995). Self-appraised problem-solving ability, affective states, and psychological distress. *Journal of Counseling Psychology, 42,* 105–115.

Elliott, T. R., & Shewchuk, R. M. (2003). Social problem-solving abilities and distress in family members assuming a caregiving role. *British Journal of Health Psychology, 8,* 149–163.

Elliott, T. R., Shewchuk, R. M., Hagglund, K., Rybarczyk, B., & Harkins, S. (1996). Occupational burnout, tolerance for stress, and coping among nurses in rehabilitation units. *Rehabilitation Psychology, 41,* 267–284.

Elliott, T. R., Shewchuk, R. M., Miller, D., & Richards, J. S. (2001). Profiles in problem solving: Psychological well-being and distress among persons with diabetes mellitus. *Journal of Clinical Psychology in Medical Settings, 8,* 283–291.

Elliott, T. R., Shewchuk, R. M., & Richards, J. S. (1999). Caregiver social problem solving abilities and family member adjustment to recent-onset physical disability. *Rehabilitation Psychology, 44,* 104–123.

Elliott, T. R., Shewchuk, R. M., & Richards, J. S. (2001). Family caregiver social problem-solving abilities and adjustment during the initial year of the caregiving role. *Journal of Counseling Psychology, 48,* 223–232.

Elliott, T. R., Shewchuk, R. M., Richards, J. S., Palmatier, A., & Margolis, K. (1997, April). *Social problem solving adjustment of caregivers of persons with recent-onset spinal cord injury.* Paper presented at the Society of Behavioral Medicine Convention, San Francisco, CA.

Elliott, T. R., Shewchuk, R. M., Richeson, C., Pickelman, H., & Franklin, K. W. (1996). Problem-solving appraisal and the prediction of depression during pregnancy and in the postpartum period. *Journal of Counseling and Development, 74,* 645–651.

Ellis, A., & Dryden, W. (1997). *The practice of rational emotive behavior therapy* (2nd ed.). New York: Springer Publishing.

Epstein, S. (1982). Conflict and stress. In L. Goldberger and S. Breznitz (Eds.), *Handbook of stress: Theoretical and clinical aspects.* New York: Free Press.

Epstein, S. (1994). Integration of the cognitive and the psychodynamic unconscious. *American Psychologist, 49,* 709–724.

Epstein, S., & Meier, P. (1989). Constructive thinking: A broad coping variable with specific components. *Journal of Personality and Social Psychology, 57,* 332–350.

Evans, J., Williams, J.M.G., O'Loughlin, S., & Howells, K. (1992). Autobiographical memory and problem-solving strategies of parasuicide patients. *Psychological Medicine, 22,* 399–405.

Ewart, C. K. (1990). A social problem-solving approach to behavior change in coronary heart disease. In S. Schumaker, E. Schron, & J. Ockene (Eds.), *Handbook of health behavior change.* New York: Springer Publishing.

Falloon, I. R. H. (2000). Problem solving as a core strategy in the prevention of schizophrenia and other mental disorders. *Australian and New Zealand Journal of Psychiatry, 34* (Suppl.), S185–S190.

Fawzy, F. I., Cousins, N., Fawzy, N. W., Kemeny, M. E., Elashoff, R., & Morton, D. (1990). A structured psychiatric intervention for cancer patients: I. Changes over time in methods of coping and affective disturbance. *Archives of General Psychiatry, 47,* 720–725.

Fawzy, F. I., Fawzy, N. W., & Canada, A. L. (2001). Psychoeducational intervention programs for patients with cancer. In A. Baum & B. L. Anderson (Eds.), *Psychosocial interventions for cancer* (pp. 235–267). Washington, DC: American Psychological Association.

Fawzy, F. I., Fawzy, N. W., Hyun, C. S., Guthrie, D., Fahey, J. L., & Morton, D. L. (1993). Malignant melanoma: Effects of an early structured psychiatric intervention, coping and affective state on recurrence and survival 6 years later. *Archives of General Psychiatry, 50,* 681–689.

Fehrenbach, A.M.B., & Peterson, L. (1989). Parental problem-solving skills, stress, and dietary compliance in phenylketonuria. *Journal of Consulting and Clinical Psychology, 57,* 237–241.

Fischler, G. L., & Kendall, P. C. (1988). Social cognitive problem solving and childhood adjustment: Qualitative and topological analyses. *Cognitive Therapy and Research, 12,* 133–153.

Folkman, S., & Lazarus, R. S. (1980). An analysis of coping in a middle-aged community sample. *Journal of Health and Social Behavior, 21,* 219–239.

Folkman, S., & Lazarus, R. S. (1988). Coping as a mediator of emotion. *Journal of Personality and Social Psychology, 54,* 466–475.

Foxx, R. M., Kyle, M. S., Faw, G. D., & Bittle, R. G. (1989). Problem-solving skills training: Social validation and generalization. *Behavioral Residential Treatment, 4,* 269–288.

Foxx, R. M., Martella, R. C., & Marchand-Martella, N. E. (1989). The acquisition, maintenance, and generalization of problem-solving skills by closed head-injured adults. *Behavior Therapy, 20,* 61–76.

Frauenknecht, M. (1990). Psychometric evaluation of the Personal Problem-Solving Inventory for adolescents (PPSI). *Dissertation Abstracts International, 52,* 141A.

Frauenknecht, M., & Black, D. R. (1995). Social Problem-Solving Inventory for Adolescents (SPSI-A): Development and psychometric evaluation. *Journal of Personality Assessment, 64,* 522–539.

Frauenknecht, M., & Black, D. R. (2004). Problem-solving training for children and adolescents. In E. C. Chang, T. J. D'Zurilla, & L. J. Sanna (Eds.), *Social problem solving: Theory, research, and training* (pp. 153–170). Washington, DC: American Psychological Association.

Freedman, B. I., Rosenthal, L., Donahoe, C. P., Schlundt, D. G., & McFall, R. M. (1978). A social-behavioral analysis of skill deficits in delinquent and non-delinquent adolescent boys. *Journal of Consulting and Clinical Psychology, 46,* 1448–1462.

Frye, A. A., & Goodman, S. H. (2000). Which social problem-solving components buffer depression in adolescent girls? *Cognitive Therapy and Research, 24,* 637–650.

Gagné, R. M. (1966). Human problem solving: Internal and external events. In B. Kleinmuntz (Ed.), *Problem solving: Research, method and theory.* New York: Wiley.

Gallagher-Thompson, D., Lovett, S., Rose, J., McKibbin, C., Coon, D., Futterman, A., et al. (2000). Impact of psychoeducational interventions on distressed caregivers. *Journal of Clinical Geropsychology, 6,* 91–110.

García-Vera, M. P., Labrador, F. J., & Sanz, J. (1997). Stress-management training for essential hypertension: A controlled study. *Applied Psychophysiology and Biofeedback, 22,* 261–283.

García-Vera, M. P., Sanz, J., & Labrador, F. J. (1998). Psychological changes accompanying and mediating stress-management training for essential hypertension. *Applied Psychophysiology and Biofeedback, 23,* 159–178.

Garland, A., Harrington, J., House, R., & Scott, J. (2000). A pilot study of the relationship between problem-solving skills and outcome in major depressive disorder. *British Journal of Medical Psychology, 73,* 303–309.

Gath, D., & Mynors-Wallis, L. (1997). Problem-solving treatment in primary care. In D. M. Clark & C. G. Fairburn (Eds.), *Science and practice of cognitive behaviour therapy* (pp. 415–431). Oxford: Oxford University Press.

Gendron, C., Poitras, L., Dastoor, D. P., & Pérodeau, G. (1996). Cognitive behavioral group intervention for spousal caregivers: Findings and clinical considerations. *Clinical Gerontologist, 17,* 3–19.

George, A. L. (1974). Adaptation to stress in political decision making: The individual, small group, and organizational contexts. In G. V. Coelho, D. A. Hamburg, & J. E. Adams (Eds.), *Coping and adaptation.* New York: Basic Books.

Getter, H., & Nowinski, J. K. (1981). A free response test of interpersonal effectiveness. *Journal of Personality Assessment, 45,* 301–308.

Given, C., Given, B., Rahbar, M., Jeon, S., McCorkle, R., Cimprich, B., et al. (2004). Does a symptom management intervention affect depression among cancer patients: Results from a clinical trial. *Psycho-oncology, 13,* 818–839.

Gladwin, T. (1967). Social competence and clinical practice. *Psychiatry: Journal for the Study of Interpersonal Processes, 3,* 30–43.

Glasgow, R. E., Toobert, D. J., Barrera, M., & Stryker, L. A. (2004). Assessment of problem-solving: A key to successful diabetes self-management. *Journal of Behavioral Medicine, 27,* 477–490.

Glasgow, R. E., Toobert, D. J., Hampson, S. E., Brown, J. E., Lewinsohn, P.M., & Donnelly, J. (1992). Improving self-care among older patients with Type II diabetes: The "Sixty Something ..." study. *Patient Education and Counseling, 19,* 61–74.

Glasgow, R. E., Toobert, D. J., Riddle, M., Donnelly, J., & Calder, D. (1989). Diabetes-specific social learning variables and self-care behaviors among persons with Type II diabetes. *Health Psychology, 8,* 285–303.

Glynn, S. M., Marder, S. R., Liberman, R. P., Blair, K., Wirshing, W. C., Wirshing, D. A., et al. (2002). Supplementing clinic-based skills training with manual-based community support sessions: Effects on social adjustment of patients with schizophrenia. *American Journal of Psychiatry, 159,* 829–837.

Goddard, P., & McFall, R. M. (1992). Decision-making skills and heterosexual competence in college women: An information-processing analysis. *Journal of Social and Clinical Psychology, 11,* 401–425.

Godshall, F. J., & Elliott, T. R. (1997). Behavioral correlates of self-appraised problem-solving ability: Problem-solving skills and health-compromising behaviors. *Journal of Applied Social Psychology, 27,* 929–944.

Goldfried, M. R. (1982). Resistance and clinical behavior therapy. In P. L. Wachtel (Ed.), *Resistance: Psychodynamic and behavioral approaches.* New York: Plenum.

Goldfried, M. R., Decenteceo, E. T., & Weinberg, L. (1974). Systematic rational restructuring as a self-control technique. *Behavior Therapy, 5,* 247–252.

Goldfried, M. R., & D'Zurilla, T. J. (1969). A behavior-analytic model for assessing competence. In C. D. Spielberger (Ed.), *Current topics in clinical and community psychology* (Vol. 1). New York: Academic Press.

Gordon, D. A., & Arbuthnot, J. (1987). Individual, group, and family interventions. In H. C. Quay (Ed.), *Handbook of juvenile delinquency.* New York: Wiley.

Goodman, S. H., Gravitt, G. W., & Kaslow, N. J. (1995). Social problem solving: A moderator of the relation between negative life stress and depression symptoms in children. *Journal of Abnormal Child Psychology, 23,* 473–485.

Gosselin, M. J., & Marcotte, D. (1997). The role of self-perceived problem-solving skills in relation with depression during adolescence. *Science et Comportement, 25,* 299–314.

Gosselin, P., Pelletier, O., & Ladouceur, R. (2000, October). *The Negative Problem Orientation Questionnaire: Development and preliminary analyses.* Poster presented at the annual meeting of the Société Québécoise pour la Recherche en Psychogue, Hull, Quebec.

Gosselin, P., Pelletier, O., & Ladouceur, R. (2001, July). *The Negative Problem Orientation Questionnaire (NPOQ): Development and validation among a non-clinical sample.* Poster presented at the annual meeting of the World Congress of Behavioral and Cognitive Therapies, Vancouver, British Columbia.

Gotlib, I. H., & Asarnow, R. F. (1979). Interpersonal and impersonal problem-solving skills in mildly and clinically depressed university students. *Journal of Consulting and Clinical Psychology, 47,* 86–95.

Graf, A. (2003). A psychometric test of a German version of the SPSI-R. *Zeitschrift für Differentielle und Diagnostische Psychologie, 24,* 277–291.

Gramling, S. E., & Auerbach, S. M. (1998). *Stress management workbook: Techniques and self-assessment procedures.* Upper Saddle River, NJ: Prentice-Hall.

Grant, J. S., Elliott, T. R., Newman-Giger, J., & Bartolucci, A. A. (2001). Social problem-solving abilities, social support, and adjustment among family caregivers of individuals with a stroke. *Rehabilitation Psychology, 46,* 44–57.

Grant, J. S., Elliott, T. R., Weaver, M., Bartolcci, A. A., & Giger, J. N. (2002). Telephone intervention with family caregivers of stroke survivors after rehabilitation. *Stroke, 33,* 2060–2065.

Greening, L. (1997). Adolescent stealers' and nonstealers' social problem-solving skills. *Adolescence, 32,* 51–55.

Guilford, J. P. (1967). *The nature of human intelligence.* New York: McGraw-Hill.

Guilford, J. P. (1968). *Intelligence, creativity, and their educational implications.* San Diego, CA: Robert R. Knapp.

Guilford, J. P. (1977). *Way beyond the IQ: Guide to improving intelligence and creativity.* Great Neck, NY: Creative Synergetic Associates.

Haaga, D. A. F., Fine, J. A., Terrill, D., Steward, B. L., & Beck, A. T. (1995). Social problem-solving deficits, dependency, and depressive symptoms. *Cognitive Therapy and Research, 19,* 147–158.

Hains, A. A., & Herman, L. P. (1989). Social cognitive skills and behavioral adjustment of delinquent and adolescents in treatment. *Journal of Adolescence, 12,* 323–328.

Hamberger, L. K., & Lohr, J. M. (1984). *Stress and stress management.* New York: Springer Publishing.

Hamilton, M. (1960). A rating scale for measuring depression. *Journal of Neurology, Neurosurgery, and Psychiatry, 23,* 56–62.

Hanna, K. J., Ewart, C. K., & Kwiterovich, P. O. (1990). Child problem-solving competence, behavioral adjustment, and adherence to lipid-lowering diet. *Patient Education and Counseling, 16,* 119–131.

Hansen, D. J., St. Lawrence, J. S., & Christoff, K. A. (1985). Effects of interpersonal problem-solving training with chronic aftercare patients on problem-solving component skills and effectiveness of solutions. *Journal of Consulting and Clinical Psychology, 53,* 167–174.

Hawton, K., Kingsbury, S., Steinhardt, K., James, A., & Fagg, J. (1999). Repetition of deliberate self-harm by adolescents: The role of psychological factors. *Journal of Adolescence, 22,* 369–378.

Hegel, M. T., Barrett, J. E., & Oxman, T. E. (2000). Training therapists in problem-solving treatment of depressive disorders in primary care: Lessons learned from the "Treatment Effectiveness Project." *Families, Systems & Health, 18,* 423–435.

Heppner, P. P. (1988). *The Problem-Solving Inventory.* Palo Alto, CA: Consulting Psychologist Press.

Heppner, P. P., & Anderson, W. P. (1985). The relationship between problem solving self appraisal and psychological adjustment. *Cognitive Therapy and Research, 9,* 415–427.

Heppner, P. P., Baumgardner, A., & Jackson, J. (1985). Problem solving self-appraisal, depression, and attribution styles: Are they related? *Cognitive Therapy and Research, 9,* 105–113.

Heppner, P. P., Baumgardner, A. H., Larson, L. M., & Petty, R. E. (August, 1988). *Problem solving training for college students with problem-solving deficits.* Paper presented at the Annual Convention of the American Psychological Association, Anaheim, CA.

Heppner, P. P., Kampa, M., & Brunning, L. (1987). The relationship between problem-solving self-appraisal and indices of physical and psychological health. *Cognitive Therapy and Research, 11,* 155–168.

Heppner, P. P., Neal, G. W., & Larson, L. M. (1984). Problem-solving training as prevention with college students. *Personnel and Guidance Journal, 62,* 514–519.

Heppner, P. P., & Petersen, C. H. (1982). The development and implications of a personal problem solving inventory. *Journal of Counseling Psychology, 29,* 66–75.

Heppner, P. P., Reeder, B. L., & Larson, L. M. (1983). Cognitive variables associated with personal problem-solving appraisal: Implications for counseling. *Journal of Counseling Psychology, 30,* 537–545.

Herrick, S., Elliott, T. R., & Crow, F. (1994). Self-appraised problem-solving skills and the prediction of secondary complications among persons with spinal cord injuries. *Journal of Clinical Psychology in Medical Settings, 1,* 269–283.

Hill-Briggs, F., Gary, T. L., Yeh, H. C., Batts-Turner, M., Powe, N. R., Saudek, C., et al. (2006). Association of social problem solving with glycemic control in a sample of urban African Americans with type 2 diabetes. *Journal of Behavioral Medicine, 29,* 68–79.

Hill-Briggs, F., Yeh, H. C., Gary, T. L., Batts-Turner, M., Brancati, F. L., & D'Zurilla, T. J. (2005). *Development of the Diabetes Problem-Solving Scale-Self Report (DPSS-SR) in a minority type 2 diabetes sample.* Manuscript submitted for publication.

Hockey, R., & Hamilton, P. (1983). Cognitive patterning of stress states. In R. Hockey (Ed.), *Stress and fatigue in human performance.* New York: Wiley.

Hosaka, T., (1996). A pilot study of a structured psychiatric intervention for Japanese women with breast cancer. *Psycho-oncology, 5,* 59–65.

Houts, P. S., Bucher, J. A., Mount, B. M., Britton, S. E., Nezu, A. M., Nezu, C. M., et al. (Eds.). (1997). *Home care guide for advanced cancer: When quality of life is the primary goal of care.* Philadelphia: American College of Physicians.

Houts, P. S., Nezu, A. M., Nezu, C. M., & Bucher, J. A. (1996). A problem-solving model of family caregiving for cancer patients. *Patient Education and Counseling, 27,* 63–73.

Houts, P. S., Nezu, A. M., Nezu, C. M., Bucher, J. A., & Lipton, A. (Eds.). (1994). *Home care guide for cancer.* Philadelphia, PA: American College of Physicians.

Hunt, J. (1963). Motivation inherent in information processing and action. In O. J. Harvey (Ed.), *Motivation and social organization: The cognitive factors.* New York: Ronald.

Ingram, R. E., & Kendall, P. C. (1986). Cognitive clinical psychology: Implications of an information processing perspective: In R. E. Ingram (Ed.), *Information processing approaches to clinical psychology* (pp. 3–21). New York: Academic Press.

Jacobson, N. S. (1978). Specific and nonspecific factors in the effectiveness of a behavioral approach to the treatment of marital discord. *Journal of Consulting and Clinical Psychology, 46,* 442–452.

Jacobson, N. S. (1984). A component analysis of marital behavior therapy: The relative effectiveness of behavior exchange and communication/problem-solving training. *Journal of Consulting and Clinical Psychology, 52,* 295–305.

Jacobson, N. S., & Follette, W. C. (1985). Clinical significance of improvement resulting from two behavioral marital therapy components. *Behavior Therapy, 16,* 249–262.

Jacobson, N. S., & Margolin, G. (1979). *Marital therapy. Strategies based on social learning and behavior exchange principles.* New York: Brunner/Mazel.

Jaffe, W. B., & D'Zurilla, T. J. (2003). Adolescent problem solving, parent problem solving, and externalizing behavior in adolescents. *Behavior Therapy, 34,* 295–311.

Jaffe, W. B., & D'Zurilla, T. J. (2006). *Personality, social problem solving, and adolescent substance use.* Manuscript submitted for publication.

Jahoda, I. L. (1953). The meaning of psychological health. *Social Casework, 34,* 349–354.

Jahoda, I. L. (1958). *Current concepts of positive mental health.* New York: Basic Books.

Janis, I. L. (1982). Decision making under stress. In L. Goldberger & S. Breznitz (Eds.), *Handbook of stress: Theoretical and clinical aspects.* New York: Free Press.

Janis, I. L. (1983). Stress inoculation in health care: Theory and research. In D. Meichenbaum & M. E. Jaremko (Eds.), *Stress reduction and prevention.* New York: Plenum.

Janis, I. L., & Mann, L. (1977). *Decision making: A psychological analysis of conflict, choice, and commitment.* New York: Free Press.

Johnson, S. M., & Greenberg, L. S. (1985). Differential effects of experiential and problem-solving interventions in resolving marital conflict. *Journal of Consulting and Clinical Psychology, 53,* 175–184.

Kagan, C. (1984). Social problem solving and social skills training. *British Journal of Clinical Psychology, 23,* 161–173.

Kahnemann, D., & Tversky, A. (1979). Prospect theory: An analysis of decisions under risk. *Econometrica, 47,* 263–291.

Kaiser, A., Hahlweg, K., Fehm-Wolfsdorf, G., & Groth, T. (1998). The efficacy of a compact psychoeducational group training program for married couples. *Journal of Consulting and Clinical Psychology, 66,* 753–760.

Kanfer, F. H. (1970). Self-regulation: Research, issues, and speculations. In C. Neuringer & J. L. Michael (Eds.), *Behavior modification in clinical psychology.* New York: Appleton Century-Crofts.

Kanner, A. D., Coyne, J. C., Schaefer, C., & Lazarus, R. S. (1981). Comparison of two modes of stress measurement: Daily hassles and uplifts versus major life events. *Journal of Behavioral Medicine, 4,* 1–39.

Kant, G. L., D'Zurilla, T. J., & Maydeu-Olivares, A. (1997). Social problem solving as a mediator of stress-related depression and anxiety in middle-aged and elderly community residents. *Cognitive Therapy and Research, 21,* 73–96.

Katon, W. J., Von Korff, M., Lin, E.H.B., Simon, G., Ludman, E., Russo, J., et al. (2004). The Pathways Study: A randomized trial of collaborative care in patients with diabetes and depression. *Archives of General Psychiatry, 61,* 1042–1049.

Kelly, J. A., Murphy, D. A., Washington, C. D., Wilson, T. S., Koob, J. J., Davis, D. R., et al. (1994). The effects of HIV/AIDS intervention groups for high-risk women in urban clinics. *American Journal of Public Health, 84,* 1918–1922.

Kelly, M. L., Scott, W. O. M., Prue, D. M., & Rychtarik, R. G. (1985). A component analysis of problem-solving skills training. *Cognitive Therapy and Research, 9,* 429–441.

Keltikangas-Järvinen, L. (2005). Social problem solving and the development of aggression. In M. McMurran & J. McGuire (Eds.), *Social problem solving and offending: Evidence, evaluation and evolution* (pp. 31–50). Chichester, UK: Wiley.

Kendall, P. C., & Hollon, S. D. (Eds.). (1979). *Cognitive-behavioral interventions: Theory, research, and procedures.* New York: Academic Press.

Kerns, R. D., Rosenberg, R., & Otis, J. D. (2002). Self-appraised problem solving and pain-relevant social support as predictors of the experience of chronic pain. *Annals of Behavioral Medicine, 24,* 100–105.

Kleinmuntz, B. (Ed.). (1966). *Problem solving: Research, method and theory.* New York: Wiley.

Kobasa, S. C., Maddi, S. R., & Kahn, S. (1980). Hardiness and health: A prospective study. *Journal of Personality and Social Psychology, 42,* 168–177.

Krasnor, L. R., & Rubin, K. H. (1981). The assessment of social problem-solving skills in young children. In T. Merluzzi, C. Glass, & M. Genest (Eds.), *Cognitive assessment*. New York: Guilford Press.

Kurylo, M., Elliott, T. R., DeVivo, L., & Dreer, L. E. (2004). Caregiver social problem solving abilities and family member adjustment following congestive heart failure. *Journal of Clinical Psychology in Medical Settings, 11,* 151–157.

Lacey, J. I. (1967). Somatic response patterning and stress: Some revisions of activation theory. In M. H. Appley & R. Trumball (Eds.), *Psychological stress*. New York: McGraw-Hill.

Ladouceur, R., Blais, F., Freeston, M. H., & Dugas, M. J. (1998). Problem solving and problem orientation in generalized anxiety disorder. *Journal of Anxiety Disorders, 12,* 139–152.

Ladouceur, R., Dugas, M. J., Freeston, M. H., Gagnon, F., & Thibodeau, N. (2000). Efficacy of a cognitive-behavioral treatment for generalized anxiety disorder: Evaluation in a controlled clinical trial. *Journal of Consulting and Clinical Psychology, 68,* 957–964.

Larson, L., Piersel, W. C., Imao, R., & Allen, S. (1990). Significant predictors of problem-solving appraisal. *Journal of Counseling Psychology, 37,* 482–490.

Lazarus, R. S. (1966). *Psychological stress and the coping process*. New York: McGraw-Hill.

Lazarus, R. S. (1981). The stress and coping paradigm. In C. Eisdorfer, D. Cohen, A. Kleinman, & P. Maxim (Eds.), *Theoretical bases for psychopathology*. New York: Spectrum.

Lazarus, R. S. (1999). *Stress and emotion: A new synthesis*. New York: Springer Publishing.

Lazarus, R. S., & Folkman, S. (1984). *Stress, appraisal, and coping*. New York: Springer Publishing.

Leadbeater, B. J., Hellner, I., Allen, J. P., & Aber, J. L. (1989). Assessment of interpersonal negotiation strategies in youth engaged in problem behaviors. *Developmental Psychology, 25,* 465–472.

Leighton, J. P., & Sternberg, R. J. (2003). Reasoning and problem solving. In A. F. Healy & R. W. Proctor (Eds.), *Experimental psychology* (pp. 623–648), Vol. 4 of the *Handbook of psychology*, I. B. Weiner (Editor-in-Chief). New York: Wiley.

Lerner, M. S., & Clum, G. A. (1990). Treatment of suicide ideators: A problem-solving approach. *Behavior Therapy, 21,* 403–411.

Levine, M. (1988). *Effective problem solving*. Englewood Cliffs, NJ: Prentice-Hall.

Liberman, R. P., Eckman, T., & Marder, S. R. (2001). Training in social problem solving among persons with schizophrenia. *Psychiatric Services, 52,* 31–33.

Liberman, R. P., McCann, M. J., & Wallace, C. J. (1976). Generalisation of behaviour therapy with psychotics. *British Journal of Psychiatry, 129,* 490–496.

Linehan, M. M., Camper, P., Chiles, J. A., Strosahl, K., & Shearin, E. (1987). Interpersonal problem solving and parasuicide. *Cognitive Therapy and Research, 11,* 1–12.

Lochman, J. E., Wayland, K. K., & White, K. J. (1993). Social goals: Relationship to adolescent adjustment and to social problem solving. *Journal of Abnormal Child Psychology, 21,* 135–151.

Logan, G. D. (1988). Toward an instance theory of automatization. *Psychological Review, 95,* 492–527.

Londahl, E. A., Tverskoy, A., & D'Zurilla, T. J. (2005). The relations of internalizing symptoms to conflict and interpersonal problem solving in close relationships. *Cognitive Therapy and Research, 29,* 445–462.

Lopez, M. A., & Mermelstein, R. J. (1995). A cognitive-behavioral program to improve geriatric rehabilitation outcome. *Gerontologist, 35,* 696–700.

Loumidis, K. S., & Hill, A. (1997). Training social problem-solving skill to reduce maladaptive behaviours in intellectual disability groups: The influence of individual difference factors. *Journal of Applied Research in Intellectual Disabilities, 10,* 217–237.

Lynch, D. J., Tamburrino, M. B., & Nagel, R. (1997). Telephone counseling for patients with minor depression: Preliminary findings in a family practice setting. *Journal of Family Practice, 44,* 293–298.

Lynch, D. J., Tamburrino, M. B., Nagel, R., & Smith, M. K. (2004). Telephone based treatment for family practice patients with mild depression. *Psychological Reports, 94,* 785–792.

MacNair, R. R., & Elliott, T. R. (1992). Self-perceived problem-solving ability, stress appraisal, and coping over time. *Journal of Research in Personality, 26,* 150–164.

Mahoney, M. J. (1974). *Cognition and behavior modification.* Cambridge, MA: Ballinger.

Mandler, G. (1982). Stress and thought processes. In L. Goldberger & S. Breznitz (Eds.), *Handbook of stress: Theoretical and clinical aspects* (pp. 49–68). New York: Free Press.

Marder, S. R., Wirshing, W. C., Mintz, J., McKensie, J., Johnston, K., Eckman, T. A., et al. (1996). Two-year outcome of social skills training and group psychotherapy for outpatients with schizophrenia. *American Journal of Psychiatry, 153,* 1585–1592.

Marsiske, M., & Willis, S. L. (1995). Dimensionality of everyday problem solving in older adults. *Psychology and Aging, 10,* 269–283.

Marx, E. M., Schulze, C. C. (1991). Interpersonal problem-solving in depressed students. *Journal of Clinical Psychology, 47,* 361–367.

Marx, E. M., Williams, J. M. G., & Claridge, G. C. (1992). Depression and social problem solving. *Journal of Abnormal Psychology, 101,* 78–86.

Masserman, J. H. (1943). *Behavior and neurosis.* Chicago: University of Chicago Press.

Mather, M. D. (1970). Obsessions and compulsions. In C. G. Costello (Ed.), *Symptoms of psychopathology.* New York: Wiley.

Maydeu-Olivares, A., & D'Zurilla, T. J. (1995). A factor analysis of the Social Problem-Solving Inventory using polychoric correlations. *European Journal of Psychological Assessment, 11,* 98–107.

Maydeu-Olivares, A., & D'Zurilla, T. J. (1996). A factor-analytic study of the Social Problem-Solving Inventory: An integration of theory and data. *Cognitive Therapy and Research, 20,* 115–133.

Maydeu-Olivares, A., & D'Zurilla, T. J. (1997). The factor structure of the Problem-Solving Inventory. *European Journal of Psychological Assessment, 13,* 206–215.

Maydeu-Olivares, A., Rodríguez-Fornells, A., Gómez-Benito, J., & D'Zurilla, T. J. (2000). Psychometric properties of the Spanish adaptation of the Social Problem-Solving Inventory-Revised (SPSI-R). *Personality and Individual Differences, 29,* 699–708.

McCabe, R. E., Blankstein, K. R., & Mills, J. S. (1999). Interpersonal sensitivity and social problem solving: Relations with academic and social self-esteem, depressive symptoms, and academic performance. *Cognitive Therapy and Research, 23,* 587–604.

McCabe, R. E., Blankstein, K. R., & Mills, J. S. (1999). Interpersonal sensitivity and social problem solving: Relations with academic and social self-esteem, depressive symptoms, and academic performance. *Cognitive Therapy and Research, 23,* 587–604.

McClelland, D.C., & Clark, R. A. (1966). Discrepancy hypothesis. In R. N. Haber (Ed.), *Current research in motivation.* New York: Holt, Rinehart & Winston.

McDonagh, A., Friedman, M., McHugo, G., Ford, J., Sengupta, A., Mueser, K., et al. (2005). Randomized trial of cognitive-behavioral therapy for chronic posttraumatic stress disorder in adult female survivors of childhood sexual abuse. *Journal of Consulting and Clinical Psychology, 73,* 515–524.

McFall, R. M. (1982). A review and reformulation of the concept of social skills. *Behavioral Assessment, 4,* 1–33.

McGrath, J. E. (Ed.). (1970). *Social and psychological factors in stress.* New York: Holt, Rinehart, & Winston.

McGrath, J. E. (1976). Stress and behavior in organizations. In M. D. Dunnette (Ed.), *Handbook of industrial and organizational psychology.* Chicago: Rand McNally.

McGuire, J. (2005). The Think First programme. In M. McMurran & J. McGuire (Eds.), *Social problem solving and offending: Evidence, evaluation and evolution* (pp. 183–206). Chichester, UK: Wiley.

McGuire, J., & Hatcher, R. (2001). Offense-focused problem solving: Preliminary evaluation of a cognitive skills program. *Criminal Justice and Behavior, 28,* 564–587.

McKay, M., Davis, M., & Eshelnour, E. (1995). *The relaxation and stress reduction workbook* (4th ed.). Oakland, CA: New Harbinger.

McLeavey, B.C., Daly, R. J., Ludgate, J. W., & Murray, C. M. (1994). Interpersonal problem-solving skills training in the treatment of self-poisoning patients. *Suicide and Life-Threatening Behavior, 24,* 382–394.

McMurran, M., Blair, M., & Egan, V. (2002). An investigation of the correlations between aggression, impulsiveness, social problem-solving, and alcohol use. *Aggressive Behavior, 28,* 439–445.

McMurran, M., & Duggan, C. (2005). The manualisation of a treatment programme for personality disorder. *Criminal Behaviour and Mental Health, 15,* 17–27.

McMurran, M., Egan, V., Blair, M., & Richardson, C. (2001). The relationship between social problem-solving and personality in mentally disordered offenders. *Personality and Individual Differences, 30,* 517–524.

McMurran, M., Egan, V., & Duggan, C. (2005). Stop & Think! Social problem-solving therapy with personality-disordered offenders. In M. McMurran & J. McGuire (Eds.), *Social problem solving and offending: Evidence, evaluation and evolution* (pp. 207–220). Chichester, UK: Wiley.

McMurran, M., Fyffe, S., McCarthy, L., Duggan, C., & Latham, A. (2001). "Stop & Think!" Social problem-solving therapy with personality-disordered offenders. *Criminal Behaviour and Mental Health, 11,* 273–285.

McMurran, M., & McGuire, J. (Eds.). (2005). *Social problem solving and offending: Evidence, evaluation and evolution.* Chichester, UK: Wiley.

Meadow, A., Parnes, S. J., & Reese, H. (1959). Influence of instructions and problem sequence on a creative problem-solving test. *Journal of Applied Psychology, 43,* 413–416.

Mechanic, D. (1970). Some problems in developing a social psychology of adaptation to stress. In J. E. McGrath (Ed.), *Social and psychological factors in stress.* New York: Holt, Rinehart, & Winston.

Mechanic, D. (1974). Social structure and personal adaptation: Some neglected dimensions. In G. Coelho, C. M. Hamburg, & J. E. Adams (Eds.), *Coping and adaptation.* New York: Basic Books.

Meichenbaum, D., & Cameron, R. (1983). Stress inoculation training: Toward a general paradigm for training coping skills. In D. Meichenbaum & M. E. Jaremko (Eds.), *Stress reduction and prevention.* New York: Plenum.

Meichenbaum, D., Henshaw, D., & Himel, N. (1982). Coping with stress as a problem-solving process. In W. Krohne & L. Luax (Eds.), *Achievement stress and anxiety.* New York: Hemisphere.

Miller, G. A., Galanter, E., & Pribram, K. H. (1960). *Plans and the structure of behavior.* New York: Holt, Rinehart, & Winston.

Miner, R. C., & Dowd, E. T. (1996). An empirical test of the problem solving model of depression and its application to the prediction of anxiety and anger. *Counseling Psychology Quarterly, 9,* 163–176.

Mishel, M. H., Belyea, M., Gemino, B. B., Stewart, J. L., Bailey, D. E., Robertson, C., et al. (2002). Helping patients with localized prostate carcinoma manage uncertainty and treatment side effects: Nurse delivered psychoeducational intervention over the telephone. *Cancer, 94,* 1854–1866.

Mitchell, J. E., & Madigan, R. J. (1984). The effects of induced elation and depression on interpersonal problem solving. *Cognitive Therapy and Research, 8,* 277–285.

Mooney, R. L., & Gordon, L. V. (1950). *The Mooney Manual: Problem Checklist.* New York: Psychological Corporation.

Morris, S. E., Bellack, A. S., & Tenhula, W. N. (2004). Social problem solving and schizophrenia. In E. C. Chang, T. J. D'Zurilla, & L. J. Sanna (Eds.), *Social problem solving: Theory, research, and training* (pp. 83–98). Washington, DC: American Psychological Association.

Mowrer, O. H. (1960). *Learning theory and behavior.* New York: Wiley.

Munoz, R., Ying, Y., Bernal, G., Perez-Stable, E., Sorenson, J., & Hargeaves, E. (1995). Prevention of depression with primary care patients: A randomized controlled trial. *American Journal of Community Psychology, 23,* 199–222.

Murphy, G. E. (1985). A conceptual framework for the choice of interventions in cognitive therapy. *Cognitive Therapy and Research, 9,* 127–134.

Mynors-Wallis, L. (2002). Does problem-solving treatment work through resolving problems? *Psychological Medicine, 32,* 1315–1319.

Mynors-Wallis, L., Davies, I., Gray, A., Barbour, F., & Gath, D. (1997). A randomized controlled trial and cost analysis of problem-solving treatment for emotional disorders given by community nurses in primary care. *British Journal of Psychiatry, 170,* 113–119.

Mynors-Wallis, L. M., Gath, D. H., Day, A., & Baker, F. (2000). Randomised controlled trial of problem solving treatment, antidepressant medication, and combined treatment for major depression in primary care. *British Medical Journal, 320,* 26–30.

Mynors-Wallis, L. M., Gath, D. H., Lloyd-Thomas, A. R., & Tomlinson, D. (1995). Randomised controlled trial comparing problem solving treatment with amitriptyline and placebo for major depression in primary care. *British Medical Journal, 310,* 441–445.

Newell, A., & Simon, H. A. (1972). *Human problem solving.* Englewood Cliffs, NJ: Prentice-Hall.

Nezu, A. M. (1985). Differences in psychological distress between effective and ineffective problem solvers. *Journal of Counseling Psychology, 32,* 135–138.

Nezu, A. M. (1986a). Effects of stress from current problems: Comparisons to major life events. *Journal of Clinical Psychology, 42,* 847–852.

Nezu, A. M. (1986b). Negative life stress and anxiety: Problem solving as a moderator variable. *Psychological Reports, 58,* 279–283.

Nezu, A. M. (1986c). Cognitive appraisal of problem-solving effectiveness: Relation to depression and depressive symptoms. *Journal of Clinical Psychology, 42,* 42–48.

Nezu, A. M. (1986d). Efficacy of a social problem solving therapy approach for unipolar depression. *Journal of Consulting and Clinical Psychology, 54,* 196–202.

Nezu, A. M. (1987). A problem-solving formulation of depression: A literature review and proposal of a pluralistic model. *Clinical Psychology Review, 7,* 121–144.

Nezu, A. M. (2004). Problem solving and behavior therapy revisited. *Behavior Therapy, 35,* 1–33.

Nezu, A. M., & Carnevale, G. J. (1987). Interpersonal problem solving and coping reactions of Vietnam veterans with posttraumatic stress disorder. *Journal of Abnormal Psychology, 96,* 155–157.

Nezu, A. M, & D'Zurilla, T. J. (1979). An experimental evaluation of the decision-making process in social problem solving. *Cognitive Therapy and Research, 3,* 269–277.

Nezu, A. M, & D'Zurilla, T. J. (1981a). Effects of problem definition and formulation on decision making in the social problem-solving process. *Behavior Therapy, 12,* 100–106.

Nezu, A. M, & D'Zurilla, T. J. (1981b). Effects of problem definition and formulation on the generation of alternatives in the social problem-solving process. *Cognitive Therapy and Research, 6,* 265–271.

Nezu, A. M., & D'Zurilla, T. J. (1989). Social problem solving and negative affective conditions. In P.C. Kendall & D. Watson (Eds.), *Anxiety and depression: Distinctive and overlapping features* (pp. 285–315). New York: Academic Press.

Nezu, A. M., D'Zurilla, T. J., Zwick, M. L. & Nezu, C. M. (2004). Problem-solving therapy for adults. In E. C. Chang, T. J. D'Zurilla, & L. J. Sanna (Eds.), *Social problem solving: Theory, research, and training* (pp. 171–191). Washington, DC: American Psychological Association.

Nezu, A. M., & Nezu, C. M. (1987). Psychological distress, problem solving, and coping reactions: Sex-role differences. *Sex Roles, 16,* 205–214.

Nezu, A. M., & Nezu, C. M. (2005). Comments on "Evidence-based behavioral medicine: What is it and how do we achieve it?" The interventionist does not always equal the intervention—The role of therapist competence. *Annals of Behavioral Medicine, 29,* 80.

Nezu, A. M., & Nezu, C. M. (Eds.). (in press, a). *Evidence-based outcome research: A practical guide to conducting randomized clinical trials for psychosocial interventions.* New York: Oxford University Press.

Nezu, A. M., & Nezu, C. M. (in press, b). Problem solving. In W. T. O'Donohue & E. Livens (Eds.), *Promoting treatment adherence: A practical handbook for health care providers.* New York: Sage Publications.

Nezu, A. M., & Nezu, C. M. (in press, c). Treatment adherence and therapist competence. In D. McKay (Ed.), *Handbook of research methods in abnormal and clinical psychology.* Thousand Oaks, CA: Sage Publications.

Nezu, A. M., Nezu, C. M., Deaner, S. L., & D'Zurilla, T. J. (1997). Problem-solving approaches: State-of-the-art [El estado de la cuestión en los enfoques de resolución de problemas] (pp. 171–179). In I. Caro (Ed.), *Handbook of cognitive psychotherapies: State-of-the-art and psychotherapeutic processes.* Barcelona, Spain: Paidós.

Nezu, A. M., Nezu, C. M., & D'Zurilla, T. J. (2007). *Solving life's problems: A 5-step guide to enhanced well-being.* New York: Springer Publishing Co.

Nezu, A. M., Nezu, C. M., Faddis, S., DelliCarpini, L. A., & Houts, P. S. (1995, November). *Social problem solving as a moderator of cancer-related stress.* Paper presented to the Association for Advancement of Behavior Therapy, Washington, DC.

Nezu, A. M., Nezu, C. M., Felgoise, S. H., McClure, K. S., & Houts, P. S. (2003). Project Genesis: Assessing the efficacy of problem-solving therapy for distressed adult cancer patients. *Journal of Consulting and Clinical Psychology, 71,* 1036–1048.

Nezu, A. M., Nezu, C. M., Felgoise, S. H., & Zwick, M. L. (2003). Psychosocial oncology. In A. M. Nezu, C. M. Nezu, & P. A. Geller (Eds.), *Health psychology* (pp. 267–292), Volume 9 of the *Handbook of psychology,* I. B. Weiner (Editor-in-Chief). New York: Wiley.

Nezu, A. M., Nezu, C. M., Friedman, S. H., Faddis, S., & Houts, P. S. (1998). *Helping cancer patients cope: A problem-solving approach.* Washington, DC: American Psychological Association.

Nezu, A. M., Nezu, C. M., Friedman, S. H., Houts, P. S., & Faddis, S. (1997). Project Genesis: Application of problem-solving therapy to individuals with cancer. *The Behavior Therapist, 20,* 155–158.

Nezu, A. M., Nezu, C. M., Houts, P. S., Friedman, S. H., & Faddis, S. (1999). Relevance of problem-solving therapy to psychosocial oncology. *Journal of Psychosocial Oncology, 16,* 5–26.

Nezu, A. M., Nezu, C. M., & Jain, D. (2005). *Psychological distress in adults with cardiovascular disease: The role of problem solving.* Unpublished data. Drexel University, Philadelphia, Pennsylvania.

Nezu, A. M., Nezu, C. M., & Lombardo, E. R. (2003). Problem-solving therapy. In W. O'Donohue, J. E. Fisher, & S. C. Hayes (Eds.), *Cognitive behavior therapy: Applying empirically supported techniques in your practice* (pp. 301–307). New York: Wiley.

Nezu, A. M., Nezu, C. M., & Lombardo, E. R. (2004). *Cognitive-behavioral case formulation and treatment design: A problem-solving approach.* New York: Springer Publishing Co.

Nezu, A. M., Nezu, C. M., & Lombardo, E. (2006). Behavioral and cognitive influences. In F. Andrasik (Ed.), *Adult psychopathology,* Volume 2 of the *Comprehensive handbook of personality and psychopathology* (pp. 36–51). M. Hersen & D. L. Segal (Editors-in-Chief). New Jersey: Wiley.

Nezu, A. M., Nezu, C. M., & Perri, M. G. (1989). *Problem-solving therapy for depression: Therapy, research, and clinical guidelines.* New York: Wiley.

Nezu, A. M., Nezu, C. M., Saraydarian, L., Kalmar, K., & Ronan, G. F. (1986). Social problem solving as a moderator variable between negative life stress and depressive symptoms. *Cognitive Therapy and Research, 10,* 489–498.

Nezu, A. M., & Perri, M. G. (1989). Social problem solving therapy for unipolar depression: An initial dismantling investigation. *Journal of Consulting and Clinical Psychology, 57,* 408–413.

Nezu, A. M., Perri, M. G., & Nezu, C. M. (1987, August). *Validation of a problem-solving/ stress model of depression.* Paper presented at the American Psychological Association Convention, New York.

Nezu, A. M., Perri, M. G., Nezu, C. M., & Mahoney, D. J. (1987, November). *Social problem solving as a moderator of stressful events among clinically depressed individuals.* Paper presented at the Association for Advancement of Behavior Therapy Convention, Boston, Massachusetts.

Nezu, A. M., & Ronan, G. F. (1985). Life stress, current problems, problem solving, and depressive symptomatology: An integrative model. *Journal of Consulting and Clinical Psychology, 53,* 693–697.

Nezu, A. M., & Ronan, G. F. (1987). Social problem solving and depression: Deficits in generating alternatives and decision making. *Southern Psychologist, 3,* 29–34.

Nezu, A. M., & Ronan, G. F. (1988). Stressful life events, problem solving, and depressive symptoms among university students: A prospective analysis. *Journal of Counseling Psychology, 35,* 134–138.

Nezu, A. M., Wilkins, V. M., & Nezu, C. M. (2004). Social problem solving, stress, and negative affective conditions. In E. C. Chang, T. J. D'Zurilla, & L. J. Sanna (Eds.), *Social problem solving: Theory, research, and training* (pp. 49–65). Washington, DC: American Psychological Association.

Nezu, C. M. (2003). Cognitive-behavioral treatment for sex offenders: Current status. *Japanese Journal of Behavior Therapy, 29,* 15–24.

Nezu, C. M., Nezu, A. M., & Dudek, J. A. (1998). A cognitive behavioral model of assessment and treatment for intellectually disabled sexual offenders. *Cognitive and Behavioral Practice, 5,* 25–64.

Nezu, C. M., Nezu, A. M., Dudek, J. A., Peacock, M., & Stoll, J. (2005). Social problem-solving correlates of sexual deviancy and aggression among adult child molesters. *Journal of Sexual Aggression, 11,* 27–36.

Nezu, C. M., D'Zurilla, T. J., & Nezu, A. M. (2005). Problem-solving therapy: Theory, practice, and application to sex offenders. In M. McMurran & J. McGuire (Eds.), *Social problem solving and offenders: Evidence, evaluation and evolution* (pp. 103–123). Chichester, UK: Wiley.

Nezu, C. M., Fiore, A., & Nezu, A. M. (in press). Problem-solving therapy for adult sex offenders with intellectual disabilities. *Journal of Behavioral Consultation and Therapy.*

Nezu, C. M., Greenberg, J., & Nezu, A. M. (in press). Project STOP: Cognitive behavioral assessment and treatment for sex offenders with intellectual disability. *Journal of Forensic Psychology Practice.*

Nezu, C. M., Nezu, A. M., & Arean, P. A. (1991). Assertiveness and problem-solving training for mildly mentally retarded persons with dual diagnosis. *Research in Developmental Disabilities, 12,* 371–386.

Nezu, C. M., Nezu, A. M., Dudek, J. A., Peacock, M., & Stoll, J. (2005). Social problem-solving correlates of sexual deviancy and aggression among adult child molesters. *Journal of Sexual Aggression, 11,* 27–36.

Nezu, C. M., Nezu, A. M., Friedman, S. H., Houts, P. S., DelliCarpini, L. A., Nemeth, C. B., et al. (1999). Cancer and psychological distress: Two investigations regarding the role of problem solving. *Journal of Psychosocial Oncology, 16,* 27–40.

Nezu, C. M., Nezu, A. M., & Houts, P. S. (1993). The multiple applications of problem solving principles in clinical practice. In K. T. Kuehlwein & H. Rosen (Eds.), *Cognitive therapy in action: Evolving innovative practice.* San Francisco, CA: Jossey-Bass.

Nezu, C. M., Palmatier, A., & Nezu, A. M. (2004). Social problem-solving training for caregivers. In E. C. Chang, T. J. D'Zurilla, & L. J. Sanna (Eds.), *Social problem solving: Theory, research, and training* (pp. 223–238). Washington, DC: American Psychological Association

Nichols, H. R., & Molinder, I. (1984). *Multiphasic Sex Inventory manual.* Fircrest, WA: Nichols & Molinder Assessments.

Nixon, S. J., Tivis, R., & Parsons, O. A. (1992). Interpersonal problem-solving in male and female alcoholics. *Alcoholism: Clinical and Experimental Research, 16,* 684–687.

Osborn, A. (1952). *Wake up your mind.* New York: Charles Scribner's Sons.

Osborn, A. (1963). *Applied imagination: Principles and procedures of creative problem solving* (3d ed.). New York: Charles Scribner's Sons.

Parloff, M. B., & Handlon, J. H. (1964). The influence of criticalness on creative problem solving in dyads. *Psychiatry, 27,* 17–27.

Parnes, S. J. (1962). The creative problem solving course and institute at the University of Buffalo. In S. J. Parnes and H. F. Harding (Eds.), *A source book for creative thinking.* New York: Charles Scribner's Sons.

Parnes, S. J., & Meadow, A. (1959). Effects of "brainstorming" instructions on creative problem solving by trained and untrained subjects. *Journal of Educational Psychology, 50,* 171–176.

Parnes, S. J., & Noller, R. B. (1973). *Toward supersanity: Channeled freedom.* New York: D.O.K. Publishers.

Parnes, S. J., Noller, R. B., & Biondi, A. M. (1977). *Guide to creative action: Revised edition of creative behavior guidebook.* New York: Charles Scribner's Sons.

Patsiokas, A. T., & Clum, G. A. (1985). Effects of psychotherapeutic strategies in the treatment of suicide attempters. *Psychotherapy: Theory, Research, Practice, and Training, 22,* 281–290.

Payne, J. W. (1982). Contingent decision behavior. *Psychological Bulletin, 92,* 382–402.

Pellegrini, D. S., & Urbain, E. S. (1985). An evaluation of interpersonal cognitive problem solving training with children. *Journal of Child Psychology and Psychiatry, 26,* 17–41.

Perri, M. G., McAdoo, W. G., McAllister, D. A., Lauer, J. B., Jordan, R. C., Yancey, D. Z., et al. (1987). Effects of peer support and therapist contact on long-term weight loss. *Journal of Consulting and Clinical Psychology, 55,* 615–617.

Perri, M. G., McAllister, D. A., Gange, J. J., Jordan, R. C., McAdoo, W. G., & Nezu, A. M. (1988). Effects of four maintenance programs on the long-term management of obesity. *Journal of Consulting and Clinical Psychology, 56,* 629–634.

Perri, M. G., & Nezu, A. M. (1992). Preventing relapse following treatment for obesity. In A. J. Stunkard, & T. A. Wadden (Eds.), *Obesity: Theory and therapy* (2nd ed., pp. 287–299). New York: Raven.

Perri, M. G., Nezu, A. M., McKelvey, W. F., Schein, R. L., Renjilian, D. A., & Viegener, B. J. (2001). Relapse prevention training and problem-solving therapy in the long-term management of obesity. *Journal of Consulting and Clinical Psychology, 69,* 722–726.

Perri, M. G., Nezu, A. M., & Viegener, B. J. (1992). *Improving the long-term management of obesity: Theory, research, and clinical guidelines.* New York: Wiley.

Pfiffner, L. J., Jouriles, E. N., Brown, M. M., Etscheidt, M. A., & Kelly, J. A. (1990). Effects of problem-solving therapy on outcomes of parent training for single-parent families. *Child and Family Behavior Therapy, 12,* 1–11.

Phillips, E. L. (1978). *The social skills basis of psychopathology: Alternatives to abnormal psychology and psychiatry.* New York: Grune & Stratton.

Phillips, L., & Zigler, E. (1961). Social competence: The action-thought parameter and vicariousness in normal and pathological behaviors. *Journal of Abnormal and Social Psychology, 63,* 137–146.

Platt, J. J., Husband, S. D., Hermalin, Carter, J., & Metzger, D. (1993). A cognitive problem-solving employment readiness intervention for methadone clients. *Journal of Cognitive Psychotherapy: An International Quarterly, 7,* 21–33.

Platt, J. J., & Scura, W. C., & Hannon, J. R. (1973). Problem solving thinking of youthful incarcerated heroin addicts. *Journal of Community Psychology, 1,* 278–281.

Platt, J. J., & Siegel, J. M. (1976). MMPI characteristics of good and poor social problem solvers among psychiatric patients. *Journal of Community Psychology, 94,* 245–251.

Platt, J. J., & Spivack, G. (1972a). Problem solving thinking of psychiatric patients. *Journal of Consulting and Clinical Psychology, 39,* 148–151.

Platt, J. J., & Spivack, G. (1972b). Social competence and effective problem solving in psychiatric patients. *Journal of Clinical Psychology, 28,* 3–5.

Platt, J. J., & Spivack, G. (1973). Studies in problem-solving thinking of psychiatric patients: Patient-control differences and factorial structure of problem-solving thinking. *Proceedings of the 81st Annual Convention of the American Psychological Association, 8,* 461–462.

Platt, J. J., & Spivack, G. (1975). *Manual for the means-ends problem-solving procedures (MEPS): A measure of interpersonal cognitive problem-solving skills.* Philadelphia, PA: Hahnemann Community Mental Health Mental Retardation Center.

Platt, J. J., Spivack, G., Altman, N., Altman, D., & Peizer, S. B. (1974). Adolescent problem solving thinking. *Journal of Consulting and Clinical Psychology, 42,* 787–793.

Plienis, A. J., Hansen, D. J., Ford, F., Smith, S., Jr., Stark, L. J., & Kelly, J. A. (1987). Behavioral small group training to improve the social skills of emotionally-disordered adolescents. *Behavior Therapy, 18,* 17–32.

Pollock, L. R. & Williams, J.M.G. (2001). Effective problem solving in suicide attempters depends on specific autobiographical recall. *Suicide and Life-Threatening Behavior, 31,* 386–396.

Poon, L. W., Rubin, D. C., & Wilson, B. A. (Eds.). (1989). *Everyday cognition in adulthood and late life.* New York: Cambridge University Press.

Pretorius, T. B., & Diedricks, M. (1994). Problem-solving appraisal, social support and stress-depression relationship. *South African Journal of Psychology, 24,* 86–90.

Provencher, M. D., Dugas, M. J., & Ladouceur, R. (2004). Efficacy of problem-solving training and cognitive exposure in the treatment of generalized anxiety disorder: A case replication series. *Cognitive and Behavioral Practice, 11,* 404–414.

Rehm, L. P., & Rokke, P. (1988). Self-management therapies. In K. S. Dobson (Ed.), *Handbook of cognitive-behavioral therapies* (pp. 136–166). New York: Guilford.

Reinecke, M. A., DuBois, D. L., & Schultz, T. M. (2001). Social problem solving, mood, and suicidality among inpatient adolescents. *Cognitive Therapy and Research, 25,* 743–756.

Roberts, J., Browne, G., Milne, C., Spooner, L., Gafni, A., Drummond-Young, M., et al. (1999). Problem-solving counseling for caregivers of the cognitively impaired: Effective for whom? *Nursing Research, 48,* 162–172.

Robichaud, M., & Dugas, M. J. (2005a). Negative problem orientation (Part I): Psychometric properties of a new measure. *Behaviour Research and Therapy, 43,* 391–401.

Robichaud, M., & Dugas, M. J. (2005b). Negative problem orientation (Part II): Construct validity and specificity to worry. *Behaviour Research and Therapy, 43,* 403–412.

Robinson, J. R., Drotar, D., & Boutry, M. (2001). Problem-solving abilities among mothers of infants with failure to thrive. *Journal of Pediatric Psychology, 26,* 21–32.

Ross, R. R., Fabiano, E. A., & Ewles, C. D. (1988). Reasoning and rehabilitation. *International Journal of Offender Treatment and Comparative Criminology, 32,* 29–35.

Ross, R. R., Fabiano, E. A., & Ross, R. D. (1986). *Reasoning and rehabilitation: A handbook for teaching cognitive skills.* Ottawa: Centre for Cognitive Development.

Ross, R. R., & Hilborn, J. (2005). *Time to think again: A prosocial competence approach to the prevention and treatment of antisocial behaviour.* Ottawa: Cognitive Centre of Canada.

Ross, R. R., & Ross, E. D. (Eds.). (1995). *Thinking straight: The Reasoning and Rehabilitation program for delinquency prevention and offender rehabilitation.* Ottawa: AIR Training and Publications.

Rothenberg, J. L., Nezu, A. M., & Nezu, C. M. (1995, November). *Problem-solving skills as a predictor of distress in caregivers of Alzheimer's patients.* Paper presented at the Association for Advancement of Behavior Therapy Convention, Washington, DC.

Rotter, J. B. (1966). Generalized expectancies for internal versus external control of reinforcements. *Psychological Monographs, 80,* 1–28.

Rotter, J. B., Chance, J. E., & Phares, E. J. (1972). *Applications of a social learning theory of personality.* New York: Holt, Rinehart, & Winston.

Rudd, M. D., Rajab, M. H., & Dahm, P. F. (1994). Problem-solving appraisal in suicide ideators and attempters. *American Journal of Orthopsychiatry, 64,* 136–149.

Sacco, W. P., & Graves, D. J. (1984). Childhood depression, interpersonal problem solving, and self-ratings of performance. *Journal of Clinical Child Psychology, 13,* 10–15.

Sadowski, C., & Kelley, M. L. (1993). Social problem-solving in suicidal adolescents. Journal of *Consulting and Clinical Psychology, 61,* 121–127.

Sadowski, C., Moore, L. A., & Kelley, M. L. (1994). Psychometric properties of the Social Problem-Solving Inventory (SPSI) with normal and emotionally-disturbed adolescents. *Journal of Abnormal Child Psychology, 22,* 487–500.

Sahler, O. J. Z., Fairclough, D. L., Phipps, S., Mulhern, R. K., Dolgin, M. J., Noll, R. B., et al. (2005). Using problem-solving skills training to reduce negative affectivity in mothers of children with newly diagnosed cancer: Report of a multisite randomized trial. *Journal of Consulting and Clinical Psychology, 73,* 272–283.

Sahler, O. J. Z., Varni, J. W., Fairclough, D. L., Butler, R. W., Noll, R. B., Dolgin, M. J., et al. (2002). Problem-solving skills training for mothers of children with newly diagnosed cancer: A randomized trial. *Developmental and Behavioral Pediatrics, 23,* 77–86.

Salkovskis, P. M., Atha, C., & Storer, D. (1990). Cognitive-behavioural problem solving in the treatment of patients who repeatedly attempt suicide: A controlled trial. *British Journal of Psychiatry, 157*, 871–876.

Sarason, B. R. (1981). The dimensions of social competence: Contributions from a variety of research areas. In J. D. Wine & M. D. Smye (Eds.), *Social competence.* New York: Guilford.

Sarason, I. G. (1980). Life stress, self-preoccupation, and social supports. In I. G. Sarason & C. D. Spielberger (Eds.), *Stress and anxiety* (Vol. 7). New York: Hemisphere.

Sarason, I. G., & Sarason, B. R. (1981). Teaching cognitive and social skills to high school students. *Journal of Consulting and Clinical Psychology, 49*, 908–918.

Sayers, M. D., & Bellack, A. S. (1995). An empirical method for assessing social problem solving in schizophrenia. *Behavior Modification, 19*, 267–289.

Scheier, M. F., & Carver, C. S. (1985). Optimism, coping, and health: Assessment and implications of generalized outcome expectancies. *Health Psychology, 4*, 219–247.

Schinke, S. P., Blythe, B. J., & Gilchrist, L. D. (1981). Cognitive-behavioral prevention of adolescent pregnancy. *Journal of Counseling Psychology, 28*, 451–454.

Schönpflug, W. (1983). Coping efficiency and situational demands. In R. Hockey (Ed.), *Stress and fatigue in human performance.* New York: Wiley.

Schotte, D. E., & Clum, G. A. (1982). Suicide ideation in a college population: A test of a model. *Journal of Consulting and Clinical Psychology, 50*, 690–696.

Schotte, D. E., & Clum, G. A. (1987). Problem-solving skills in suicidal psychiatric patients. *Journal of Consulting and Clinical Psychology, 55*, 49–54.

Schotte, D. E., Cools, J., & Payvar, S. (1990). Problem-solving deficits in suicidal patients: Trait vulnerability or state phenomenon? *Journal of Consulting and Clinical Psychology, 58*, 562–564.

Schulz, P., & Schönpflug, W. (1982). Regulatory activity during states of stress. In H. W. Krohne & L. Laux (Eds.), *Achievement, stress, and anxiety.* New York: Hemisphere.

Schwartz, M. D., Lerman, C., Audrain, J., Cella, D., Rimer, B., Stefanek, M., et al. (1998). The impact of a brief problem-solving training intervention for relatives of recently diagnosed breast cancer patients. *Annals of Behavioral Medicine, 20*, 7–12.

Seligman, M. E. P. (1975). *Helplessness.* San Francisco: Freeman.

Seligman, M. E. P. (1999). The President's address. *American Psychologist, 54*, 559–562.

Seligman, M. E. P., & Csikszentmihalyi, M. (2000). Positive psychology: An introduction. *American Psychologist, 55*, 5–14.

Selye, H. (1983). The stress concept: Past, present, and future. In C. L. Cooper (Ed.), *Stress research: Issues for the eighties.* New York: Wiley.

Shaw, W. S., Feuerstein, M., Haufler, A. J., Berkowitz, S. M., & Lopez, M. S. (2001). Working with low back pain: problem-solving orientation and function. *Pain, 93*, 129–137.

Shisslak, C., & Crago, M. (1987). Primary prevention of eating disorders. *Journal of Consulting and Clinical Psychology, 55*, 660–667.

Shure, M. B. (1981). Social competence as a problem-solving skill. In J. D. Wine & M. D. Smye (Eds.), *Social competence.* New York: Guilford.

Sidley, G. L., Whitaker, K., Calam, R. M., & Wells, A. (1997). The relationship between problem-solving and autobiographical memory in parasuicide patients. *Behavioural and Cognitive Psychotherapy, 25*, 195–202.

Simonian, S. J., Tarnowski, K. J., & Gibbs, J.C. (1991). Social skills and antisocial conduct of delinquents. *Child Psychiatry and Human Development, 22*, 17–27.

Siu, A.M.H., & Shek, D.T.L. (2005). The Chinese version of the Social Problem Solving Inventory: Some initial results on reliability and validity. *Journal of Clinical Psychology, 61*, 347–360.

Skinner, B. F. (1953). *Science and human behavior.* New York: Macmillan.

Smith, E. R. (1994). Procedural knowledge and processing strategies in social cognition. In R. S. Wyer, Jr. & T. K. Srull (Eds.), *Handbook of social cognition* (2nd ed., pp. 99–151). Hillsdale, NJ: Lawrence Erlbaum.

Snyder, R. C., Bruck, H. W., & Sapin, B. (1962). *Foreign policy decision-making.* New York: Free Press.

Spaccarelli, S., Cotler, S., & Penman, D. (1992). Problem-solving skills training as a supplement to behavioral parent training. *Cognitive Therapy and Research, 16,* 1–18.

Spiegler, M. D., & Guevremont, D. C. (2003). *Contemporary behavior therapy* (4th ed.). Belmont, CA: Wadsworth.

Spitzer, R. L., Endicott, J., & Robins, E. (1978). Research diagnostic criteria: Rationale and reliability. *Archives of General Psychiatry, 36,* 773–782.

Spivack, G., Platt, J. J., & Shure, M. B. (1976). *The problem-solving approach to adjustment.* San Francisco: Jossey-Bass.

Spivack, G., & Shure, M. B. (1974). *Social adjustment of young children.* San Francisco: Jossey-Bass.

Spivack, G., Shure, M. B., & Platt, J. J. (1985). *Means-Ends Problem Solving (MEPS). Stimuli and scoring procedures supplement.* Unpublished document. Hahnemann University Preventive Intervention Research Center, Philadelphia, Pennsylvania.

Sprafkin, R., Gershaw, N. J., & Goldstein, A. P. (1980). Structured-learning therapy: Overview and applications to adolescents and adults. In D. P. Rathjen & J. P. Foreyt (Eds.), *Social competence: Interventions for children and adults.* New York: Pergamon.

Staats, A. W. (1975). *Social behaviorism.* Homewood, IL: Dorsey Press.

Steinlauf, C. (1979). Problem-solving skills, locus of control, and the contraceptive effectiveness of young women. *Child Development, 50,* 268–271.

Sternberg, R. J., & Wagner, R. K. (Eds.). (1986). *Practical intelligence: Nature and origins of competence in the everyday world.* New York: Cambridge University Press.

Sternberg, R. J., Wagner, R. K., Williams, W. M., & Horvath, J. A. (1995). Testing common sense. *American Psychologist, 50,* 914–926.

Straw, M. K., & Terre, L. (1983). An evaluation of individualized behavioral obesity treatment and maintenance strategies. *Behavior Therapy, 14,* 255–266.

Ström, L., Pettersson, R., & Andersson, G. (2000). A controlled trial of self-help treatment of recurrent headache conducted via the internet. *Journal of Consulting and Clinical Psychology, 68,* 722–727.

Tarrier, N., Yusupoff, L., Kinney, C., McCarthy, E., Gledhill, A., Haddock, G., et al. (1998). Randomised controlled trial of intensive cognitive behaviour therapy for patients with chronic schizophrenia. *British Medical Journal, 317,* 303–307.

Taylor, S. E. (1991). *Health psychology* (2nd ed.). New York: McGraw-Hill.

Telch, C. F., & Telch, M. J. (1986). Group coping skills instruction and supportive group therapy for cancer patients: A comparison of strategies. *Journal of Consulting and Clinical Psychology, 54,* 802–808.

Teri, L., Logsdon, R. G., Uomoto, J., & McCurry, S. M. (1997). Behavioral treatment of depression in dementia patients: A controlled clinical trial. *Journals of Gerontology Series B—Psychological Sciences and Social Sciences, 52B,* 159–166.

Tisdelle, D. A., & St. Lawrence, J. S. (1986). Interpersonal problem solving competence: Review and critique of the literature. *Clinical Psychology Review, 6,* 337–356.

Toobert, D. J., Glasgow, R. E., Barrera, M., & Bagdade, J. (2002). Enhancing support for health behavior change among women at risk for structure heart disease: The Mediterranean lifestyle trial. *Health Education and Research, 17,* 547–585.

Toomey, R., Wallace, C. J., Corrigan, P. W., Schuldberg, D., & Green, M. F. (1997). Social processing correlates of nonverbal social perception in schizophrenia. *Psychiatry: Interpersonal and Biological Processes, 60,* 293–300.

Toseland, R. W., Blanchard, C. G., & McCallion, P. (1995). A problem-solving intervention for caregivers of cancer patients. *Social Science and Medicine, 40*, 517–528.

Tracey, T. J., Sherry, P., & Keitel, M. (1986). Distressed and help seeking as a function of person-environment fit and self-efficacy: A causal model. *American Journal of Community Psychology, 14*, 657–676.

Trower, P., Bryant, B., & Argyle, M. (1978). *Social skills and mental health.* London: Methuen.

Turk, D. C., Salovey, P. (1985). Cognitive structures, cognitive processes, and cognitive-behavior modification: I. Client issues. *Cognitive Therapy and Research, 9*, 1–17.

Tversky, A., & Kahnemann, D. (1981). The framing of decisions and the psychology of choice. *Science, 211*, 453–458.

Tymchuk, A. J., Andron, L., & Rahbar, B. (1988). Effective decision-making/problem-solving training with mothers who have mental retardation. *American Journal on Mental Retardation, 92*, 510–516.

Ullmann, L., & Krasner, L. (1969). *A psychological approach to abnormal behavior.* Englewood Cliffs, NJ: Prentice-Hall.

Unutzer, J., Katon, W., Callahan, C., Williams, J. W., Hunkeler, E. M., Harpole, L., et al. (2002). Collaborative care management of late-life depression in the primary care setting: A randomized controlled trial. *Journal of the American Medical Association, 288*, 2836–2845.

Unutzer, J., Katon, W., Williams, J. W., Callahan, C., Harpole, L., Hunkeler, E. M., et al. (2001). Improving primary care for depression in late life: The design of a multicenter randomized trial. *Medical Care, 39*, 785–799.

Urbain, E. S., & Kendall, P. C. (1980). Review of social-cognitive problem-solving interventions with children. *Psychological Bulletin, 88*, 109–143.

van den Hout, J. H. C., Vlaeyen, J. W. S., Heuts, P. H. T., Stillen, W. J. T., & Willen, J. E. H. L. (2001). Functional disability in non-specific low back pain: the role of pain-related fear and problem-solving skills. *International Journal of Behavioural Medicine, 8*, 134–148.

van den Hout, J. H. C., Vlaeyen, J. W. S., Heuts, P. H. T., Zijlema, J. H. L., & Wijen, J. A. G. (2003). Secondary prevention of work-related disability in nonspecific low back pain: Does problem-solving therapy help? A randomized clinical trial. *The Clinical Journal of Pain, 19*, 87–96.

Wade, S. L., Wolfe, C., Brown, T. M., & Pestian, J. P. (2005). Putting the pieces together: Preliminary efficacy of a web-based family intervention for children with traumatic brain injury. *Journal of Pediatric Psychology, 30*, 437–442.

Wallace, C. J., & Liberman, R. P. (1985). Social skills training for patients with schizophrenia: A controlled clinical trial. *Psychiatry Research, 15*, 239–247.

Wege, W. J., & Möller, A. T. (1995). Effectiveness of a problem-solving training program. *Psychological Reports, 76*, 507–514.

Weinberger, M., Hiner, S. L., & Tierney, W. M. (1987). In support of hassles as a measure of stress in predicting health outcomes. *Journal of Behavioral Medicine, 10*, 19–31.

Weisskopf-Joelson, E., & Eliseo, A. (1961). An experimental study of the effectiveness of brainstorming. *Journal of Applied Psychology, 45*, 45–49.

White, R. W. (1959). Motivation reconsidered: The concept of competence. *Psychological Review, 66*, 297–333.

Whitlatch, C. J., Zarit, S. H., & von Eye, A. (1991). Efficacy of interventions with caregivers: A reanalysis. *The Gerontologist, 31*, 9–14.

Wilkinson, P., & Mynors-Wallis, L. (1994). Problem-solving therapy in the treatment of unexplained physical symptoms in primary care: A preliminary study. *Journal of Psychosomatic Research, 38*, 591–598.

Williams, J. G., & Kleinfelter, K. J. (1989). Perceived problem-solving skills and drinking patterns among college students. *Psychological Reports, 65,* 1235–1244.

Williams, J. W., Barrett, J., Oxman, T., Frank, E., Katon, W., Sullivan, M., et al. (2000). Treatment of dysthymia and minor depression in primary care: A randomized controlled trial in older adults. *Journal of the American Medical Association, 284,* 1519–1526.

Willis, S. L., & Marsiske, M. (1993). *Manual for the Everyday Problems Test.* Unpublished manuscript, Pennsylvania State University, University Park, Pennsylvania.

Wills, T. A. (1986). Stress and coping in early adolescence: Relationships to substance use in urban school samples. *Health Psychology, 5,* 503–529.

Witty, T. E., Heppner, P. P., Bernard, C., & Thoreson, R. (2001). Problem solving appraisal and psychological adjustment of persons with chronic low back pain. *Journal of Clinical Psychology in Medical Settings, 8,* 149–160.

Wodarski, J. S., & Wodarski, L. A. (1998). *Preventing teenage violence: An empirical paradigm for schools and families.* New York: Springer Publishing.

Woicik, P. B., Conrod, P. J., & Pihl, R. O. (2002). *Validation of a four-factor model of substance abuse risk and the substance use risk profile scale.* Manuscript submitted for publication.

Woolfolk, R. L., & Lehrer, P. M. (Eds.). (1984). *Principles and practice of stress management.* New York: Guilford.

Wrubel, J., Benner, P., & Lazarus, R. S. (1981). Social competence from the perspective of stress and coping. In J. D. Wine & M. D. Smye (Eds.), *Social competence.* New York: Guilford.

Yang, B., & Clum, G. A. (2000). Childhood stress leads to suicidality via its effects on cognitive functioning. *Suicide and Life-Threatening Behavior, 30,* 183–198.

Yerkes, R., & Dodson, J. D. (1908). The relation of strength of stimulus to rapidity of habit formation. *Journal of Comparative and Neurological Psychology, 18,* 459–482.

Zarit, S. H., Anthony, C. R., & Boutselis, M. (1987). Interventions with caregivers of dementia patients: Comparison of two approaches. *Psychology and Aging, 2,* 225–232.

Zebb, B. J., & Beck, J. G. (1998). Worry versus anxiety: Is there really a difference? *Behavior Modification, 22,* 45–61.

Zigler, E., & Phillips, L. (1961). Social competence and outcome in psychiatric disorder. *Journal of Abnormal and Social Psychology, 63,* 264–271.

Zigler, E., & Phillips, L. (1962). Social competence and the process-reactive distinction in psychopathology. *Journal of Abnormal and Social Psychology, 65,* 215–222.

Index